D0913305

Stealing Sunlight

J. Mc. G. S.

May 2004
reread
April 2007

reread
3-20-12

reread 11-12-13

Stealing Sunlight
Growing up in Irishtown

Angeline Kearns Blain

A. & A. Farmar

© Angeline Kearns Blain 2000

First Published in 2000 by
A. & A. Farmar
Beech House
78 Ranelagh Village
Dublin 6
Ireland
Tel: + 353 1 496 3625
Fax: + 353 1 497 0107
Email: afarmar@iol.ie

All rights reserved. No text may be reproduced in any medium or storage system without permission from the publishers.

ISBN 1-899047-71-9

Printed by GraphyCems
Navarra, Spain

In memory of Neddy Kenny,
who fed our family in desperate times.

Acknowledgements

I want to thank Anna and Tony Farmar for receiving this manuscript with kindness and respect, and for doing such a great job on editing the book. A thank you also to Renée Golden, my agent and lover of literature, and Haywood Williams for her help in the early stages of the project.

My family and relatives have been very supportive while I worked on this project. My son, Stephen Lyon, has been particularly encouraging. I would also like to acknowledge my brother Frank Jr, his wife Bridie, their children and grandchildren. A special hug to my six-year-old granddaughter, Katie Lyon, who lives close by, and makes no bones about loving her granny. My husband, Michael Blain for his love and labour, and for taking me on trips to the Oregon Coast!

Finally, I want to acknowledge the people who made this memoir possible –all the friends and neighbours who lived in O'Brien's Place and George Reynold's house.

Angeline Kearns Blain
June 2000

Contents

Part 1: O'Brien's Place

The neighbourhood

We were born and raised, my three brothers and I, in a single room in one of the dilapidated whitewashed tenements which were strung along O'Brien's Place like dingy bedsheets. O'Brien's housed impoverished people—discards as far as the Irish government cared. The hidden laneway was behind the beautiful Victorian houses on Northumberland Road in Dublin. A wall that seemed to tower overhead separated O'Brien's from the dwellings of the rich.

The rooms in the tenements were rented out by the week. They had no plumbing or electricity. The communal water tap and lavatories were outdoors at the back. The landlords who owned the hovels never made an appearance in the laneway. Their stand-in, Mr Ferguson the rent collector, showed up in O'Brien's every Friday evening to bag their loot. To a young child, Mr Ferguson seemed as morose and grey as a sack of cinders.

Ma and Da had moved into Number 10 O'Brien's in 1927 soon after they were married. Da had migrated to Dublin in 1926 from his home in Castleblayney, County Monaghan, to join the Irish Free State Army. Ma and Da's first child, a boy, shrivelled in and out of life in the space of three weeks: died of pneumonia, died from the cold, died from the bone-dampness of being born in O'Brien's.

Da was a wireless operator in the army. Headquartered in Collins Barracks, he got sent out on manoeuvres all over the countryside. Most of the time, Ma hadn't a clue as to his whereabouts; she complained about the army keeping Da away from us. 'They're always sending yer Da on damp excursions and leaving me holding the bag,' went her frequent complaint. Lower-ranking men in the army like Da were paid a pittance, so when he went soldiering Ma begged and borrowed to keep us from dying young.

Counting in my head the houses from the top of the lane to the bottom, about fifty people ranging from the very young to the very old lived in O'Brien's. Living in such close quarters meant neighbours poked their noses into each other's businesses. A tree branch couldn't shake over O'Brien's without someone running their fingers through the leaves.

Children played games in the laneway and the place huffed and puffed with elders shuffling about. O'Brien's heave-hoed with family-men going about their business, tongue-clicked with housewives smacking their lips over gossip, and glistened with girls coming of age. Lads in the laneway scraped sparks from the cobblestones as they sauntered the lane in their hobnailed-boots, hoping for a glimpse of a girl or the chance of a job.

Our room had grey plastered walls that no wallpaper would adhere to due to dampness. Ma tried to cover the bare walls with flowered wallpaper but it fell down in strips onto the floor. The dingy whitewashed ceiling was crisscrossed with cracks and petals of plaster fell from the ceiling. A narrow one-paned window let light into the room. An assortment of decayed floorboards covered the earthen floor. The door, shrouded in countless coats of old paint, grunted resentment each time someone came into or went out of the room. A dugout hole at the bottom of one wall served as a fireplace, our only source of heat and only means of cooking.

A double bed leaned against the wall; Ma, baby Noely and myself slept at the top of the bed and when Da was home he and my brothers Frank and Bob cuddled at the foot. A kitchen table stood in front of the fireplace, and a small brown painted cupboard held our few utensils. A kitchen chair and a couple of wooden crates were scattered about the room.

A picture of Jesus hung above the fireplace on a nail as long as a poker. The face of Jesus gazed upon us with eyes as forlorn and bewildered as an immigrant from a far-off land. Ma had inherited the framed picture from her dead mother, Kate O'Connor. Ma constantly muttered to the icon about not having any money to buy food or fuel or medicine for her children as if the thing had ears and might correct her plight.

When we had no money to buy either turf or coal to burn in the fireplace, my older brothers and I scoured outside the neighbourhood for anything we thought would burn in the grate. Ma appreciated our scavenging. She used all we took from dustbins as a source of fuel: odd shoes, twigs, pages of newspapers, rubber rungs from wheels of a baby's pram, slats from wooden crates, pieces of coal, coke and blobs of dried-out horseshite.

Wintertime pinpointed the misery of poverty. Without money for fuel to start a fire in the grate or for a tallow candle to light on a dark evening, Ma lost the will to tell yarns. Without any stories to take the mind off reality, hopelessness deepened. Then the bed beckoned. The six of us would cover up under a pile of old blankets and go into our separate worlds 'til sleep blotted out the dreariness and stilled our pangs of hunger. Ma's usually optimistic face crumbled to smithereens.

Rats lived in the walls of our room and under the floorboards. Their squeaks and scurryings caused my head to blaze inside. I prayed for mornings to come. Sensing my fear of the rats Ma held my hand throughout the night assuring me that God was strong and had a good mother who watched over us.

If family members needed to relieve themselves in the middle of the night, the bucket proved a necessity. Fear of falling down in the outdoor darkness or stepping on a rat in one of the outhouses was real. The dark, reeky lavatory stalls churned the stomach. Only a desperate person could hold their nose and keep from breathing long enough to relieve themselves. There was the worry of falling on slippery piss-soaked floors patterned with blobs of green and yellow phlegm, coughed up hard by children, mothers, fathers and old people.

Yet sometimes I chose to go outside. In spite of the assurance of my brothers—'We're not looking. Ma will break our necks if we do!'—the shame of relieving myself in front of them was unbearable and it was easier to face the pits than go to the toilet indoors. At night Ma took a lighted candle with us. It wasn't unusual to find a rat lapping in a dark corner of the toilet. Ma spread newspapers over the hole before I sat down. While she waited for me, light from the candle flickered across the hieroglyphic shite marks painted on the walls. The disgusting art to my mind, even then, were attempts to beautify.

Granny Martin and Jamey, her unmarried son, had the room across the hall from us. The Brays lived upstairs. Johnny Duggan, an old-age pensioner, had a room across the landing from the Brays. He used to mutter to himself, 'Sure we're like sardines in a can without tamata sauce.' Those within earshot dittoed Johnny's chant.

Ma set the time of day by Johnny's rambling back and forth above our ceiling. In early morning he thudded down each of the squeaky stairs on his way out to the backyard to empty the slopbucket. Ma wouldn't stir out of bed 'til she thought Johnny had emptied the bucket and filled his tea kettle from the water tap. She thought he wouldn't want a woman to see his bucket of slop being emptied. As soon as Johnny heaved himself back up the stairs with his empty slopbucket and tea-kettle of water, Ma darted out of bed to start a new day. By the time she had a fire blazing in the grate, the morning light had recoiled out of the window as if pulled by a fist and shadows dimmed the room.

The tenements rang with the clang and clatter of slopbuckets being emptied in the lavatories and kettles being filled with water from the backyard tap. Women lugged buckets down flights of stairs in the dim light. Ma and the other women acted embarrassed while they waited their turn to empty the slopbuckets filled with piss and shite into one of the two lavatories. Oftentimes, plumbing in the overused lavatories broke down and days would pass before the landlords sent someone out to fix them. Every family had a slopbucket.

During winter the lavatories and the tap froze. On such mornings Granny Martin called out to Ma, 'Yoo hoo Mary, can ye light some newspaper and hold it under the tap to unfreeze it. Thank

God for ye, Mary O'Connor.' The blobs of phlegm dotting the backyard iced over like faded flowers under a glass-domed funeral wreath.

On summer nights smells from the lavatories seeped into the hallway and drifted under the doorways in the building. Anyone with half a nose had more than a nodding acquaintance with the smells of urine, faeces and vomit. Whenever possible Ma kept a fire of some kind smouldering all summer long to keep hell out.

Even when I was a young child, I wondered why we were so poor. Da's pay came through the post every two weeks but his wage did not cover the cost of rent, fuel, candlelight, food or new clothing for any of us. Ma wore the same shabby skirt and jumper and broken shoes for years. Her threadbare coat lost all of its warmth.

We never knew where the army sent Da. Although most of the people in O'Brien's lived hand to mouth, none of the unemployed men joined the army for a job. The army tried to recruit single young men, but the paltry wages offered enticed none in O'Brien's. The young men, like their unemployed fathers, hoped to find jobs in a factory or in the Dublin gasworks, or in Guinness's brewery.

Women begged and borrowed from each other. Outgrown clothing got passed around among families. Women lent each other whatever they had that might be pawned for a shilling or two to buy food for hungry children; they shared whatever they could from a bit of soap to a pinch of tea to a piece of a candle to a sod of turf.

The Angelus bells from our parish church Saint Mary's pealed over O'Brien's Place twice daily. The bells stopped Ma in her tracks. The half-starved woman acted as if the Angelus filled her face with food. Looking at me, Ma said, 'Ye came into the world the hour the Angelus bells rang at twelve, midday. I planned to call ye Kathleen, but coming in on the Angelus the way ye did, meant I had to name ye Angeline after the bells. D'ye know that?'

Ma knew how much I liked her to tell me the story behind my name, but not the part where the priest insisted that she christen me Angela, instead of Angeline Bridget. Angeline, according to the code, wasn't a Christian name. Ma called me Angeline in spite of what appeared on the baptism certificate. She called me Angeline for eighteen years, until I emigrated to the United States where a customs official clipped my name to Angie .

While growing up in O'Brien's I'd count the strokes of the Angelus to tick off my current age. Young and old alike were supposed to bow their heads and say the Angelus prayers when the bells clanged at noontime, and at six o'clock in the evenings. Crabby old men in O'Brien's pretended they were stone-deaf to the clatter of the bells and continued their toss-the-penny game in the laneway to the chagrin of the pious, like old Mrs Legg.

Granny Martin and the other women stood around the running tap chirping like a flock of birds. The chatter of the women matched the chatter of the wild birds who nested in the treetops above the high stone wall that separated O'Brien's from the mansions on Northumberland Road. There were berry-red robins, green linnets, yellow and blue finches, dusky brown sparrows and pitch-black starlings.

Da identified the birds while looking out of the window of our room. He knew his onions when it came to birds because of having grown up around the Black Lake in Castleblayney. He peeled eyes towards the treetops in hopes of seeing a jackdaw, a bird he remembered as being common in the fields and farmlands of his youth on the border of Ulster. Granny Martin, Granny Doyle, Granny Gale, Granny Carey, Granny Ross and Granny Murphy saved pieces of stale bread to toss in the laneway for the wild birds, and the old women quibbled and quarrelled among themselves over which bird was which and whose breadcrumbs the flocks favoured.

Kids knew not to climb over the wall. The people on the other side had embedded hundreds of pieces of broken glass from one end of the wall to the other. The sharp fragments, so carefully placed, were meant to cut in the cruellest way and act as a signal to keep us confined to the slums. The smashed glass in colours of opaque emerald green, amber and blue came from broken bottles, ashtrays, vases, jamjars, traffic lights, windowpanes and mirrors. On bright days, the sun skiddered the length of the wall turning the ugly edges into the image of fairy-lights strung all the way out to Christmas.

Down the lane from O'Brien's, the government built Lansdowne Place, new semi-detached houses with indoor plumbing, electricity, front and back gardens and garages. They were set aside for police officers and other law-enforcers. We called the police 'bluebottles' because of the navy blue uniforms they wore. They worked out of the police station in Pearse Street. The police and detectives were from Limerick, Kerry and Cork. Eamon de Valera favoured the rural husky types over the more wiry Dubliners.

Granny Martin eyed the comings and goings and offered a mouthful about the new housing and its occupants a spit away from our slums. Granny commented 'the bluebottles and dicks talk like their gobs were full a marbles' and 'such blow-ins wouldn't let a fly land on them without charging 'em rent'. The police officers and detectives never had a cross word for any of the children in O'Brien's as they scooted up and down the laneway on bikes or rode in motorcars, but the same couldn't be said for their wives. The wives would not give the time of day to anyone in O'Brien's as they took a shortcut through our neighbourhood on their way to morning mass at Saint Mary's on Haddington Road.

The wives ran out of their front doors if they saw kids from O'Brien's coming into their neighbourhood. They came towards us and lifted their floral aprons in front of them to shoo us back to our hovels. The wives raged at us for being in their neighbourhood and especially if we came to play with their kids. The coppers' cross-eyed kids, even the ones who didn't wear glasses, were not allowed to play with us though some wanted to play cops and robbers.

Standoffs between the lawmen's wives and the kids in O'Brien's became common. Da told me that after the English had been defeated in Ireland, Irish men, women and children were free to go anywhere they wanted. I took his word as gospel.

I bounced my ball out of O'Brien's and into the copper's turf without as much as 'ye please'. As I was bouncing and cocking my leg over the ball on the pavement, one of the wives flew out of her house and yelled at me to take myself back home, before she called the authorities. I'd been so completely involved in seeing how many times I could cock my leg over the bouncing ball, that the sound of her harsh voice caused me to trip and fall down on the pavement. I eyed the tall skinny woman glaring down at me, her face as red as a rose. She acted as if I had no right to exist not only where she lived but in the world itself. I got up and retrieved the only tennis ball to be had in O'Brien's, then headed down the lane, but not before I gave a bit of guff.

'Fly back to Kerry or Cork on yer broomstick ye auld bitch,' I shouted.

'You're ill-bred, ill-mannered, uneducated and unsightly. Do you hear that, my good girl?'

'I heard ye. Do I look deaf, ye auld faggot?' I told her that Granny Martin had her, and other blow-ins like her, pegged. And I shouted at her that I lived in a free country, and my da was a soldier in the Irish army serving his country.

After hearing such cheek, the copper's wife hurled back:

'For a girl, you're as bold as a pig, as bold as a pig.'

'Well, if I'm as bold as a pig, ye're a ringer for Olive Oyl in Popeye the Sailor Man!'

With that, she raised a hand to give me a slap, but I darted down the lane before she got the chance.

When word got out in O'Brien's that lorries full of cut turf were arriving from the country for the fireplaces of the police and detectives at government expense, and us without the money to buy turf, resentment bubbled in our pores.

The wives supervised the unloading of the turf from the trucks sod by sod. Their kids and the lorry drivers filled wheelbarrows with turf and wheeled the overflowing barrows into the back gardens where they stacked the black sods as high as a wall. As the unloading went on, we took our positions behind corners, lamp-posts and hedges armed with buckets, cardboard boxes and gunnysacks. The wives stood guard by the trucks. Kids from O'Brien's ran in circles around the parked trucks, distracting the wives. While this went on, the kids in the vanguard rushed to the lorries, loaded their arms with turf, and ran like hell back to O'Brien's.

The shouts from the wives brought their cross-eyed kids scurrying to their rescue. We warned the kids we'd beat them up and bury them if they prevented us from getting some turf. The country kids hid behind their mammies' skirts at such threats, and we filled our sacks with turf and ran like March hares back to our mammies.

The grannies came out into the laneway to see all the commotion over the turf. They gummed their lips in pleasure at the turf knowing it would be shared with them, all except for old Granny Legg. All she did was tut-tut on about what robbers we were. She complained out loud about having the misfortune to live among robbers in a wicked world. 'Yez all have committed a sin by robbin' other people's turf,' she accused. Eyeballing the kids, she continued, 'Tell the priest in yer next confession that ye robbed turf from innocent people.'

Granny Murphy, in spite of her lumbago, gave a little skip at being offered a bucket of turf for her fireplace. Granny Martin patted my brother Bob's head after he filled her bucket. Then she cooed on that Bob was 'a darlin' sonny-boy and the spittin' image of his mammy'. Legg continued lashing out over the turf. Her jabbering caused Granny Martin's cage to rattle. She tried to put Legg straight in her thinking about the turf.

'Looka here, Legg, ye been rattling like pots and pans over a bit of robbed turf for no good reason. The only reason the government gave them coppers lorries full of turf and little houses with gardens and everything else, is 'cause they're coppers, and nothin' else. Cler'ta God, look at Mary O'Connor, and the four mouths she's ta feed, livin' like a widda with her husband, what's 'is name, gallivanting all over the country for de Valera. Does de Valera give her any turf for nothin'? If ye want to scuttle about wrongdoing scuttle about de Valera, keeping poor people poor, and loading coppers down with everything.'

If you wanted a sparring-partner Granny Martin fitted the bill. Da used to say that she had a tongue in her head like a prongfork, and when she used it to inflict pain, she did a better job than any devil dancing in hell.

As Legg left our doorway to head back to her room, Ma asked her if she didn't want a sod of turf. Legg looked at Ma, then at the rest of us, with distaste. The old woman pulled up her stiff coat collar and tugged down her long grey coat, put her hands up the sleeves of the coat and shuffled off, still complaining that she lived in a wicked, wicked world. Ma felt sorry for the contrary windbag who measured everything by her own yardstick, and never saw another person's side of a coin.

The grannies headed into their respective rooms along O'Brien's either hugging an armful of turf tight to their flattened old breasts or carrying the sods in a bucket like bricks of gold. Feelings of good fortune ran through us all due to getting the free turf, stolen or not. It had been a grand day, and as Granny Martin would have it, the devil with anything else.

Why hadn't Da joined the garda instead of the army? Or what if he had linked arms with the IRA? In the eyes of most who lived in O'Brien's the outlaws were miles higher in their estimation than any soldier in the national army. Soldiers like Da were seen as foolish rather than heroic, and on top of that worked for so little.

An older lad in the laneway asked my brothers, on seeing Da in his green uniform, 'can he tell the difference between his arse and his elbow?' The loudmouth in a roundabout way said Da served in the wrong outfit. Da didn't see it that way. He talked about a vision that Eamon de Valera, had for us all. Da said that Dev wanted a land where people would be pious and prosperous.

'What's he waiting for then?' interjected Ma.

'Listen to the rest,' said Da irritated. 'Dev wants an Ireland that will be bright with cosy homesteads, whose field and villages will be joyous with the sound of industry, with the romping of sturdy children, and the laughter of comely maidens.'

'How de ye know all that?' asked my brother Frank.

'I read it in the newspaper.'

'Does he notice places like O'Brien's that are strung across the city?' Ma wanted to know. She got hot and bothered at the ridiculous promises de Valera and his ilk made to poor people which they never kept. As for Da, he continued to believe in de Valera's notion of fairyland, fool that he was.

Da talked with fondness about his former home in Castleblayney, or 'Blayney' as he preferred to call the place. His parents owned three small shops in the town of Castleblayney at one time. Da's father died young. According to Da, his mother, Minny, set her heart upon his becoming a priest. He spent time in some seminary studying for the priesthood before he made off for Dublin and joined the army. After he backfired on his mother's wish for him, she gave him up for dead. Granny Kearns refused ever to set eyes on him again. She disowned him completely and the rest of us along with him. Da had two sisters, Kathleen and Sissy. Sissy wrote to Da a few times, but Kathleen gave him up for dead. It rattles the brain, even now, that Granny Kearns possessed such an iron will, and a chiselled stone heart.

Da spoke all his life with a Northern accent. The neighbours in O'Brien's respected his ability to read and write, and considered him the most educated person in O'Brien's. Some of them used to ask him to write letters and fill out forms for them because they could neither read nor write.

I asked Ma how she met Da. Da jumped in with the story.

'One bright sunny morning as the leaves were splitting the trees, I went for a walk along O'Connell Street, Dublin, where I happened to see your mother, Mary, and her friend, Lela Boylan, strolling over the bridge. They gave me a grin and I gave them a grin. I kept turning my head back in their direction, and they were looking back in my direction. I walked back towards them, and they waited for me to catch up. I told them I was new to Dublin from the country and didn't know my way around. Lela and your mother walked my feet off.

'I loved Mary from the first glance. She liked me, too. It wasn't long before we were courting. We decided to get married if we could find a place to live. There was a great shortage of places for newly-married couples. We were lucky to find a room in O'Brien's Place where all of you were born. That's our love story, isn't it, Molly O?'

Da had a variety of names for Ma. He call her 'Moll', 'Mary', 'Molly O' and his girl. Da called me 'Titch' or 'Duck' when I was in his good books. Otherwise, he referred to me as 'Miss Sour Puss' or 'Miss Prim'.

I turned five years old the night Noely fell into the world. He wasn't much bigger than a milk bottle. From the start he seemed dawny as if indigo coursed through his veins instead of crimson blood. On cold mornings Noely's face and tiny hands were the colour of a slate North Sea. Ma sucked and held his hands in her mouth 'till crimson overcame the indigo blue. She blew warm breath over his face 'till life stirred and he opened blue eyes the exact colour of Da's.

Noely's bowel slid out of his bum like a red balloon. It took Ma hours to squeeze the red balloon back up inside Noely's tiny arsehole. The baby cried hard until she got it back in place. Although puny, when disturbed Noely opened the heavens.

Every morning Ma washed Noely in the big soup dish Bob had found in a dustbin and brought home to her. Noely slept in a wooden orange crate during the daytime. On warm afternoons Ma took him outside in the orange crate and sat it on the ground under our window. All the kids came over to gawk at Noely as he lay chewing on his hand or kicking his wee feet in the air.

Granny Martin took her chair outside and sat by the orange crate as Ma went about doing things. Ma loved Noely and constantly sang into his ear bars from an old folksong:

'Auld Johnny Raw, I'll beat ye on the paw if ye should touch me babby. Auld Johnny Raw, I'll beat ye on the paw if ye touch me babby.' The sound of Ma's singing caused Noely's ears to split apart.

Noely wore hand-me-down clothing given to Ma by neighbours whose own babies had outgrown the garments. Noely didn't get to feel the slick of anything new on his body 'til years went by. He, like the rest of the children in the laneway, wore others' castoffs. The women in the laneway also shared and passed on clothing to each other. The men in O'Brien's would rather have been dead than wear each other's rags in public.

Girls steal sunlight

The men in the laneway gathered to themselves, to each other, that is. They liked to bunch together in the evenings at the top of O'Brien's, older men, younger married men and single lads in their teen years. They either puffed on 'coffin nails' (cigarettes) or chewed on pipe-stems. They argued out loud, laughed out loud, and discussed matters for hours. The men nodded to our mothers if they passed by, but they never invited a woman to join in their chat. The gathering of the men in O'Brien's, evening after evening, seemed mysterious, secretive and exciting. I knew little about men with Da on the march most of the time and too, older women tried their best to see that girls continued to know little about men.

Old Master John, as the elder, who lived a few doors down from us, lorded over the other men's conversations. Master John had worked for years at the Dublin gasworks until he got the sack. Ever since his lay off, he cursed the owners of the gasworks.

I can still hear them at the corner, Master John arguing loudly about the way things were in the bloody country, ranting about the lives of working men in Ireland, booming out, 'For Christ sake, the workers haven't anything going for them here. Young lads and workingmen have it better in England, begob.' After every statement, Master John puffed out his chest, sucked on a pipe, puckered his crabby face and jettisoned a dirty spit from between sealed lips taking aim at the wall.

Danny would say, 'Ah, yeah, we know, Master John about how things are better in the wide blue yonder.' When a conversation got too hot or never made it off the ground, one of the bunch would begin a singsong. Danny sang a verse the men had made up to the tune of 'God Save The King'.

God save our glorious.
Half a loaf between the four of us.
Thank Jaysus, there's no more of us.
God save the king.

Liam Rafferty, trying to one up over Danny, sang his version of the hymn 'Hail Glorious Saint Patrick', the most famous hymn in Ireland.

Hail Glorious Saint Patrick
Will ye lend me ten bob?
I'll pay it back t'ye
When I get a good job.

Now Thou are high
In the mansions above,
On Éireann's green valley
Piss down a few bob.

On Éireann's green valley,
On Éireann's green valley,
On Éireann's green valley
Piss down a few bob.

After the singsong, Danny Wall chimed in, 'If ye heard the stories I have about the way blokes can make a fortune in America, ye'd be off tomorrow.'

'Oh, yeah, we heard about them stories about making a fortune in America, but who can come up with a bleeding shilling to get outta O'Brien's, for Christ sake?' Billo added with a spike of impatience in his tone.

'That's the difference between America and England, be japers', said the younger Carey, relishing the idea of becoming a millionaire.

'Yis, there's millionaires born in American ever day begob,' said Christie Jenkins.

'Begob, it's all true,' scuttles old Master John as if he knew on the gospel.

Master John shut down the men's chatter as he caught me loitering nearby.

'Looka her! What d'ye think ye're doing sailing around where men are talking, young wan? Git off with ye this very minute. Ye're a brazen girl, cocking yer ear into what men are saying among themselves. Don't ye know better than to come near or go beyant where men are gathered? What are ye up ta anyway?'

'I'm looking for a match that hasn't been lit along the gutter for me ma to light the fire with.'

'What's that fer an answer?' he scowled. 'Where's yer mammy? Is she in her home or gossiping with the rest a them instead of mindin' yez, and lettin' ye wander under our feet? Yerra, what is the country coming to with young wans like you cocking an ear into men's conversations?'

I always knew I'd be in for it when Master John got wind of me scouting about. Any time I passed him in O'Brien's he gave me the look of a lemon. I knew it wasn't proper for a girl to listen into the conversation between men, but curiosity coaxed.

As I headed back to our room, any sorrow I felt about Master John getting the boot from the gasworks evaporated. He acted like all the others who held that girls stole sunlight from the day.

First communion

When I was six I started First Babies in the parish national school, Saint Mary's on Haddington Road. The parish was one of the most affluent in Dublin. It had two national schools: one for boys and one for girls and it also operated a private girls' school for the offspring of the rich. The nuns in the girls' schools made every effort to keep the private and national school children apart. The girls in the private school were not slapped by the nuns; girls in the national school were targets for the nuns' rage and frustration.

I could hardly wait to start school. Ma laundered and mended my dress and Da nailed down the soles on my shoes with a mouthful of tacks. They had no money to buy me a school satchel, so I made do with a lady's handbag that Mrs Purdy let me have. I hated having to carry a handbag because it looked ridiculous, but orders demanded that a kid must carry a satchel. The kids asked if I were an old lady when they saw me with Mrs Purdy's handbag slung over my shoulder.

Ma walked me up to the school on my first day. It was behind the church, circled by a high wrought-iron fence. All the kids entered the school grounds by going through a high iron gate. No parents were allowed in with the kids. I asked Ma to wait outside the gate until school was over. I had gone everywhere with her, and now I had to leave her behind.

My teacher, Miss Blake, taught First and Second Babies. She came from somewhere in the country, and was hard to understand. There were about fifty children in my class, seated by pairs in desks lined in rows.

After looking the class over, Miss Blake told us the most important thing we needed to learn was how much God loved us and how we turned God away when we sinned. The first lessons would be the prayers said in the holy Catholic Church: the Hail Mary, the Our Father and the Glory Be.

Ma had taught me how to say the prayers. In fact, she had taught me how to say the Hail Mary in Irish. She still knew bits and pieces of Irish she had learned from her own mother. We spent all morning saying the prayers over and over. One of the small girls had an accident and pissed in her knickers and it ran onto the floor. As soon as Miss Blake saw the puddle, she stopped praying and told us that if we had to go to the lavatory, we needed to raise up our hand, and ask her for permission to go to the cloakroom, where the toilets were located. A shower of hands shot up in the air.

Miss Blake taught us our numbers by using an abacus. We learned our colours from her stringing coloured wooden spools on a rope. The teacher passed out a small black slate-board to each child and a stick of white chalk. When she wrote a number on the board we were supposed to copy it down on our slates.

Miss Blake told the class that if anyone did not listen to her with both ears and all their minds, she would smack them on the hand with her cane. She kept the long smooth bamboo cane on her desk. All the little girls became fearful of her words and sat like little soldiers in their desks. When we were not writing down our numbers, we were supposed to sit up straight with our hands behind our heads. We were not to talk to each other in the classroom and any girl who talked with another would be punished.

One girl forgot and talked to the one beside her. Miss Blake made her march up to the front of the class and hold out her hand. Miss Blake brought the stick down with force and slapped the small hand until the child cried out in pain. The act of cruelty dumbfounded me and does even to this day.

Miss Blake arranged the girls in the classroom according to a variety of birds: the better-off looking girls sat up in front and were the bluebirds. The second group sat in the middle of the room and were red robins. The third group of girls, myself included, sat at the back of the room. We were dusky sparrows.

One morning Miss Blake talked to the class about the importance of good nutrition. She informed all the poor kids that good food is fuel for a growing body and that the mission of the body was to carry us all through life. With that, she called on me to tell the rest of the class what I ate for breakfast, dinner and tea. After what seemed like an eternity, I stood up, both eyes blinking a mile a minute.

'Me mammy makes what she always makes in the morning, dip-bread and mugs a tea. Me mammy buys a quarter of a pound of brown drippin' in the pork shop—some call it lard—Ma calls it drippin'. She lets the fry-pan get hot over the fire, drops in a lump a drippin' and lets it melt in the pan. Then she cuts off a slice of bread from a loaf and drops the slice in the boiling grease. Ma lets it brown on one side then the other, flips it out of the pan, and gives it t'me with a mug of tea.'

'How often do you eat it?' Miss Blake wanted to know.

'In the mornin', for our dinner, and if there's any bread and drippin' left over, we get it for our tea.'

When I got through telling the class about Ma's dip-bread she nodded for me to sit down in my seat, then she pointed her finger at Joan, and asked her to tell the class what she had for her meals.

Joan told the class that her mother made the same dip-bread for all of them. Miss Blake found out that most of the girls in the class ate dip-bread for most of their meals. Miss Blake ended the lesson on good food by telling us all to eat more eggs, poultry, fish and beef. All the kids shouted out '*Go deimhin!*'—the Irish for 'Sure'.

One day Miss Blake called me to the front of the room and told me to hold out my hand. She took her cane off the desk, grabbed the tips of my outstretched hand and brought the cane down as hard as she could. She gave me three slaps with the cane on the hand before I cried. The teacher was the only woman ever to strike me with a stick. She slapped me because I had no penny copy book to write in. After the hammering, I developed a terrible case of eye twitches. Every time I came to school and entered the schoolroom, my eyes blinked out of control. Ma and Da thought I'd been looking at the sunlight too much. I kept my face down and my hands clasped behind my head to avoid meeting the teacher's eyes in the classroom.

Miss Blake prepared the class to make their first holy communion. According to the teacher, this was the most important day in a child's life. Jesus Christ would come into our hearts for the first time through the sacrament of holy communion. In order to receive the sacrament, we first had to learn about going to confession. Going into the confession box and confessing our sins for the first time was scary. The teacher told us she would play the part of the priest to rehearse us all for the real thing.

Miss Blake took a chair and sat down beside the cupboard in the classroom. She opened one of the doors of the cupboard and hid behind it. As each child went up to the cupboard and knelt down on the floor, Miss Blake flipped the cupboard door aside, like a priest sliding back the slide in the confession box. 'Bless me Miss Blake, for I have sinned, I mean Father,' I uttered. Then I told her my list of sins: being disobedient to my father and mother, fighting with my brothers, saying curse words and robbing an apple from the greengrocer's in Bath Avenue. Miss Blake pretended to give me absolution for my sins, then handed out the penance: 'Say three Hail Marys.'

But after going through months of the rigmarole to make my first holy communion, Ma said I'd have to postpone it until the following year because there was no money to buy me a communion outfit. The families of boys and girls who were going to make their first holy communion were expected to buy their child a set of new clothes for the occasion. A girl had to have a new white frock and white veil, new underwear, new shoes and socks, a new coat, white gloves and a handbag along with a religious silver medal to wear around the neck. It cost a lot of money to outfit a child for the occasion, and Ma and Da hadn't a penny to spend on such stuff.

Ma told me to tell Miss Blake that I had to be held back. I told Ma I would not tell such a thing to the teacher, and that I hated her and Da for having nothing and that I wished they weren't my mother and my father! Ma got a terrible hurt look in her eyes at my outburst, but I felt no mercy.

The next morning Ma, with Noely Joseph in tow, came to the school to talk to Miss Blake. As soon as one of the children in the classroom opened the door in answer to Ma's knuckle knock, Noely Joseph swooped into the empty space and dashed into the classroom. He had on his long red gansey that Ma gathered between his legs and fastened with a safety pin, to keep his bare arse covered. His small bare feet slapped over the floorboards and as soon as he spotted me in my desk, he came over and brushed his head and face across my shoulder, then ran like mad among the empty spaces between the rows of desks. His unevenly cut hair spilled down his shoulders and fell over his forehead. The children squealed loudly as he raced by on sturdy bare feet. He only slowed down to offer a splattering raspberry, causing some of the kids to take cover for fear of getting splashed. After five minutes of the dance, my friend Sylvia grabbed Noely and pulled him across the room and into the hallway where Ma waited.

The teacher went into the hallway to talk to Ma. Some of the kids asked me if the woman in the hallway was my mother. I wished that I could have said No, because Ma looked so shabby and poor. Yet Noely licked and kissed her hand that firmly held his arm. Later on Ma told me that Miss Blake had been like a lady to her. The teacher told Ma that she didn't know two adults and four growing children could live in one small room. She also told Ma that the few shillings she received from Da's army pay could surely not cover food for a family of six.

Miss Blake told Ma that it would be a shame to keep me from making my first holy communion with the rest of the class but she said she understood why I would have to wait another year. Miss Blake did not encourage Ma to seek some kind of charitable help from the Society of the Saint Vincent de Paul to help pay for my first communion outfit. She told Ma in confidence that the Catholic charity would expect her to get down on her knees before they offered her crumbs.

I hated the thought that all the kids in the classroom would know that my family was too poor to dress me for the most important day of my life. And all the kids in O'Brien's would find out about me not making my first communion, and think it was because I didn't know my catechism. Da said that all the fuss and bother about making poor children wear special outfits for communion and confirmation was enough to drive families out of the Church and into the clutch of the Protestants.

The next day at school, Miss Blake told me to stay after class. She told me that she and her sister were going to buy me my first communion clothes. She gave me a note for Ma to explain what she intended to do. The following afternoon after school, Miss Blake took me into the city to get me ready for the biggest day in my life.

I felt awkward and shy being with the teacher outside the classroom. I wondered what the kids at school would think if they found out that Miss Blake dressed me for communion.

We went to Cassidy's shop and looked at their display of communion dresses in the window. Miss Blake told me to pick out the one I liked. I selected the white flimsy georgette dress with the tucked top. Miss Blake said I had made a good selection and she liked the long veil I chose that had a wreath of tiny lily-of-the-valley. I picked out a royal blue coat with a black velvet collar to wear over the dress, and they also bought me some new underwear, white socks, and a pair of black patent leather silver-buckled hornpipe shoes.

I knew we were only to wear white shoes, but I grabbed the dancing shoes and asked her if I could have them instead of the regular white. She nodded Yes, and asked if the shoes were the first new pair I ever had, and I answered Yes. I selected the last stitch of the outfit, a white shoulder-bag. After all the lovely new clothes were wrapped up, we carried our parcels to the religious shop to buy the holy communion medal for me to wear around my neck, and after that we headed for the tram to take us back to the corner of Haddington Road.

When the tram-car stopped at Haddington Road, I spotted Ma and Noely sitting on the street bench waiting for us. Ma thanked Miss Blake for her kindness and goodness for getting me ready for holy communion. The teacher told Ma not to mention it. On the walk back to O'Brien's Ma asked all about the shopping trip with Miss Blake. She said that she and Da felt they had let me down because of having no money to get me a communion outfit, and me their only daughter. Ma felt a dismal failure.

Miss Blake had prepared us well for going through our first confession. The night before first communion, Ma heated kettle after kettle of water on the grate and poured the water into the basin and washed every inch of my body with soap and water. She scrubbed my hair until it shone. The next morning she dressed me in all the lovely new clothes. She gave me a lump of tissue paper and told me to open it up. I pulled out a long length of white satin hair ribbon. Ma tied the ribbon around my head and fashioned it into a butterfly bow.

Ma and Noely walked with me up to Saint Mary's to make my first communion. After we got to the church, Ma and Noely sat in the back, while I joined the rest of the kids in the pews.

The nuns separated the national-school children and the private-school children in the church. They tied white ribbons around the arm of each private-school kid before they got into the pews. The white ribbons were meant to distinguish the rich from the poor, so that no one would make a mistake about such an important fact. When it came time to approach the altar rail and receive the eucharist, the body and blood of Jesus Christ, from the hands of the priest, the nuns made sure the rich kids were first. After they were finished, we were filed to the altar rail and received the bread of life.

Miss Blake had taught the class a special prayer to say while we waited to receive the eucharist. I never forgot it.

Jesus, thou art coming, holy as thou art.
Thou, the God who made me, through my little heart.
Jesus, I believe it, on thy holy word.
Kneeling, I adore thee, as my king and lord.
Take my body, Jesus, eyes and ears and tongue.
Never let me, Jesus, do thee any wrong.
Take my heart and fill it, full of love for Thee.
All I have I give you. Give yourself to me.

When the ceremony ended, I joined Ma and Noely again and we walked slowly back to O'Brien's, but not before Ma stopped at one of the shops to buy some fairy cakes to take home with us in honour of my making my first holy communion. Somehow, Da had come up with a shilling to pay for the fairy cakes.

While my first communion outfit seemed the height of fashion, Bishop Wall had on the loveliest gear I'd ever seen, when the nuns herded all of us to see him laid out at his wake. The nuns led us from the school ground to the bishop's mansion, a quick march of ten minutes away. All the schoolchildren were to see the remains of the man, and pray at his bier. When we filed into the mansion, the smell of lilies and beeswax tickled the nose. We were ushered in by a priest to where the bishop was on display. He looked as if every crease in his body had been ironed out as he posed on the white pallet on top of the bier.

The bishop wore a long sleeved white priest's surplice under a scarlet robe embellished with gold trim. The cuffs of his surplice showed under the robe revealing the finest of tatted Irish silk lace, delicate as cobwebs. His long scarlet robe came down to the tip of his red velvet slippers garnished with silver threads and fronted with gold tassels as dainty as any worn by Cinderella. A three-pronged red and gold decorated mitre, studded with coloured gems, and bands of braid, sat on the bishop's head.

In spite of the splendid garments and dancing slippers on his feet, in spite of the cartloads of tall waxy lilies, the long-stemmed white carnations and the yellow roses arranged in the Chinese vases, in spite of the majestic bier, and the majestic room he waked in, the bishop smelled like a dead cat. As I said my three Hail Marys for the bishop's soul while I circled his bier, I could only mourn the thought of him being buried in the grave with all the lovely gear on him, especially the red velvet, gold tasselled slippers with the little heel. I did a double circle around the bier again to take in the lovely vestments and the jewels on his feet. I fantasised about robbing the clothes off the bishop and his shoes.

I knew what I would do with the bishop's stuff if I could get it home to our room in O'Brien's. I'd rip out the stitching from his robe, and fashion it into a lovely frock for Ma and me to wear. I'd strip the white frothy lace from the cuffs of the surplice and sew the lace round the neck of the frock. I'd make a pair of fancy knickers for Ma and me out of the surplice adding touches of lace on the legs. I'd remove the tassels from the Bishop's slippers and set them aside. I'd be greedy and keep the slippers for myself to dance in up and down the lane. I'd poke a hole through the top of the bishop's mitre with the poker, and sew the tassels from the slippers to the mitre. Then if we ever got electric light in our room, I'd say to Ma, 'Close yer eyes and open yer hands.' I'd put the bishop's mitre in Ma's outstretched hand and say, 'Sunrise! Here is the fanciest lampshade in the whole of Ireland.' As I was pondering all I would do with the bishop's clothing my movements must have come to a standstill, as a firm hand grabbed my elbow and scuttled me out of the room.

More than one kid remarked after paying their respects, that the bishop was a ringer for Captain Hook, except he hadn't a beard and he had both of his arms.

Bridie and I raced back to O'Brien's after viewing the bishop's body. We were glad to be alive and out in the pouring down rain.

The army legacy

I heard Ma inside our room singing as I rattled the doorknob. She knew bars from a lot of songs.

She was a miller's daughter fair . . .
La, la, la, la, la, la.
Came a fisher lad one day . . .
La, la, la, la la, la, la.

'There y'are,' said Ma on seeing me. She was down on her knees scrubbing the floor with a scrub brush and a bucket of soapy water laced with Jeyes' Fluid disinfectant. Ma sang more and more as the days drew near for Da to come home on leave. We all waited for him to come home because he never came empty-handed. He always saved half his army rations in his haversack for us. And while he was home on leave, Da never ate anything without first checking with Ma to see if everyone else had their fill. The few cans of stew and baked beans he managed to put in the haversack for us were like gifts from God. My brothers and I fought over the empty tin cans because a few beans or a peck of stew might be still inside the cans.

I remember some of the times Da came home on leave from the army to see us, especially the last time when it seemed his head had lifted off his shoulders. He jumped up on the chair and onto the table. Then he tried to jump across the table. He began to dance all over the place boasting that Ireland now had a Fred Astaire. He began to croon like a lovesick swain, 'Dinner for one, please, James.

No, Madame will not be dining. Yes you may bring the wine in. Dinner for one please, James.'

When he got through dancing and singing, he became a wrung-out washrag and flopped down on the bed, trying to pull Ma with him. She told him to leave off in front of the children. Then he jumped from the bed, grabbed me and twirled us both around the room until we nearly hit the wall.

Da prided himself on looking the part of the Irish soldier. He kept his uniform pressed, shined the rows of brass buttons on his uniform with Brasso polish 'till the buttons shone like a cat's eye in the dark. He polished his army boots 'till the leather looked like liver. Da couldn't sit still. When it came time for him to return to the barracks, he packed and repacked his haversack. He seemed so young, even then, as he stood to attention in the moss-green wool uniform, hat perched on the side of his head and his blue eyes glowing as he spoke of his love for Ireland.

Ma beamed on him even though he left her without a penny in the house. Before leaving for the barracks, Da gave Ma his new army topcoat to use as a cover for the bed, and hoped the sergeant wouldn't notice the missing coat.

Da enjoyed his time in the army except when the Germans dropped two bombs meant for England on the north side of Dublin. He told me about it.

'At the time I was stationed at the Phoenix Park barracks. I remember it, Titch, as if it were yesterday. May 31, 1941, the day the German Luftwafte bombed the North Strand of Dublin. Our army outfit was the first to arrive at the scene of the bombing. There was people piled under the rubble moaning with pain. One old granny stands out in my mind. She was lying under a pile of plaster and she called out to me. She wanted me to find her little bit of silver that she had saved in a small blue and white striped jug that she had on her mantelpiece. The mantelpiece was in bits. The poor old creature worried more about her few shillings than about her own self. I knew that she was seriously injured, and I directed a priest towards where she lay. She died soon after that. I came across a cot that was still standing on its legs. A babby was in the cot. I thought the poor little thing was asleep until I lifted it up. It was then I discovered that it was stone dead. The babby was no more than five or six months old. He had been sleeping in his little cot when the bomb fell on the house. How can I ever blot it all out of my mind the scenes of that day? The sights of death and injury. I wish I didn't remember, Titch.'

After this last leave, Ma received a letter in the post from an official in the army informing her that Da had been put into the army hospital in Phoenix Park. Ma took me with her to the hospital. She went in to see Da and came out and told me they said he had 'mental exhaustion'. She said she had never heard of anyone going into the hospital for mental exhaustion.

Ma took me along every Sunday to see Da and Frank and Bob stayed at home and watched Noely Joseph. The walk from O'Brien's to the Phoenix Park took all morning. Ma made onion sandwiches to take with us to eat on the way. Sometimes our neighbours gave us the bus fare to go see Da.

Da lay propped up in bed dressed in blue and white striped pyjamas. He looked as if he had got over a case of the measles judging from the splotches on his face. He seemed flushed and jittery. Ma thought his jitters came from his not having anything to drink in the hospital.

Da saved most of his meals at the hospital for Ma and me. He saved all the dessert for me.

Besides other sick Irish soldiers, Da pointed out that the ward also housed a group of German airmen, prisoners of war, shot out of the sky in their planes by the British as they flew over the Irish Sea. A crew from an Irish fishing trawler had pulled the Germans out of the sea, and ferried them back to Dublin. The Irish army planked the sick and injured Germans in with Irish soldiers in the Phoenix Park hospital. According to Da, after the Germans recovered from their injuries the Irish government would hand them over to the English government. He hoped the British would show some mercy towards the Germans.

Da said that the Germans shared chocolate bars and cigarettes with him and all the other Irish soldiers in the ward. A couple of the Germans asked Da about me after a visit. He told the men I was his only daughter. One Sunday, Da gave me a lovely, buttercup-yellow woven basket that the Germans had made for me. The prisoners had collected empty packs of cigarettes, Sweet Afton packs, and wove a basket from the packs.

Da told us that the Germans said I reminded them of their own kids back home, and the younger bloke with the busted leg saw in me the sight of his sister. None of the prisoners knew if any members of their family still remained after the Allied bombing, according to Da.

The beautiful two-handled basket seemed like a heavensent gift to me. While I nursed the basket on my lap, Da whispered for me to wave down the ward and tell the German men 'thanks'. Some of the prisoners could speak a little English, Da pointed out. As I held the basket up in the air and called out 'Thank you' the sad-faced Germans broke into smiles, and clapped their hands in appreciation.

I showed all the neighbours in O'Brien's my lovely yellow basket. While some examined the jewel, I let them know about Da being in the army hospital full of smashed German soldiers. After hearing the account, Granny Redmond rushed in and out of her room and handed me a newly-laid brown hen's egg to put in the bottom of the basket. 'The egg's for yer mother.' Ma later told Granny Redmond that she'd take the fresh egg to Da in the hospital. 'Eat it yerself,' said Granny. 'Me and the kids will have it for dinner,' Ma assured her. In order to dispel any sombre feelings, Ma joked to Granny Redmond that an egg without salt was like a kiss from a beardless man. Her joke floated over my head. The ways of men and women were mysterious for a girl of my age.

When he left the hospital the Irish army gave Da a medical discharge. Da, still sick and now unemployed, caused havoc. The army washed their hands of any responsibility towards Da, his wife and children. The government gave Da a monthly army pension of three pounds for the six of us to live on. Ma realised her family had landed on spikes. She searched for work as a washerwoman, a dishwasher or whatever would bring in a few shillings to keep us from starving.

Da stayed in bed for a long time after he got home. He sat up in the bed and stared into space all day. He never moved or spoke to anyone except Ma. I didn't understand his strange behaviour. The red flush on his face began to fade. Once when he broke through his feeling of despair he called me to the bed and said, 'Wee Titch, my wee duck, what is going to happen to your father?' Sometimes his body shook like a willow before a storm. Ma covered him with a blanket.

I felt Da's isolation and pain although unable to voice a word. I'd sit by the bed and blow warm breath across his cold hands trying to warm him. All he said was he hoped I'd have a future, live to see better days, and pleaded, 'Titch, never sell your hens on a wet day.'

It seemed a long time before Da began to get well. He often fell on the floor in some kind of fit, his body twitching and eyes rolling back in his head. Ma dropped to her knees beside him and cradled him in her arms until he regained his senses. It seemed ages before he even left the room and went outdoors.

All the time, Ma fended for us and took care of Da, who didn't seem to have the sense of Noely Joseph. When I stayed with him alone he started to act strange. He'd get out of the bed and slap me as hard as he could with the palm of his hand on my buttocks leaving me black and blue. Other times he pushed me down on the bed and tickled 'til I screamed for him to stop, but he continued. If I cried he cupped his hand over my face until no sound escaped.

I didn't want to tell Ma about his bad behaviour and worry her more, but when I refused to stay alone with Da in the room, Ma smelled a rat. I showed her my bruised thighs and she went white with rage.

She confronted Da about the beatings. Ma told me that she told him never to lay a finger on me again or she'd saw his heart in two. Afraid of the madman, I followed Ma everywhere like a waddling duck.

Da was getting an army pension of three pounds a month but before Ma could cash Da's pension, she first had to have it signed by the parish priest in Saint Mary's. Da got angry at such an arrangement. He complained that his army pension should have nothing to do with the Catholic Church. But without the priest's signature, his pension cheque could not be cashed.

Month after month, Ma had to go up to the church and wait for a priest to sign Da's pension. It often meant waiting around the corridor of the church for an hour or so. Da didn't have the physical stamina for the ordeal of taking his cheque up to the priest to sign. The priest always quizzed Ma and me, as he signed the pension, whether we said our prayers rigorously and attended Sunday mass. He quizzed Ma on whether she kept her children away from seeing films that had been condemned by the Church. He'd ask whether she said the rosary in the family, and if she ever served her family meat on a Friday. Similar interrogation went on for half an hour.

After the priest signed the pension cheque, Ma rushed all the way to the bank in Baggot Street to cash it. Then she hurled herself all the way back to O'Brien's to get the four of us ready for school, and look after Da.

Da wondered if the coppers went through the same hoops in cashing their pensions as soldiers were forced to.

In disgust, Da shouted that Irish Free State soldiers were treated like the scum of the earth by the nation, while priests and lawmen were sucked up to. Ma paid all the bills due out of the pension. She purchased all kinds of things on credit from the pedlars who came into O'Brien's to sell their wares. And sometimes she had to meet with our rent collector, Mr Ferguson, especially if arrears were due. Without Da's monthly army pension, small as it was, we would all have likely perished.

It seemed unreal that with Da finally on the mend Ma should get sick. I asked her what caused the pain? 'Me body is sick and injured,' she replied going no further. I told her I wanted to see what caused the pain. She continued to give me the deaf ear. I persisted until she pulled off her vest and showed me bunches of red festering sores under her armpits and under both of her breasts. The terrible sight and the agony they caused made us both cry. She screamed when she had to pee. My brothers did not know the cause of Ma's injuries either. Her sickness remained a mystery.

Da was beside himself regarding Ma's illness. I overheard him telling her that he would kill himself if it would undo the damage. He begged Ma to go to see a doctor at an outpatients clinic that he knew about. Ma refused to go near such a place. She asked Da what would happen if any of the neighbours were to see her going into or coming out of the clinic. She whispered that she would rather die than bring shame upon the heads of her four innocent children. She also asked Da what people in the public health service would do if they found out about her ailment. Would they come and take us away because of her illness?

All the questions left me in a state of bewilderment. I sensed that the conversations between Ma and Da were not for our ears, and that the injuries to Ma's body were unlike any other.

Da told Ma in no uncertain terms to rid her head of rubbish about what anyone thought. He told her over and over under his breath to stop acting foolish and see a doctor. The excruciating pain of having to pee finally drove Ma to the clinic for medical help.

After her first visit to the clinic, she wobbled home. Her face looked like grey ash and her blue eyes looked as dead as a doornail. I asked what caused her to wobble. She said her thighs hurt from two walloping penicillin injections that the doctor had given her. I asked her to show me the places where the needles went in. Ma pulled up her skirt, and I saw the walnut sized bumps on each of her thighs from the penicillin injections and the red inflamed rings around them.

She asked me to take Noely Joseph outside so she could lie down 'til the fireworks went out of her head. She warned me not to let Noely chase after any strange dogs because she feared one might bite him and give him rabies. I took Noely outside and held his hand. He spotted a straggler dog wandering into O'Brien's, sniffing the gutters in hopes of finding a finger of food. The straggler, like other mangy dogs, came into O'Brien's with an empty belly and usually left in the same condition. Noely tugged us both towards a mangy mutt entering the lane. 'Here, goggie, goggie, goggie,' he said, holding a small hand towards the mutt hoping for a lick.

Sometimes, Ma lost composure and burst into tears in front of us all. Her tears hit us like buckshot. The sight of Ma crying stunned Da, Frank, Bob, myself and Noely Joseph. We looked and felt like wounded animals in a trap unable to do anything. Ma restrained her tears when she realised the pain it caused. She had only to look at Da to realise that if she did not hide her pain, she'd soon have a ghost on her hands.

Da told me to go with Ma to the clinic and make sure she got home all right. Ma protested against taking me near such a place. I begged her to take me along because I loved her and wanted to help. She bade me wait at the top of Upper Mount Street while she went to the clinic. As I waited for her, I played cat's cradle with a length of red yarn. I figured out how to use the yarn to cat's cradle the shape of a parachute, a scissors, a fan and the gates of heaven. After I got weary of cat cradling, I circled around a lamp-post until I got dizzy. Then I put my forehead against the metal post to blot out what was happening to my mother in the clinic. The hard metal felt soothing against my head as I waited for her to come.

After Ma got through with the treatment, she'd limp to the top of the street where she'd find me waiting. I'd take her by the hand and walk her home in baby steps.

One morning after she came out of the clinic, cradling her arm sore from the penicillin injections, she mulled aloud about one of the doctors at the clinic. The doctor had comforted Ma by telling her that she had no reason to feel any shame, that she hadn't brought whatever ailed her on herself, and that she had to stop blaming herself and making herself sick from shame. He also told Ma that the army doctor who took care of Da in the hospital in Phoenix Park should have made her aware of Da's sickness.

After Ma got finished airing her head about what the doctor said, I asked her if Da gave her the terrible sores that made her cry out with pain. 'Yes,' she said.

'Ma, do ye want me to kill him? Shoot him?'

'Kill who? shoot who? What are ye talking about?' she asked with horror.

'I'm talking about the auld fella. I'm talking about Da! I know how to shoot him. All I have to do is get a rifle and cock it over me knee to break it apart. Then I take two bullets out of me vest, put them in the barrel and cock the gun back shut. I aim it at his eye and pull the trigger. Out will pop a puff of smoke, and he'll fall down dead in a jiffy.'

'My God, what are ye saying? Do ye know what ye just said?'

'I know how to kill him,' I repeated.

'My God what is the world coming to? Where did ye learn all about shooting from?'

'I learned it from the pictures, that's where,' I told her with irritation.

'But ye love yer daddy and he loves you!' she continued as if to herself. 'No one in the whole of Ireland would believe a girl would say such a thing. My God, to think about a seven-year-old girl from O'Brien's Place shooting her father!'

'I won't kill him if ye don't want me to.' Then I asked her if she still had a heart for him.

She sighed with a weariness and said, 'I have half a heart for him. I used to have a whole heart for him, but now it's half a heart.'

'I only have half a heart for him too,' I fired back, trying to be on the same wavelength.

It took a lot of visits to the clinic before Ma's terrible sores faded. She had to bathe them in a mixture of hydrogen peroxide and warm water three times a day. She dabbed under her arms and under her breasts with the mixture. Then she lifted her skirt and squatted over the basin to finish her treatment, her face grimacing with pain. She burned all the soiled cotton wool in the fireplace.

Trying to be helpful, I offered to empty the washbasin and burn the dirty cotton wool, but Ma would not let me lay a finger on either. Nor would she let me kiss her until all the lesions had disappeared. Ma explained her reluctance by telling me that when I got to be a *cailín mór*, a big girl, she'd tell me more.

Johnny Duggan

If Da had a friend outside of Ma, it had to be Johnny Duggan from upstairs in our building. When Johnny passed Da in the hallway, he'd call out, 'Morra, Frank. There y'are. How are ye? Did that army outfit break yer spirit?' His room sat directly above ours and the old man's constant shuffling back and forth across the floor caused specks of plaster to fall down on us like snowflakes. He and Granny Martin were my favourite neighbours in O'Brien's. I felt lucky they lived in the same tenement as ours. Granny Martin had an eye for the elderly Johnny but in a reverential way. To her eyes Johnny fitted the picture of a saint in street clothes. 'Ye only have to look into his countenance to see his goodness,' she'd say. No one ever had a bad word to say about the elderly bachelor. Johnny chuckled at Da while eyeballing me and noted 'She's a girl who nails things in her head.'

Johnny said the same things over and over to Da. People like Johnny, who repeated the same thing, were accused of 'boiling their cabbage twice'. Sometimes a girl had to clip her tongue in order to be respectful to elders like Johnny who boiled his cabbage constantly. Kids who backcheeked or showed disrespect to elderly people in O'Brien's got their ears clattered.

The elderly, heavyset Johnny stood head and shoulders in height above the rest of the men in O'Brien's Place. He had the frame of an oak, said Granny Martin. Johnny's only perceivable flaws were all the purple splotches on his big face. Ma thought his splotches were connected to a heart problem. Granny Martin called the purple splotches 'portwine marks'.

Granny Martin thought portwine marks came as a result of a pregnant mother eating radishes before the birth of her baby. One

Saturday Granny Martin took me with her into Moore Street, to buy cheap vegetables. 'D'ye see that poor woman?' said Granny pointing to a dealer women selling oranges and apples. The dealer woman had the biggest portwine mark I'd ever seen. It completely covered one side of her face. The dealer woman's birthmark and Johnny Duggan's streaky blotches were like night and day.

I had an opinion about what caused Johnny's portwine birthmarks. Once he showed a few of us kids the way he lassoed and captured the grey and inkblue wild pigeons. He had learned how to capture them after seeing a Hopalong Cassidy picture at the cinema. Johnny made a lariat out of a piece of cord and fashioned one end into a loop. He put the loop on the outside windowsill trailing the tail of the cord into the room. Then he dabbed clear coloured glue into the loop. He broke off a chunk of white bread from a loaf and rolled the chunk in his big hands 'til it crumbled like rice.

'Ye use white bread because pigeons are just like youse, they don't like brown bread,' he noted. He lowered the window and held the end of the cord. We watched and waited for the sight of a pigeon from behind a lace curtain blackened over the years by soot.

A pigeon flying over O'Brien's noticed the breadcrumbs on the windowsill and came in for a landing. It landed first on the outer ledge of the windowsill. The grey and navy-blue feathered pigeon bobbed its head then tip-toed into the loop to peck up the crumbs. As the bird pecked up the crumbs it circled in the loop getting its feet sticky with glue.

The bird looked about then looked down at its feet now sticky with glue and caked in breadcrumbs, as if to ask 'What in jeepers is going on here?' While the pigeon pondered, Johnny Duggan yanked the cord from inside the room and lassoed its legs. He raised the window, and whipped in the flabbergasted bird. We heard Johnny crack its neck, and the pigeon went limp. Its tiny head tippled over to one side. 'Me dinner,' boasted Johnny, his face as red as the reddest balloon.

My brother Bob thought God must be raging at Johnny for polishing off so many pigeons as if pigeons were on a par with fish and chips. What a shock to realise that Johnny—the saint in street clothes—had the mind and appetite of a cannibal. Had not his cannibalising of so many inky-blue pigeons caused the purple spidering on his face, which for all the world resembled pigeon tracks? We were sure of it.

Johnny left his room every morning to attend the seven o'clock mass at Saint Mary's in rain or shine. The man burst with religion and his devotion to the blessed virgin verged on rapture. He had a homemade altar to the blessed mother in his room. Myself, Fanny and Angie Bray pestered Johnny to let us come into his room and see the altar.

Johnny's altar to the virgin stood in the middle of the wall. Constructed from discarded wooden crates from Cantrell and Cochrane's mineral water works, the altar looked like a pile of rubble that would topple at a touch. A chalk statue of the blessed virgin, arms open wide, stood in the middle of the pile. Over the years, grime had turned the image into an aborigine. Her eyes were closed from soot.

Johnny had outlined the virgin's mouth with coral lipstick, and smudged a dab on each side of her face. He had placed a glass jamjar on each side of the altar and stuffed them with crinkled paper flowers, the kind sold in Woolworths for a penny a piece. Buttends, left over from burned out candles, were stuck to the wooden crates like flattened moths.

Johnny turned to Fanny, Angie and myself and said as he pointed to the statue of the virgin, 'Everything on me altar is blessed by her. She has the power to bless this box of Friendly Matches I'm holding in me hand. Our Lady is the queen of Ireland.'

The four of us dropped to our knees before the altar to pray. After the prayers, Johnny walked over to the mantelpiece and took down a blue shaving mug. He dipped two long fingers into the mug and fished up a threepenny bit. He handed the coin to Fanny and told her to exchange it for three pennies. She was to keep a penny for herself, give a penny to her sister, and a penny to me. While we thanked Johnny for letting us see his altar and for giving us a penny, his eyes darted towards the window. He jammed the three of us out the door, but not before I saw the rope jigging on the floor and the sound of a pigeon pecking its beak on the windowpane.

It seemed like a miracle that anyone would give away a three-penny bit with money being so scarce. The things a penny could buy at the corner shop! A penny could buy a fizzbag with a straw or four honeybee camels or a peppermint drumstick or a long whip of black liquorice or a handful of dolly mixtures. Or you could try your luck and put the penny in the slot-machine and hope for a fortune. How many times did the three red cherries nearly, line up in a row to pay out ten shillings? How many times did a girl cup her hand under the spout of the slot-machine waiting for God to deliver?

One Friday morning Johnny didn't come thudding down to empty the slop. This should have been a warning something was amiss. Johnny didn't leave the room all day. Ma thought he might have stayed in bed because it was so cold out. When he failed to make an appearance all the way to Sunday, Ma's antenna went up. Then on Sunday afternoon, drops of water began to fall from our ceiling, and it smelled bad.

Could it be from Johnny's bucket? wondered Ma. She called Granny Martin into the room and pointed to the ceiling. Granny Martin saw the seepage coming through the ceiling and guessed the worst. 'Merciful Jaysus, O merciful God, what ails Johnny?' she cried out. Ma added, 'Heart a God, Heart a God! Granny Martin, somethin's the matter with Johnny!'

Ma and Granny shouted up the stairs to the Brays who lived across the landing from Johnny. 'Mrs Bray, Mrs Bray are ye in?' they yelled. Mrs Bray and her grown children, Daisy and Mickey, ran down the stairs at the sound of the alarm.

The Bray family worked at odd jobs all over the city. Fanny and Angie were usually the only ones at home during the day. Mrs Bray stood with folded arms taking in the whole picture. She suggested that someone call the police. Mrs Bray, Ma, and Granny Martin went up the stairs and knocked on Johnny's door.

'Run down the lane and get a copper to come,' said Mrs Bray. My brother Frank jumped in and told everyone he'd go and bring back a copper.

While we waited for Frank to bring back a policeman, silence fell over our tenement. Granny Martin pulled her shawl tight about her. Ma made the sign of the cross. Frank finally appeared with Sergeant Duffy in tow. The sergeant took the stairs in two until he reached the upstairs landing. He rapped on Johnny's door and called out, 'Mr Duggan are you in there? Mr Duggan do you hear me?' Not a sound came back from behind the door.

Sergeant Duffy told Ma and Granny Martin that he thought Johnny had died. He wanted to know if Johnny had any ailments that anyone knew of. Granny Martin said only his portwine marks. Ma told him that Johnny never complained to her about anything being wrong with him.

Sergeant Duffy said he'd be off to find a doctor and put in a phone call to the morgue from Ryan's pub. Some men came and knocked Johnny's door down. Johnny lay spread-eagled on the floor in the middle of the room, the slopbucket now empty at his feet. The men put Johnny in a wooden crate and lowered the crate out of his window to the ground, and hauled Johnny's body off to the morgue.

Later in the week, Sergeant Duffy came to our hallway and told us that Johnny had died from a massive stroke. Johnny had no family that anyone knew of. Someone mentioned he had a brother who had emigrated to America, years ago. Everyone in O'Brien's went to the rosary for him at Saint Mary's. Ma tried to comfort me about Johnny's death by letting me know that as soon as Johnny's head hit the floor his soul lit for heaven. Granny Martin said Johnny had returned home, and that was that.

Grannies

Granny Martin and her son, Jamey, were a cosy twosome in their room and a half. For the sake of modesty, Granny Martin had fixed-up a snug nest for Jamey in one corner of the room. He slept on a couch behind a flower-patterned curtain.

Granny Martin's eldest son, the Panther, had electricity installed in the room for his mother and Jamey. The Panther made his living as a moneylender and bookmaker. He worked the greyhound dog races at Shelbourne Park and Harold's Cross, and in between times he made loans to poor people. The Panther's younger brother Jamey remained a bachelor and continued to live with Granny Martin.

Jamey sold the evening newspapers on O'Connell Bridge and he never got home until late. His mother often got lonely and asked me over to keep her company. I'd spend the evening with Granny by the fireplace and marvel that she had so many lovely things. The Panther lavished nice things on his mother. He had her room replastered and wallpapered. The wallpaper had little Dutch boys and girls and windmills all over in the colours of blue and red. The son also had someone lay linoleum over the bare floor. The room looked like a palace compared with our chickencoop that squeaked with six people fighting over an inch of space to call their own.

Winter evenings stirred Granny Martin's memories, which fell from her head like confetti, especially memories of her only daughter, Emily, her 'jewel and darling', who had died at the age of twelve from meningitis. Granny kept a charcoal sketch of Emily at ten years of age hanging on the wall over her bed.

Granny told me that Emily went so quick—her love, her child, her only girl—then she'd sob. The sight of Emily, seemingly so healthy, broke the heart of anyone who looked at the picture. Granny would say that it seemed only yesterday that Emily's arms were round her waist, and she'd sob some more. When tears ceased over the loss of Emily and Granny Martin dried her eyes and mine, it was time for tea and cakes.

Granny loved fairy cakes, small round cakes filled with jam and slathered with sugar icing. Granny joyfully mauled the small cakes with her gums, advising me in between mauls to take care of my teeth, or I'd end up gummy like her. She served the cakes and tea on blue willow pattern china. She liked a drop of whiskey in her tea, and on occasion would drop a dollop in mine. While we sipped our tea out of the lovely china cups and polished off every crumb of the cakes, memories continued to pour. Granny only had a sliver of memory left about her long, dead husband, Nacker. 'Ah, he died long ago. Lots a water spilled 'neat O'Connell Bridge since Nacker toppled down dead on the floor,' she said.

Wednesday evenings were the only evenings I hadn't a welcome at Granny Martin's. The Panther, dropped in for his dinner every Wednesday evening before he headed off to the greyhound races at Shelbourne Park.

Granny Martin seemed to lose her marbles every Wednesday the way she fussed and fretted about finding the best bit of lean corned beef and the freshest green head of cabbage for the Panther's dinner. She slow-simmered the corned beef all day in a big black pot then about an hour from the time her son was to arrive for his dinner, she dropped in the spuds and cabbage. The smell of the corned beef simmering all day filled our hallway and it nearly caused me to faint with hunger.

When the Panther stepped into our hallway on a Wednesday evening he bellowed out for the benefit of his mother behind the door, 'Yum, yum! Pig's bum, cabbage and potatoes.'

'That you, Paddy darling?' she'd yell. 'Yer bit a grub is ready!'

After he'd eaten Granny Martin's grub, the Panther set up business in our hallway. People from O'Brien's lined up to borrow money from him. Some said, the begrudgers, as his mother called them, that the Panther charged more than an arm and a leg in interest on money he lent out.

Ma had borrowed from the Panther, and like so many others, she waited in dread for him to finish his dinner, hoping that in the light of Jesus, he enjoyed the grub and it would put him in a good mood. For every ten bob Ma borrowed from him, she paid back five shillings extra. She'd been paying off the Panther since I knew her. He got real mean if anyone reneged on a payment. The men in the laneway feared him and sent over their wives to deal with him when they needed to borrow some money. Ma feared him.

After he got through with taking in payments and giving out loans, the Panther often pitched me a penny. He knew Granny liked him to toss a penny my way. 'Did Paddy give ye a hansel?' she'd ask as he headed out the hall door, pockets a jingle.

Kids in O'Brien's teased Granny Martin due to the rhyming possibilities of her last name. It drove her to distraction when impertinent kids sat under her windowsill and wailed,

Granny Martin, Granny Martin,
The cat's fartin.
Where, where?
Under the chair.
Where's the chair?
On the grass.
Where's the grass?
Up yer arse!

Granny Martin would rip from her room and streak into the laneway calling out after the kids that they were whore's melts.

Kids also teased Jamey Martin about the way he sounded when he sold the newspapers. Jamey sing-songed to all passersby, 'Git yer early Mail and early 'erald '. His mother said that her Jamey walked the length of O'Connell Bridge to earn a few shilling in all kinds of weather. When he came home at night he usually had a stack of unsold papers under an arm and one hand in his trouser pocket, the fingers counting the nightly earnings. Granny Martin made more of a fuss over the Panther, but Jamey kept her on tippy toes the rest of the time. Unlike his talkative mother or his older brother, the Panther, Jamey latched his gob. He never spoke a word to anyone as he went in and out of our building or on his way to the lavs to have a piss. When it came to his mother though, he'd stars in the eyes.

Granny cleaned her room from head to toe once a week. She'd run me around to the shop on the corner to buy a bar of blacklead. I'd watch as she put the bar of blacklead on a saucer, pour a few drops of water on the bar to soften it, wrap her two fingers with an old sock, rub the sock on the blacklead, and apply the sock to blacken the wrought-iron grate, firescreen and black kettle. She rubbed and rubbed until sweat dampened her brow. She continued her polishing until she saw her face reflected on the side of the kettle.

Sometimes Granny annoyed me, but she especially annoyed me over her bed. The brass frame glittered and shone like an altar rail. Granny had three palliasses tied on top of the bed like steps of stairs. She kept a small ladder hooked over the end of the bed and used it to get in and get out. No one ever saw the bed unmade. Only the outer linens were ever revealed. She covered the bed with a lovely soft white bedspread that draped down to the floor. It was edged with puffy white pompoms that looked like rows of snowballs. She had four plump pillows covered in soft white cotton that cuddled at the head of the brass bed like lambs on a hillside.

The overall look of the bed with its gleaming brass frame, the soft white bedspread trimmed in snowballs, and the cuddled pillows caused a girl to yawn and long for sleep. Nobody, not even Jamey or the Panther dared lay a finger on the bed, nor could a child brush against it. 'Don't touch me bed!' she'd bawl, wagging a finger in front of my nose. 'Granny Martin, I'm only dancing me fingers along the spread.' 'Keep yer hands in yer pockets, that's a good girl.'

One night Granny decided to get ready for bed while I was still in the room. She took off the bedspread and put it on the back of a chair. She stripped off the pillowcases and put them over the bedspread. Then she kicked off her black boots and climbed up the ladder in her stockinged feet. When she reached the top of the ladder, she turned towards me, then toppled backwards into a dirty nest sending skimpy old feathers flying everywhere.

'Why do ye sleep up there, Granny?'

'Haven't I told ye a half dozen times? I can't shut an eye unless I'm off the floor. Are ye a gillygoosey or d'ye pay no attention? Sssh! Saah! Switch me light off and go across to yer mother, Mary O'Connor, til morn.'

Sometimes Granny checked on her burial stuff that she kept in a cardboard box inside a dresser drawer. She expected my complete attention as she took out the box and untied the string. Then she'd take out her blue burial shroud with the long cord, her white laying out sheet, a small glass dish for holy water, two copper pennies to be placed over her eyes, a pair of candles, and a box of matches, and she'd put them all on the table for me to admire.

After she had checked and rechecked to make sure all was in order, she'd tell me to help her fold her shroud, and she'd put everything back in the cardboard box and return it to the middle drawer of her dresser.

The frequent sight of the blue shroud, the laying-out sheet, the two pennies, the holy water dish, the tallow candles, and the box of matches depressed me, so I would try to distract Granny Martin by directing her attention to the birds chirping on her windowsill, but she'd rather tut-tut over the burial things.

I started to catch on when the mood overcame Granny to check on her burial things one more time. She'd stare at the middle drawer in the dresser where she stored the stuff. As soon as I spied her eyes locking onto the drawer, I'd pretend I had to use the outdoor lavatory, that I had to do my number two and not my number one, so it would be a while and she would not chide me for the delay.

Granny insisted on having everything in order for her burial because she didn't want either the Panther or Jamey to worry about anything if she died. She expected to die first. Little did she know that Jamey would be the first to topple.

When the winter flu hit hard one year, Jamey got pneumonia. His hard hoarse cough echoed all throughout the tenement. He coughed his lungs up from morning 'til night.

Granny Martin called in a doctor and paid him five shillings for the visit, a fortune at the time, but it did no good. She fixed Jamey cabbage soup, whiskey soup and oxtail soup. She dowsed him down with castor oil, and made hot dough poultices to place on his chest, but nothing cleared up the phlegm that had hardened in Jamey's chest. Da said only a pick-axe could hack out the congealment in Jamey's lungs. Jamey died before the first speck of spring returned to O'Brien's.

Granny Martin cried like a banshee. Her whole friendly being dwindled to despair. She let her usual careful appearance collapse: her white hair, that used to be neatly coiled, was now dishevelled round her shoulders like a pale fog. Granny Martin was lost to the world. She stopped gussying-up her bed, refused to utter a word to anyone, hissed at the priest trying to tell her Jamey was now better off, and even pushed away the fairy cake Ma bought me to give her.

Some in O'Brien's thought that Granny Martin was finally wrecked. The old widow walked up and down the laneway babbling and chatting out loud to herself about Jamey: how she needed to wash and darn his wool socks, put a new button on his striped shirt, and get him a nice crusty pan loaf to go with a hardboiled egg for his tea; take his one old boot to be mended and re-studded at Nick's shoe shop, first thing in the morning. Then she stopped in her tracks and told all the world that her son Jamey had never been like some in the laneway—like cornerboys. He'd worked 'til he got walloped with the pneumonia, Granny gurgled. When she wailed, Granny Martin opened her mouth wide and I could see her only tooth rooted alone like a miniature lighthouse on a shelf in the bay.

Other days, Granny Martin stood in our hallway gawking up and down O'Brien's waiting to catch the familiar sight of Jamey coming home from selling his newspapers on O'Connell Bridge.

'God help us,' Ma remarked on noticing how Granny Martin's keen green eyes were becoming more and more clouded. The neighbours and Ma continued to beg Granny Martin to take a bite to eat or drink a sup of tea, but she refused, and acted with annoyance at being approached. Jamey's death wrecked her as her only daughter's death must have long ago.

Things didn't start to get better for Granny Martin until Granny Doyle sauntered into our building. Granny Doyle lived in a room in the same building as the O'Dowd's. She knocked on Granny Martin's door every afternoon at two on the dot. At first Granny Martin ignored Granny Doyle's gentle knock, her louder knock, her annoyance knock, but she could not ignore her front door any longer when Granny Doyle tried to heave it off the hinges. After some talk,

Granny Doyle had Granny Martin put on her coat, led her out of the room, into the hallway, and in the direction of Ryan's pub.

Granny Doyle never made any bones about her fondness for a drink or two. She firmly believed that a drink would sweep the cobwebs out of the mind, and she challenged Granny Martin to take her advice. Every day for the rest of our days in O'Brien's Place, Granny Doyle and Granny Martin were seen linking arms as they shimmied over the cobblestones on their way to Ryan's.

The pair of old ladies became the best of friends. Granny Martin nearly gained back her old self. In fact, she became fashion conscious. She stopped wearing her black woollen shawl going to the pub. She wore her best long skirt that came down to the tip of her high laced ankle boots. She wore her Sunday hat with its mountain of feathers. Granny Martin must have liked the idea of parading around with a pigeon's roost on her head.

Granny Doyle draped her ample figure in layers of black clothing. She pounded the lane in her hobnailers with determination in her stride. Unlike the even-tempered Granny Martin, Granny Doyle had a reputation for being a bit of a rip-roarer when crossed. Some in O'Brien's called her a 'cross auld heifer' but anyone foolish enough to cross her the wrong way had to be fond of a stay in hospital.

Granny Doyle's husband, Nutley, had died before she moved into a room in O'Brien's. She told stories about what a great and good man Nutley had been. Until his death, Nutley worked as a cleaner on the trains in Westland Row railway station. Somehow he had managed to acquire a scale model of a real train engine. The model engine became the pride and joy of the Doyles who never had any children. Granny Doyle kept the model on a table in front of her window. Everyone in O'Brien's stopped to look at the engine. Once in a kid's life Granny Doyle would let him or her in to look at the engine firsthand, but not before she pushed them to the back of the room. She did not want a kid to breathe or cough near the model for fear of causing rust. And no one could touch the engine.

Then, God help us, Georgie Wright, a husky boy of nine years old, broke into Granny Doyle's room while she was away in the pub and made off with the engine. Startled eyes watched Georgie puffing down the lane in broad daylight with Nutley's engine glued to his chest. Georgie's mother found him and the engine under the bed in their room. The poor woman, who was pregnant at the time, with trembling lips told the onlookers that her Georgie must be undergoing a dose of brain fever, and that he had no idea that he had lifted Granny Doyle's engine off the table and taken it out of the room.

We waited for Granny Doyle to get back to her room. None of us went near her building. Bomber Rafferty later gave us an account of what he had heard. He'd been in bed sleeping having worked the night before: 'Thunderin' Jaysus, the roar she let off when she saw Nutley's engine gone. Jaysus, I thought sometin' terrible happened, like Nutley had returned from the dead or somethin'. She nearly slit both me ears with her shrieks of "Where's the engine? Where's Nutley's engine? Where's me dead husband's pride? Whoever took that engine, when I find them, I'm going to cleave their head off!"'

How Georgie ever got up the nerve to take the train back, God only knows. Some of us followed him as he returned the engine. Granny Doyle gave him a tongue-lashing the likes of which was never heard before or since in the laneway, ever! She roared into his face, 'I'll melt the heart out of ye, Georgie Wright, or anyone else young or auld, Protestant or Catholic, who dares lay a finger on my Nutley's engine. Jaysus be t'Christ I won't be responsible for me actions. I'm lettin ye off easy Georgie Wright because of the state of yer mother. Only for that ye'd go home without a head.'

Then she followed Georgie as he headed home, his head glued to the ground. The tongue-lashing lasted until Georgie ran into his hallway and into the room. The continuing uproar caused Granny Doyle's chins to sway like the tide. After the outburst, a neighbour took Granny Doyle back home afraid that the hysterical woman might have a stroke.

Granny Legg, or the 'garboil' as Granny Martin preferred to call her, caused more strife in O'Brien's than anyone else who lived there. Legg, well on in age, lived alone in one room. She never went anywhere without her walking cane and used the stick to point out evil in the world. She used to lift the hem of our dresses with her stick while she complained how in modern times a girl's frock barely covered the knees. She hooked up the edge of my dress with the crook of her cane, while ranting, 'Cover them knees if ye're over seven. Shame, shame, shame!'

All the kids did a bunk when they saw the old biddy heading in their direction, hellbent on some cause. Ma and other mothers told their kids to show respect for elders in O'Brien, but keeping a civil manner around Legg, with the tip of her walking stick under my frock, required me to have the patience of a saint. I mocked the biddy by muttering a limerick under my breath:

Old wigger, old wigger, how dare you presume
To piss in the bed with the po in the room?

Da taught me the raunchy limerick with the same nonchalance he had me memorise the sacred Agnus Dei.

Granny Legg nagged at Granny Lynch, pestering her for years to explain her relationship to the woman she lived with. Granny Lynch told everyone Kitty was her niece, but Legg insisted to whoever happened to be in earshot, that Kitty bore no resemblance to any Lynch, or anyone on the other side of the family, for that matter. Kitty and Granny were the most resourceful and remarkable females I knew; for example, neither one ever made a fuss or gushed over babies, or went 'goo goo' into an infant's face as the new mother tried to show off her treasure. Instead Granny Lynch and Kitty would gaze at a baby, look at its mother's faded face, and inhale in unison as if to exclaim, 'Sweet mother of God!' The pair's seeming indifference to infants and eligible menfolk in O'Brien's appeared fishy to the hardboiled Legg.

Unlike anyone else in O'Brien's, Granny Lynch and Kitty rented out a postage-sized fenced plot of scrub behind the laneway. No one in the lane dared to set foot in the place. Granny Lynch scrawled on the front of the entrance, in black heavy pencil, 'KEEP OUT'. The two worked from morn to eve to raise pigs and chickens on the plot.

About twice a year, Granny Lynch appeared in the middle of O'Brien's wearing a long apron over her clothes. A butcher's set of slaughtering tools was girdled around her waist. Kitty stood by, and handed Granny a sharpening stone which she used to sharpen the blade of the knife 'til it glittered like ice, then nodding to onlookers, she headed for the plot of scrub, selected a baby pig and chopped off its head. After the kill, Granny Lynch came back into the laneway looking like a deranged demon, her grey wispy short hair spiked like nails; the agate blue eyes busting out of their sockets; the determined mouth rigid as a horseshoe. Kitty carried the carcase of the limp pink creature, Granny held the head like a trophy. The two women sold the carcase to the butcher's shop in Bath Avenue, for badly needed cash. And as I passed their doorway, I spied Granny Lynch as she pitched the smiling head into a pot of water nestled down deeply on a bed of red coals while Kitty stood by with a head of cabbage at the ready.

Granny Lynch seemed fierce and independent compared to all the others in O'Brien's. She also had the reputation of being the most religious person in the neighbourhood. She attended the devotion to the sacred heart of Jesus, devotion to the blessed virgin Mary, devotion to Saint Joseph, and prayers for the pope, the bishop and the priests. I saw her at them all.

Granny Lynch kept an eye out for anyone from O'Brien's who attended the devotions at Saint Mary's church. I used to go to all the evening devotions at Saint Mary's just to get out of our stifling room and to be alone. The quiet and spaciousness of the church became a refuge when life in our room seemed unbearable.

The beautiful church with its coloured glass windows and all the images of the saints, angels, and Jesus and Mary were as familiar to me as Ma, Da, Frank, Bob, and Noely Joseph. Best of all, none of the plaster images could talk or argue, and the sing-song voices of the priests sent me asleep in the pew.

My presence in the church did not go unnoticed by Granny Lynch, who thought me a remarkably religious child. As I roused myself after the devotions, Granny Lynch, on her way out of the church came over to me and wriggled a penny into my hand. She never invited me to sit with her in the pew.

Things happen in threes

Ryan's pub served as the drinking spot for Bath Avenue, Lansdowne Road, an occasional toff from Haddington Road, and the people in O'Brien's. The publican, a tall robust man, had a wife and three kids. The family lived in rooms above the pub. The three children attended private school somewhere in the city; they were not allowed to play with the kids in O'Brien's. Granny Martin, a regular to the pub, declared that fairies would never make it their business to cart off the plain looking Ryan kids. The mother never gave an eye to any of our mothers in the lane.

The publican's manner with his customers bordered on the curt. At closing time, he bellowed for all to hear: 'Time, gentlemen, please'—his way of telling drinkers to clear out of the pub.

Ma used to get me to run round to the pub to tell Da that he needed to come home. He never liked to be fetched from his perch on the stool among his cronies. I'd tell Da that Ma had his bit of grub ready for him and that if he didn't come it would be his own fault if the food burned to a pitch.

The dimly lit pub reeked of porter, unwashed men, pipe and cigarette smoke, sawdust and stale farts. Elders mulled over their frothy necked pints as they sat on barstools belly-up to the long counter, as if they had all the time in the world. The younger men drank with others their own age at various spots across the pub. The younger men yapped the loudest and lowered their pints the fastest as if they were on the run. Men like Da looked at their drink as if it were the final one, knowing all too well that a line-up would follow, come hell or high water.

Kids often got a slap across the head for coming into the pub and calling their relatives home, but a few fathers and uncles called out to the counterman to pour a bottle of lemonade or orange squash for a son or a nephew.

Sitting on the high barstool next to Da, I felt as if I was on a tree top. While I slowly sipped the lemonade, I listened to the noise of all the chatter going on in the pub. I smelled the drink, took in the smell of sawdust scattered underfoot, inhaled the clouds of choking pipe and cigarette smoke, squeezed my nose at sour farts and observed the obvious signs of objection on some faces at the sight of me seated in the men's part of the pub. Da asked if I were ready yet to run home. I turned to him and said, 'Ma can bloody well wait her time 'til we are good and ready to leave.'

The Guinness's brewery lorry parked at the top of O'Brien's twice a week to deliver barrels of porter to Ryan's pub. All the kids in the lane gathered around the lorry when it parked. We liked to watch the driver set up the ramp on the back of the lorry to roll down the huge wooden barrels of porter onto the street. Then he would roll each one into the storage area behind the pub. The same man delivered the barrels of porter every time. We pestered him to let us ride in the back of the lorry as he headed down O'Brien's on the way back to the brewery.

The afternoon that Herbie O'Dowd joined the rest of us for a jaunt in the lorry had been a wet one, though that morning the rain had burst from the clouds in spurts instead of the usual widespread downpour. The lorry driver told us to jump on and sit down in the back of the vehicle, and he walked to the cab of the lorry, started it up and proceeded to drive down O'Brien's. The ride had hardly begun when Herbie O'Dowd fell over the side of the lorry. We felt the back wheels bump over Herbie as if he were a sack of spuds. We all screamed and the lorry driver threw on the brakes. He sprang from the cab of the lorry, ran down one side of the vehicle and asked what had fallen off. Gracie told him that Herbie O'Dowd had fallen over the side. We all got off the back of the lorry and walked a few yards back, and there on the cobbles lay a grey bundle.

The kids' screams on seeing Herbie brought out the neighbours who came running to see what had happened. The mothers knew that their kids often got a hitch on the Guinness lorry, and wondered if the bundle on the cobbles belonged to one of them. The lorry driver and a couple of women went to find Herbie's mother, Violet, who at the time was hanging a load of washing on the clothesline. She dropped the white shirt she had ready to peg on the clothesline when told about Herbie.

Herbie's mother sat down on the street with the small boy's head and trunk in her arms. She cried, 'Herbie, Herbie,' as she cradled the silent child in her arms. Everyone knew Herbie had been killed in the accident. Herbie, the small boy whose father cut his brown hair so unevenly the kids joked that his da probably used a knife and fork to cut his hair, the boy with gleaming blue eyes and a gurgling laugh, now lay crumpled and broken in his mother's arms, a slick of red blood dribbling from his mouth.

Herbie's four sisters and four brothers joined their mother in forming a ring around him until his father could be reached. Then Herbie got lifted up and carried home.

Mrs O'Dowd, Ma, Granny Martin and Mrs Bray prepared Herbie for his burial. All the children filed in first to see Herbie laid out on the white sheet in the bed. He looked as if a bully had punched him black and blue. His mother dressed him in an altar boy's surplice that covered him from the neck to the tip of his bare blue toes. Someone had tied Herbie's pudgy hands together with a green rosary as if to haul him away against his will. On the table next to the bed stood a jamjar filled with spring scented white and yellow daises.

Herbie's father and brothers carried the coffin on their shoulders to Saint Mary's church. Everyone in O'Brien's, some with infants in arms, walked behind Herbie's coffin. After arriving at Saint Mary's the priest came forward from the door of the church to lead the way inside. He directed that the coffin be placed on a bier where it would remain overnight.

We all joined the priest in saying a rosary for Herbie and in the prayers for the dead. After the prayers, the priest and Herbie's family left the church. When the last mourner had left the church, the electric lights were switched off. Herbie had to stay all alone on his perch without a mammy or daddy's hand to latch. I wondered why the powerful men of God would not allow one electric bulb to stay lit throughout the night, as Herbie's mother wished for, just one lit bulb to dispel the vast darkness. Morning light would flow through the floral stained glass window bedecked with sprays of green shamrocks and flame over Herbie's perch.

The owner of Ryan's pub advised Mrs O'Dowd to sue Guinness's brewery over Herbie's death. She refused. Herbie's mother knew if she made a fuss about Herbie's death the brewery might fire the lorry driver. Mrs O'Dowd did not want that to happen because the driver had a family. Probably Guinness's Brewery never knew their involvement in the tragedy in O'Brien's Place.

Ma hadn't many comforting words to offer over the death of Herbie. All she said was, 'It's a bitter, bitter blow to his poor mother. Bitter as bile.' Too bitter for words to comfort.

Herbie's sister Bridie I listed as one of my best friends. She told me that after her brother died, the whole family knelt to say a rosary every evening to send up to Herbie. She said that her mother knew he was in Heaven praying for everyone on earth.

Da said that things happen in threes. In the space of a year Herbie got killed, and the oldest son in the O'Neill family in O'Brien's hung himself in one of the outdoor lavatories in the back of the tenement they lived in.

No one could recall in all their days of living in the laneway that anyone had died by their own hand. All kinds of reasons as to why Jack O'Neill killed himself circulated. Da wondered if he hung himself because of unrequited love, whatever that meant. Others thought that he might have been a member of the IRA and wanted out. There was no getting out of the IRA. When a young man joined the organization, that was that 'til doom's day! He could have been despondent over not finding work, the doctor told his mother.

'Maybe the chap just lost his mind,' asserted Granny Martin.

'Catholics are not supposed to kill themselves,' fumed auld Legg. Granny Martin told her to whist, and stop being a garboil!

'Whatever caused Jack O'Neill to hang himself in the lav, he would not have done it had he known the grief it caused his mother,' said Ma. And finding O'Neill with a rope around his neck and hanging from a spike that he himself had nailed into the wall nearly took the life out of young Andy Duffy.

Andy had gone into the lav to do his morning's duty when he found the body swinging from the spike. The sound of the ambulance tearing down O'Brien's aroused the rest of us to what had happened, and to the sight of two strange coppers pedalling their bikes down the lane. The coppers went into the lav with a notebook open and a ready pen. Then they came out of the lav and told the ambulance driver that the chap was dead from a broken neck. They took Jack out on a stretcher, covered the body with a sheet, and put it into the back of the ambulance.

Mr O'Neill and some of the other women held Jack's mother back from seeing her son. As soon as the ambulance door had closed, Mrs O'Neill broke away and fell to her knees behind the ambulance, and wailed, 'Jack, Jack, my son. What have ye done? What have ye done with yerself?' Then she began to sob and pray. The ambulance slowly pulled away, and she remained on her knees on the ground.

There wasn't any wake for Jack O'Neill, and that seemed strange. Some of the neighbors began to use a word I never heard of: 'suicide'. The word had terrible meanings. I heard that anyone who committed suicide could not have a Mass said for them or have a Christian burial. And stories about what had happened to people like Jack who took their own lives became a sort of pastime, for a while. One story went that O'Neill was doomed to walk the face of the earth 'til God forgave him for taking his life, because only God could decide when a person was to die. And if Mrs O'Neill mourned the loss of her son day and night, her intense mourning would cause Jack to return to O'Brien's as a ghost. It was unwise for anyone to mourn for too long, because the dead person would be kept from their rest and return.

None of the kids would go near or use the lav after Jack hanged himself. They held their shite and piss now more than ever. And no one wanted to pass the lav at night in fear of seeing the ghost of O'Neill. Within six months, Andy saw his ghost roaming the laneway like a lost soul drooping in sorrow. I never went near that lav again, either. Jack could appear even when you were wiping your arse, and God! then what?

The third death passed the lane by. Da was wrong, as usual. But then I learned there were other ways a person could leave the world. And Molly Molloy left the world in a very strange way.

The Molloy sisters lived together in a room in O'Brien's. The two spinsters lived in a room beside Neddy Kenny, a bachelor. Molly, the older of the Molloy sisters living beside Neddy, went mad. When her sister Katy came out of the doorway to tell the neighbours what had happened to her sister we were sent to fetch chairs for the grannies. They sat down to listen to what Katy had to say. And, from the look on her face, she wasn't going to rush it.

Molly had told her sister that God had appeared to her in the room dressed like a Highland piper. God told Molly that he wanted another few kids; He wanted twins this time instead of a single one. God wanted Molly to be the mother of the twins. We all knew that Molly would have made a wonderful mother, in years gone by, because she had something nice to say to kids and offered them sweets if she had any. According to Katy, Molly kept waiting for the twins to arrive without success, and got downhearted. Then she refused to empty her slopbucket. She started to save her shite and let it collect in the slopbucket. When she had collected enough of the stuff, Molly began to mould little figures out of the shite, and she set them on the mantelpiece to dry and harden. Katy thought the figurines must have been meant to be a line of saints or sinners, but Molly informed her they were her own darlin' girl and boy babbies, and she the mother, and still a virgin to boot!

When Katy got through with her story about Molly going mad, not a voice piped up from those gathered round. The account of Molly's madness stunned all within earshot. Only the stir of hands making the sign of the cross, and making a sign of the cross on the foreheads of children close by, broke the silence.

Neddy Kenny complained about a queer smell of rotten cabbage, forcing Katy to do something about her sister. Katy sighed a sigh of relief as we watched Molly skipping out of the doorway, all smiles and humming 'I Love A Lassie', as one of the ambulance attendants elbowed her into the waiting ambulance to cart her off to Grangegorman, the Dublin madhouse.

Neddy Kenny kept to himself. Unlike most of the men in O'Brien's, he had a steady job in the gasworks. Some nicknamed him, 'the bantam cock'. My mother came to find out that under Neddy's sombre and snappish manner lay a heart of gold. The tenderness he showed our family will never be forgotten. In some way or another he took a shine to Ma, although the two never spoke more than the two words, 'Good mornin' or 'Good evenin'.

One Friday evening, Neddy Kenny knocked on our door and asked to talk with Ma. He told her that he wanted to buy the family a loaf of bread three times a week, until the mister got back on his feet, if he ever did by the look of the things. With that he thrust a loaf of fresh bread, wrapped in brown tissue paper, into Ma's arms, tilted the cap on his head and turned heel. Ma turned to face us with the fresh loaf of bread cradled in her arms, and her face as red as a beetroot. Neddy Kenny told Ma that he felt sorry for her having such a hard life, and her with a good word for most. He said that he noticed her and me going to mass early in the morning on his way to work at the gasworks, and wondered if the poor mother and child had a crust of bread.

It seemed amazing that Neddy Kenny could give a care about our family, when none of us had ever spoken to him, except for the usual nod or comment on the day as we passed in the lane. Despite his own hard life and circumstances, Neddy kept his promise to Ma and supplied our family of six with a loaf of bread three times a week, and if Neddy had to leave O'Brien's for some reason, he made sure to pay the shopkeeper to deliver the bread until he returned. The bread came as a blessing.

Ma and I went to seven o'clock mass, and then set off for Ma's part time job at Ryder's Cement Company in Upper Baggot Street, where Ma worked as a cleaning-woman. I helped her sweep the floors, dust office furniture, wash and scrub the lavatory and sink, wax and polish the long, long hallway in the corridor, empty wastebaskets, shake out the carpets, and set out the tea cups and saucers for office staff. Ryder's paid Ma ten shillings a week for the backbreaking labour.

Neddy Kenny had remarked to one of my brothers that Ma worked herself into the ground. Neddy proved right about Ma. She got sick, and the doctor said it was yellow jaundice. A couple of weeks earlier, Ma had cut her hand on a piece of glass. Ma's skin turned yellow, even the whites of her eyes were the colour of a banana. She had a fever and could hardly get out of bed, but she did. Da and the rest of us helped all we could. I don't what would have became of us had it not been for Neddy Kenny's bread, and the sharing of a little bit of this and a little bit of that from other neighbours in O'Brien's. Ma told me that Neddy's kindness scalded her heart. His kindness will scald my heart 'til the day I die. He made me believe in the unexpected goodness of people, when it seemed that those who spoke on God's behalf would let our family shrivel from the face of the earth.

Behind the wall

One day, I asked my friend Bridie if she ever wondered what lay behind the wall that separated O'Brien's from the mansions on Northumberland Road. I told her that I had a way of finding out if she happened to be interested. All we needed to do was throw our tennis ball over the wall. Then we could walk up to Northumberland Road and ask the owner of the garden the ball had landed in if we could go and fetch it. 'Simple as that?' asked Bridie. She tried three times before she threw the tennis ball high enough to sail over the wall. We figured out what back garden it probably landed in. Then we set off for Northumberland Road. After we arrived, Bridie pointed to the third house in the row where she thought the tennis ball must have landed.

The three-storey stone house with a downstairs basement was a ringer for the others along Northumberland Road, except for the bright red door. The windows that faced the street glistened like sheets of rain caught by the sun. From the open windows, edges of lace curtains blew in the breeze like licks of ice cream. Dark green hedges grew behind the black wrought-iron railings surrounding the outside of the house. We unlatched the squeaky gate and walked up the flagstone path that led to massive stone-cut steps all the way to the front door. A half-shell shaped window stood above the door. A figure of a miniature white horse stood behind the window. We decided not to bang the big brass door knocker. Instead, Bridie stood on tippy-toes to press the brass bell that looked like a titty.

We waited for a response to the bell. It seemed that any sound that came from such a small bell for such a big house would be lost to the ears of those inside. After what seemed ages, we heard the clack of quick footsteps coming closer and closer towards the door. The big door opened by inches. A young servant girl dressed in a black and white uniform answered the door. She stared at Bridie and me. She asked in a countrified way what it was we wanted, and said that all deliveries were to be made downstairs in the basement.

'We're not here to make deliveries. We live behind this house in O'Brien's Place. We accidentally let our tennis ball fly over the back wall of this house, and we were wondering if we could go into yer back garden and get our ball,' I said. Bridie nodded her head to the servant girl with every word.

'Go downstairs to the basement, and talk to the maid down there and see what she has t' say,' said the lovely servant girl. 'Don't come up to the front door again. And do not press on this bell.' We told the narky servant we'd do neither again. Her unfriendly manner almost put us off heading down to the basement, but soon Bridie knocked on the door below.

An older servant girl wearing a grey scullery maid's uniform answered our knock. She listened as Bridie repeated the recitation that I had given to the person upstairs. The maid sniffed us both. She either thought we smelled bad or else she had a bad case of catarrh, and needed to eat more onions.

'Take no more than five minutes,' she whipped out, opening the side gate that led into the back garden. As soon as we stepped through the garden gate, Bridie and I were transfixed at what lay in front of our eyes. It was an acre of newly mowed grass, green as an emerald, and as luxurious as velvet. There were cut-outs here and there on the lawn that choked with flowers of every colour imaginable. The stone walls around the garden were all cobwebbed with trailing branches from flowering bushes in flaming reds, pale pinks, and bright yellows. A white filigree round house stood on one side of the lawn like an uncut wedding cake.

The warm August afternoon sun dipped down on our heads as we walked along the garden path taking in the beautiful sights. The beauty of it all lit the senses. My heart pounded as I tried to replace the rancid smells of the tenements with the perfume from the flowers and cut grass. Bridie and I realised there were areas beyond the flowers. We came to an orchard. The ripe smell from apples and pears in the orchard made us hold our bellies.

The branches of the apple and pear trees were buckled down with fruit: swaying pears begging to be suckled; wobbly apples swinging downwards like the balls on young boys. Scores of apples and pears lay rotting on the ground under the trees. Bees as big as duck-eggs hovered over the fallen fruit as if in a stupor. Ma's voice echoed in my ears as I gazed on the clumps of rotting fruit, 'Wilful waste makes woeful want.'

We heard the voice of the servant girl call us back to the house. I told Bridie I was going to nick some apples and pears to take home with me. 'Where will ye hide 'em?' 'Up the leg of me knickers. The elastic in the leg of me knickers will hold in an apple and pear.'

'Mine will too,' said Bridie, and she stuffed two apples up the leg of her knickers. Then we carefully walked back up the garden path with our load of apples and pears bouncing about inside our drawers.

We told the servant girl that we could not find the ball, and asked if we could come back again the next day to hunt for it. While the servant girl rolled our request over in her head, I could feel the elasticity in the leg of my knickers giving out. Down fell the apples and pears towards the feet of the servant. With heart in mouth and blushed with shame, I waited for the greatest chastisement of my life. The maid remained silent and stone-faced for a split second, then she hauled us both by the back of the collar and dragged us towards the door. She hammered after us, 'You're the boldest and brassiest girls in Dublin city! Off with you!'

On the way back to O'Brien's, Bridie reached her hand under her frock and into her knickers. She brought out an apple and handed it to me, then she reached back inside her knickers for the other apple. We chomped into delicious apples that smelled unmistakably of warm arse. We were both glad to get back home. The mystery of what lay behind the wall had been solved, one less headscratcher to figure out.

Wakes and births

Like the rest of the kids in O'Brien's, we were exposed to death as a natural thing. All the kids attended the wakes in the laneway, and looked upon them as special occasions and opportunities to mingle with the adults in the neighborhood.

When Mr Rosin was on his deathbed, his sister, Josie, asked Ma if she could do anything to ease the pain of her brother. Mr Rosin couldn't do his pee which caused him great pain. Ma told us how she rubbed the elderly man's belly with warm oil and kneaded it until he flowed like a fountain, but he died before the week ended, anyway.

As was the custom, the women in O'Brien's prepared Mr Rosin's body for his wake. They washed his body, combed his hair, and cut his finger and toe nails. Then one of the men in the neighbourhood came over and gave Mr Rosin a shave. Confidentially, Ma told us that Josie asked her and the other women to put a pair of woolly long johns under her brother's shroud, because he constantly complained of the cold and dampness.

I asked Ma why she was not afraid to touch a dead person. I asked her if the body felt as cold as marble. I asked her if she really could tell when a person was dead and if she feared being haunted by the ghost of a dead person.

Ma answered all my questions by saying, 'Ah! dead people are harmless. They can't do anyone any harm. Any harm they did is over with. It's the livin' ye have to contend with.'

All the neighbours in O'Brien's went to pay their last respects to Mr Rosin. Men, women, and school-age children were expected to go to see the body and offer a prayer for the departed soul. The relative of the dead person knew which adults and children dropped by to say a prayer for the departed. Sometimes children stayed up half the night with the parents at a wake.

Mr Rosin lay waked on an iron bed on a white sheet in his brown habit of Saint Francis, and looked as flat as a pancake on the bed. Someone had placed two round copper pennies over Mr Rosin's eyes to keep them shut. He had an Irish penny over one eye and an English penny on the other, and at first gawk he looked like he had on a pair of motorcycle goggles.

Each of us was invited to dip a feather into the bowl of holy water and sprinkle it below Mr Rosin's face while we said our Hail Marys. Fifteen-year-old Mary Jenkins, known to be a bit awkward, dunked the feather too deeply into the dish and soaked up too much holy water on the feather. She flipped the feather over Mr Rosin's face until he looked like he'd been caught in a shower of rain. We half expected the dead man to sit up in the bed and tell the awkward lummox to get home with herself.

Some in O'Brien's said that they knew beforehand when a death was going to take place in O'Brien's. They would say they had heard the wailing of the banshee. Everyone knew that the banshee foretold the death of someone in advance.

As the evening drew on at Rosin's wake, the neighbours began to tell stories about the banshee. Even Da, half-drunk as he was, sprang to life when talk about the banshee got started. Da set the tone for the rest of by reciting a part of a poem or story he memorised about Ireland's famous ghost woman.

T'was the banshee's lonely wailing
Well I knew the voice of death,
On the night wind slowly sailing
O'er the bleak and gloomy heath.

Unlike the Dubliners present, Da often referred to the banshee as being the 'Lady of Death'.

Ma noted to all present that the banshee only came to wail and cry for the descendants of all the auld Irish families that had the letter 'O' in front of their names, like her own maiden name, O'Connor.

'Does the banshee travel over the ocean to wail for all who left Ireland?' asked Una Goggins from two doors down.

The Goggins' family had notions of emigrating to England so the father could find work and their six kids could attend a school where Catholic nuns would not batter the kids for being poor.

'Be a long haul for the banshee to travel to England, America, Canada and even Australia to wail for Irish immigrants with an "O" in front of their names,' piped Carrie Murphy.

'Ye made a brilliant point there, Carrie,' gushed Billo in an attempt to butter up to Carrie.

'The banshee strides in the night,' said Sean Murphy getting his two pennies worth in.

'Who's seen the banshee in this room with their own eyes?' asked Nellie.

'Well, I'll tell ye,' said Nellie. 'I did,' and Nellie proceeded to give an account of that time: 'She appeared to me all dressed in white looking like a child angel standing be the wall. The wall behind the small child lit as bright as a star. I wasn't afraid. No. not a bit.'

Then Liam told of his experience with the banshee: 'She looked like an auld ugly woman with long, grey stringy hair hanging down all the way to her bum. She screamed and cursed as she glided a comb through her hair. Shivers ran up and down me spine as I watched her from the corner of me eye. I ran like hell.'

Next, a couple of know-it-alls described their sighting of the banshee in O'Brien's: 'We were coming back from the cinema, the Shack, after seeing the picture, *She Wore a Yella Ribbon* with John Wayne and Maureen O'Hara. It's a great picture and ye all should see it. When we got to O'Brien's we heard an unmerciful wailing like a hundred skinned cats. The banshee stood in the middle of the lane, screaming to herself in an awful way while brushing her hair. She saw us gawking and flung the comb at us. The comb nearly hit Frank Kearns and meself. We were so afraid, we nearly dropped our shite. If the comb hada hit us we were both dead. That's the way the banshee kills people.'

Hearing stories about the banshee over cups of tea and bottles of porter shortened the wake, but soon my three brothers and I began to fall asleep on the floor.

Ma and Da decided, after seeing the four of us passed out on the floor, it was time to head back to our room and go to bed. We all enjoyed Mr Rosin's wake, and hoped the gates of heaven had opened wide to receive him.

Parents in O'Brien's hadn't any qualms about informing us about the mysteries of death. But dare any one of us ask how we got into the world, and all we got was a deaf ear. Mammies and daddies were struck dumb when it came time to the mystery of birth.

Bundles of new babies were born to families in O'Brien's. Dolores, Maureen, Bridie, Annie, Gracie, Bernadette, Patricia and myself were now at the curiosity stage about where all the babies came from.

Something or someone had to know how the bundles of babies got to O'Brien's, usually in the spring. I asked Ma time after time how babies got into the world and she ignored the question. I'd say to her, 'Ma, Mrs Thing-a-bob had a fat belly last week and now she has a babby.' Ma would eye the question, but never spring an answer. 'Ma, why does God give poor people babbies and nothing else?'

Ma didn't like the tone of this question I could tell, and reminded me that a baby lights up the barest room and that each one brings its own kind of love into the world. I continued to press her to answer how babies came into the world. 'God sent them down from heaven,' she answered, and that was that.

Ma's told their kids that they were found under mushrooms, under turnips, and under cabbages. I knew these fishy stories about our birth were cover-ups to keep us in the dark about why Mrs So and So had a big belly last week and now had a baby and her big belly disappeared—disappeared as if by magic.

Da, his ear cocked into our conversation, interrupted and said, 'Some things aren't for little pig's ears.' I bent Granny Martin's ear trying to satisfy my curiosity about babies.

Granny Martin acted like Ma, saying, 'Ye're wanting to know more than yer head is ready to hold. Get out iv the hallway with yer skipping rope, and stop pestering poor people with questions that have no answer.'

But old Master John let the cat out of the bag when he was overheard to say as Mrs Murphy passed by, 'There goes another belly-a-pups.'

Ma helped in the delivery of babies in O'Brien's. This didn't sit well with Da, especially when a knock sounded on our door in the middle of the night or early morning. 'Yoo hoo, in there, Mary. Mary O'Connor. Are ye awake?' Up sprang Ma scattering all the covers onto the floor. She knew the knock woke me and everyone else. Ma would whisper in my ear, 'Another babby will be in O'Brien's by the time ye get up in the morning.'

Selecting a godmother for a new baby often depended on who had money to pay the priest for the christening. It cost ten shillings to have a baby baptised in Saint Mary's on Haddington Road. Ma reluctantly turned down offers to be a godmother because she hadn't any money to pay the priest.

Usually, infants were baptised three days after they were born. After a baby was baptised, the godmother took it all around O'Brien's to show to the neighbours, and hoped the neighbours, if they could, would put a small coin in the baby's blanket. By the time the baby had been ogled by every housewife and granny in the laneway, the godmother had collected a good bit of money for the new mother.

Most babies got threepenny bits tucked into their blanket, and sometimes as much as ten shillings would be collected to help out the new mother and baby. Had anyone ever put more than a three-penny bit into the baby's blanket the heavens would have opened, and the godmother would have lost the use of her legs.

If a family could afford it, neighbours were invited to the chris-tening. The new parents handed out cups of tea or bottles of porter to the grown-ups. Kids were treated to lemonade and sweet sugar biscuits. All the kids at the christening promised to take care of the new baby when it got old enough to play in the laneway.

Granny Martin, Granny Carey and Granny Sullivan believed they could predict a baby's future by looking closely at its features. If a baby boy shifted its head more to one side than the other it meant the child would grow up to be a sailor. Granny Sullivan believed a baby boy with bright eyes would become a scholar. She also pre-dicted that a baby boy who kept its fist balled-up for more than a week went on to become a stubborn and contentious man. Granny Carey predicted a baby boy who opened his fists soon after birth grew up to be a missionary with outstretched hands towards heathens.

The grannies also predicted what the future had in store for baby girls by studying their features. A bawling baby girl would become a nagging housewife. A smiling baby girl would be close to the Church and probably become a nun. A quiet baby girl had to be watched because quiet indicated someone who could hatch things in the mind, and a gurgling baby girl, God help us, went on to become a chatterbox and the neighborhood gossip.

The old women also believed that if newborn babies were not closely watched over, fairies would come and steal them away. Or the fairies would replace a human baby with one of their squalling imps. And the grannies pointed out that beautiful babies and beautiful younger children had to be guarded more than plainer types, because the fairies were tempted to steal and carry the beautiful types back to their unseen world. The grannies believed that in order to guard the lovely ones from the unseen ones, every infant and child in the whole of Ireland had to be baptised in the Catholic Church. The sign of the cross had more power than any fairy, the old women attested.

Girls and boys come out to play

The summer evenings in O'Brien's were a blessing for all. The children stayed out late to play, the mammies gathered outside in a group to talk with each other, and the grannies had kids bring out their chairs to sit on while they joined in on everything. The long bright summer evenings made it possible for the women to take their knitting outdoors. They brought out their workbaskets that held skeins of wool and knitting needles. Grannies crocheted lace to edge handkerchiefs or pillow tops. Granny Murphy expertly worked on what she described as a popcorn border for a pillowcase to give to her grandgirl (granddaughter). All that was knitted or crocheted would be stored away until Christmas. Great knitters like May and Lally helped other less experienced knitters.

May instructed Mrs Hayden on knitting a matching pair of jumpers for her daughters, Bernadette and Pat. Lally encouraged others to try their hand with more fancy stitches such as the hobnail, the cable, fan-and-feather, the blackberry stitch, and the colourful fair isle patterns that Lally could pull from her head like magic.

Lily preferred to crochet. She started on an apple-pink dress for her two-year-old daughter, Clara. May knitted a mile a minute and never let a stitch fall off the needles as she carried her instructions to all the knitters. Small girls like me got to unravel wool from worn-out jumpers and scarves. We got to use the salvaged wool for whatever we wanted to knit. We used pairs of wooden skewers that we had begged from the butcher for use as knitting needles. May and Lally got us started on scarves. They taught us how to set up our stitches on the skewers, and knit in rows of plain and purl, the beginning stitches for everyone. Using the wavy navy blue wool that I had unravelled from a jumper, I decided to knit Da a scarf to keep him warm in the winter to come. I asked May if, when I got to the middle of the scarf, she'd teach me to include the blackberry stitch. And she did.

'May! Lally! knit us a house!' went the joke of the evenings. The constant chatter of the talkative women kept pace with all the clicking sounds of the knitting needles that were hopefully churning out unforgettable woolly treasures.

The women discussed the high cost of food in the shops, who might be in the family way, if things were ever going to get better in Ireland, if Hitler and the Germans would take over the world, take over Ireland, take over O'Brien's Place.

The unmarried girls talked about their craving for nylon stockings, fashionable frocks, and wanting to dress and look like Lana Turner and Betty Gable, two Hollywood 'dotes' if there were 'dotes' in the world.

On a more serious side, mothers talked about how they intended to take their babies to one of the new 'baby clubs' that had opened up for the poor of Dublin. The baby clubs offered free medical examinations for new babies, issued vouchers for free milk and cheese for nursing mothers, and offered help with toddlers. Some of the mothers explained how they had observed with their own eyes the blossoming of 'dawny babies' who became robust on account of all the help the new baby clubs offered.

After the mothers got through talking about dawny babies, Maura told us about a baby born with a pig's head.

'The hullabaloo began when a poor mother and her children knocked on a swank's halldoor to seek a bit of charity. My pal, Ella, worked for the swank in the scullery and gave me the inside scoop. The swanky wan told the poor mother to clear off with herself and take the swine with her.

'Soon after, the swanky wan gave birth to a baby with a pig's head. Its parents tried to make it drink from a silver cup but it knocked it skyhigh, and when they insisted the offspring eat of gussie goosie dishes, it had knpitions. The thing began to squeal and oink, oink, oink 'til dawn rolled twice around Dublin city.

'Finally, the parents ordered a cattle trough to be fetched to the fancy residence. Ella got orders to save apple and potato peelings, turnips, wilted cabbage heads and slops and put the whole mess into the trough for the hog-headed baby, who slobbered it up like a greedy pig.

'The poor woman and children who asked the swank for a bit of charity were Jesus and angels dressed in rags, out testing the waters. A priest baptised the thing on the shoulder not wanting to eye the head wearing an Easter bonnet.'

As the evenings wore out, all the knitting got put back into the workbaskets and time came to help the grannies take their chairs inside. Time for the pubs to close. Time for daddies to come home. Frank, Bob, and Noely Joseph pestered Ma to come home, and tugged on the sleeves of her jumper 'til she'd make the move.

I'd put four corks from four porter bottles on the ends of my skewers to keep the knitting from falling off. I had to finish the scarf before Christmas, and I knew time ducked fast, as fast as playtime in the lane.

The sounds of the girls and boys playing in the laneway endures in my memory. Some of the games were just for girls although girls and boys played kick-the-can together. Small girls played chanies from the first warm day of spring 'til the chill of autumn. Chanie-ware came from pieces of broken floral chinaware and coloured glass ornaments tossed into ashbins. We went out of O'Brien's to find our chanies because no one had any fancy dishes or fancy coloured glass ornaments, except for Granny Martin, and she never broke any of her nice things. She promised to give me her blue willow-pattern china set when she died.

We rummaged through the ashbins along Haddington Road, and Pembroke Road to find our treasures. The broken pieces of china and glassware were carried home in tin cans. Pieces of china or glass bigger than two inches were broken into smaller bits, then all of the bits were sorted by colour and design and put into empty shoe-polish cans for display. The rarest colours and floral designs were the most prized, and went into special tins. A combination of tiny specks of coloured glassware and chinaware became dolly-mix-tures. After all was arranged, we put a price on each of the tins of make-believe sweets.

The many-faceted glass chips-amber, blue, pink, red, green, and white crystal held the sun's gaze as it shone upon our displays. Chanie shops ringed the laneway in O'Brien's like a necklace.

Plain pieces of white china broken down into various sizes were used as makebelieve currency. Before any buying or selling began, we linked our voices in chorus to sing out, 'Buy away! Buy away! The new shop's open. It won't be very long 'til the new shop shuts!'

The girls competed with each other to find the most ornate pieces of broken delft and brilliant glass scraps. The best of both were put into a box and also sold as dolly mixtures.

Dolores, Fanny, Bernadette and Gracie wanted to buy my mixtures in exchange for two handfuls of the plain delft we used as money, but I would never part with the treasures I had collected. Ma let me sleep with my box of sharp dolly-mixtures because she knew how I prized the small gems.

To decide how much each piece of white delft was worth in pound-notes, a measurement was taken. The width of two fingers across the piece of delft had the value of a two pound-note. Three fingers meant it was worth three pound-notes, and so on. The buyer and the seller both had to agree on how many pounds were in each piece of the white delft. Skinny-fingered girls measured out more pound-notes in their pieces of delft than fat-fingered ones.

Throwing balls up against the wall was another game played only by the girls. The balls were thrown against the wall to the rhythm of special songs, like 'The Drunken Sailor'.

Another rhyme to chant while throwing the ball was all about the 'glimmer man'. The glimmer man came round to O'Brien's Place to make sure that the neighbours who had gas-rings for cooking only used them at certain times of the day because gas was rationed on account of the war. Anyone who got caught with a glimmer of gas on when they weren't supposed to, got a ticker from the inspector. Ma and some of the other women often told us to keep an eye out for him.

Keep it boiling on the glimmer
Here comes the glimmer man
And out goes the glimmer.
If you see him don't let him in.
Ha ha ha, and that shook him.

Boys never played chanies or wanted to join us throwing the ball against the wall. These were sissy games for girls and that simply went without saying. The boys had their own games. They played with hoops from old bikes, which they made move along the lane with a stick. The faster the hoops went, the wilder the shouts from the boys.

All the while the girls were playing their games, young boys marched up and down the lane pretending to be soldiers. They made their soldier hats out of used newspapers which they folded into the exact shape of a real soldier's hat and they wore it on the side of the head and each carried a stick over his shoulder as his rifle. They sang out with might and mockery this song, as they paraded the laneway.

Hitler's granny has a shop down in hell an'
She's selling ammunition
And she's doin' very well.
A ha'penny fer a bullet and a penny fer a shell,
Hitler's granny has a shop down in hell.

The name 'Hitler' came up often. Boys who played soldier would shout out, 'Heil Hitler', as they marched by. None of us knew who Hitler was except we did know that a war with him in it was taking place somewhere far away from O'Brien's Place.

If the favourite games of the boys was playing soldiers or cowboys, the most popular game of all for the girls was skipping. Gracie Gale had the best skipping rope in the lane. It was a long heavy piece of thick rope that because of its weight never tangled up. The girls knew plenty of skipping songs to sing as they jumped the rope. The most popular skipping song was this dark little ditty:

There was an auld woman and she lived in the woods
Weela, weela, wala.
There was an auld woman and she lived in the woods
Down be the River Saula.
She had a babby three months old,
Weela, weela, walya.
She had a babby three months old,
Down be the River Saula.
She stuck a penknife through its heart
Weela, weela, wala,
She stuck a penknife through its heart
Down be the River Saula.
Three hard knocks came a knocking on the door

Weela, weela, waula.
Three hard knocks came a knocking on the door
Down be the River Saula.
They took her to the county jail
Weela, weela, waula.
They took her to the county jail
Down by the River Saula.
And that was the end of the woman in the woods
Weela, weela, waula.

'That song's about a girl who had a babby before she got married,' figured out Bernadette. 'That's why she stuck it with a penknife and got hauled off to jail.'

Another skipping song was this one:

Skinny malink malojeon
Legs, umbrella, feet
Went to the pictures and couldn't get a seat.
When the pictures started
Auld skinny malink farted.
Skinny malink malojeon
Legs, umbrella, feet.

By the time we had gone through our repertoire our ma's would be screaming for us to get home for tea and perhaps they'd get a rest from the jaded voices. Next day might be the time to play another 'girls only' game, called, 'Here's the Gypsy Riding'.

In playing 'Here's the Gypsy Riding', eight to ten girls held hands and formed two lines, far apart from each other, but facing each other. A girl was picked to play the gypsy, and she stood in the middle of the two lines and skipped back and forth singing out loud

Here's the gypsy riding, riding, riding.
Here's the gypsy riding Y. O. U.'

The other girls would sing back,

'What are you riding here for, here for, here for?
What are you riding here for, Y. O. U.'

Their answer from the gypsy would be,

'I'm riding here to marry, to marry, to marry.
I'm riding here to marry Y. O. U.'

And they would sing back to her,

'Marry wan of us, Sir, us, Sir, us, Sir,
Marry wan of us, Sir, Y. O. U.!'

The gypsy would reply,

'Ye're all too dirty, dirty, dirty,
Ye're all too dirty, Y. O. U.!'

They would return,

'We're just as clean as you, Sir, you, Sir, you, Sir,
We're just as clean as you, Sir, Y. O. U.'

Another game that had its own song was 'swingin' round the lamp-post'. The song went like this:

My mother said, I never should,
Play with the gypsies in the wood.
If I did, she would say,
Do not dare to disobey!
Where have ye been all day long?
Down in the ally, playing with Sally,
Picking-up cinders, breaking winders, all day long!

The tallest, skinniest lamp-posts were along Haddington Road. A rope would be folded in two and placed around the lamp-post, the two ends of the rope pulled into the middle of the rope, and the two ends of the rope tied together. Then the rope got shifted up the lamp-post and pulled tight. A girl would get inside the length of the rope 'til her bum reached the knotted ends, slide her feet backwards on the ground, push her body towards the post and spin round the pole 'til dizzy. My brother Bob could shimmy up the tallest lamp-post, and he'd slide the rope up for us 'til it almost reached the middle of the pole. He often had a swing himself.

He liked to engage me in brain teasers like the one that went, "If Do, Ray, and Me went into the madhouse, and Do and Ray came out, who was left inside?" Or our favourite, which we took turns at, which began, 'As I was going up Haddington Road I happened to see a pile of dead cat guts, rat guts, spider guts, and piles of horse shite sitting in the road!' 'I one it,' the first one would say, and the second, 'I two it' followed in turn with 'I three it' 'I four it', 'I five it', 'I six it" 'I seven it' and no one wanted to follow, with 'I eight it'!

Children weren't the only ones to play games in the laneway of O'Brien's Place. Married men and older single fellas had their games to play. On Sunday morning after mass the younger men and the older went round the back of the lane to play toss-a-penny.

The idea behind toss-a-penny was for each of the men and young fellas to pitch a penny towards the back wall and try to get the penny to land as near the wall as possible. The one who pitched the penny closest to the wall won the game. He got to pick up all the other thrown pennies as his winnings. If any girls even looked at the men tossing their pennies, the older men told the younger ones to shoo us away. They told us small girls to go home to our mammies. While the lads were talking like this to us, they ogled the bigger girls. A couple said that girls brought bad luck by hanging around, and that girls were meant only to be fetchers, to do the bidding of men.

One day I sat on the kerbstone with some other small girls to watch the men toss the pennies. Two older boys, on orders from the elders, came over and told us to be off with ourselves. Bridie and I didn't budge. The boys lifted their legs in front of us, and grunted farts in our direction. The funk of their farts lifted us off the kerb and sent us scurrying home to our mothers. Bridie and I could not understand why men acted like they did towards girls and grown women.

There was talk in O'Brien's about a young girl who had been assaulted by a man in a field behind Beggar's Bush barracks the past autumn. The girl used to walk around the streets selling bundles of kindling. She lived with her family down by the Grand Canal. All anyone knew about her was her name, Peggy, and that she was thirteen years old. Teresa told me that she overheard her brothers Sean and Liam talking in hushed tones about the attack.

According to her, the man who assaulted the girl must have lost his mind because after he did whatever he did, he cut off all her curls. A copper took the girl to the hospital. Only inward damage, they said she had suffered, except for the loss of her hair, and she'd be up on her legs in no time. I had dreams about the girl being attacked, her curls scattering in the wind like milkweed.

Both men and women in O'Brien's followed the horses. Having a flutter on the nags appealed to them all. Master John stood in the midst of the others with the butt of a pencil in his mouth trying to figure out the horses. The fellas that could read the newspaper guided their eyes down the list of possible winners.

The Grand National brought out all the chance takers. Men and women in O'Brien's put a bet on one or another horse in the race. Granny Martin, Mary Clay, Ma, Magi, Lucy and Polly pooled their pennies together to bet on a pony. Da read out the list of horses running in the Grand National for the neighbours who could not read. The women selected the horse they wanted to bet on by its name. Romantic names like the Rose of Avonmore or the Lady of Spain were enough to guarantee the mothers and grannies that either would be a winner.

The lowest bet allowed on a horse by the bookmaker was a shilling. The name of the horse and the amount of the bet had to be written on a piece of paper. Women were not expected to enter the bookie's shop, a place only for men, so after Da wrote down the women's bets, he took them over to the bookie's shop and placed their bets. The mothers and grannies clustered together outside the doorway and waited with great anticipation for news of the horse who had won the Grand National.

'Here comes Paddy from the bookie's,' said Sadie.

'I hope our jennet came in first,' said Polly.

Paddy announced the winner of the horse race. It was Master McGrath.

'Master what?' inquired Granny Sullivan, a hand cupped to her ear.

'Master McGrath,' repeated Paddy, adding that the Rose of Allendale had arrived dead last.

Granny Sullivan and the rest of the women who had put a bet on the Rose of Allendale were left up the creek. But in the spirit of

O'Brien's, they told Paddy they would have no trouble picking a winner in next year's race.

Before he went off on his bicycle, Paddy said, as if a bit of cheering-up was needed, he'd got a great tip about picking a winner from one of the jockeys. The trick was to watch the horses before they leave the starting gate. 'Watch for the horse who drops a big shite. That's the one to put yer money on. It's lighter on the legs,' he said.

'Git outta here,' screamed the women in mock rage.

Christmas

Da found a job as a furnace stoker in a milk factory and his pay provided for a few extra treats for Christmas. The kids in the lane looked forward to Christmas and Santa Claus coming down the chimney.

The small shops on Bath Avenue were decorated for the holiday. The Christmas display in Cullen's shop window got all the kids' attention. The owner turned the front window into a winter wonderland: cottonwool for make-believe snow, silver sparkle for icicles, and strings of coloured fairy lights framing the window. There were boxed sets of English toy soldiers, dressed in brilliant red regimental uniforms, hard plastic toy cars and motorcycles along with toy drums, whistles, and cowboy guns. Several dolls were displayed in their boxes, and the doll that captured my heart I named Nora.

Nora had glassy eyes fringed with thick, black eyelashes. She'd a ruby mouth, dimpled cheeks, and pasted-on lacquered black hair. Bernadette, Gracie and Bridie also had their eyes on the doll. Nora wore a green plaid taffeta dress trimmed with red and yellow ribbon, ankle socks and patent leather shoes.

The shop owner, Mr Cullen, invited kids from O'Brien's to put down a deposit on any toy in the shop window. The kids were to let their mammies know which toy they had put a deposit on, and Santa Claus would pick up the toy from Cullen's and deliver it on Christmas morning.

By the time Christmas Eve rolled around, I had six pennies paid as a down-payment on Nora which left a balance of nine shillings and sixpence. I took Ma down to Bath Avenue to show her the doll. Ma warned me not to set my heart on the idea that Santa Claus would be bringing it to me for Christmas. She said she'd love him to, but not to set my heart on it.

Mr Cullen also had red Christmas paper bells, paper chains and boxes of Christmas cards for sale for the holiday. He had three big cardboard boxes on the counter full of cards. The penny box had cards with red robins carrying holly in their beaks. The two-penny box displayed cards with images of German gingerbread houses caked with snow, and the three-penny box was full of religious cards with pictures of the manger scene, the holy family, and the lone figure of the blessed virgin dressed in blue. I spent hours looking through the cards, but nobody in O'Brien's ever sent cards to each other.

Back in our room, Ma bristled with the Christmas spirit. It showed on her face. She got all excited about making a Christmas pudding. Because of the war going on and the shortage of things, we had to tramp all over Dublin to collect the ingredients she needed for the pudding. Ma got her shopping bag and we were off.

We walked from O'Brien's to Findlater's shop in Baggot Street. Ma talked the man behind the counter into selling her half a pound of raisins and a quarter pound of currants. Then on to O'Grady's to buy a yard of white calico to wrap the assembled pudding in. Next we had to tramp down to Cullen's for sixpence worth of dried candy peel, sixpence worth of dried red cherries, and three pennies' worth of crystallized ginger.

Then we walked into Mooney's to get what Ma considered the most important thing to go into a pudding, some fat sultana raisins. Ma knew one of the shop girls behind the counter in Mooneys. She would put in a little extra this and that. The girl measured out the sultanas and put them into a bag, then Ma asked her to weigh out twopence worth of cinnamon, ground cloves, ginger, nutmeg, and allspice.

Then it was off to Boland's Bakery to get day-old-bread to crumble for the pudding. On our way home to O'Brien's, we stopped to rest by the canal on a street bench. We looked up at the silver barrage balloons floating above the canal. The balloons were floating in the sky above Dublin, to tangle German planes which flew over the city.

A bomb shelter had been build near the canal, and I asked Ma if we could look inside the square cement structure. A couple of civil defence men had come into O'Brien's to tell everyone that if they heard the air-raid siren they were to run and hide in the shelter Ma and I were standing in now, holding our noses. The civil defence men also passed out gas-masks to everyone who lived in O'Brien's. The scary black rubber masks came packed in brown cardboard boxes. Ma took the six boxes and piled them in a corner of our room. The civil defence man warmed us that Hitler might gas everyone in Dublin. Ma said Hitler and people who made war were mad.

The stench inside the bomb-shelter took the breath away. The place had no windows, except for a slice of light that entered through some cracks. Cement pews were built next to the walls. The place looked like a tomb. Only stray dogs and cats from around the area entered the place, and only then to shite and piss all over the floor. Ma said what a terrible thing it would be to die in such a place without the light of day.

The next day, she began to assemble the pudding. Ma had me crumble the stale loaf of bread with my fingers, and drop the crumbs into an empty washbasin. Frank and Bob seeded the sultanas, Ma reminding them frequently that the fruit was meant for the pudding and not for their mouths. Noely Joseph and Ma put three cups of flour, a dash of baking soda and some salt into the washbasin on top of the breadcrumbs. Noely dumped in a cup of brown sugar, Ma added a cup of treacle, a cup of suet, the currants, the sultanas, and the other dried fruit. Frank grated a carrot, an apple and a potato and slid the lot on top of everything in the washbasin. I poured in the mixed spices.

Ma dived her hand into the washbasin and mixed the mixture until she got it to her satisfaction. Da added a few dribbles from a bottle of porter. Ma dived in again with her hands and mixed the lot once more. I spread the square of calico on the table, greased it, and sprinkled it with flour.

After that, Ma tumbled the mixture from the washbasin into the middle of the cloth, grabbed the edges of the cloth, tied them together with string, and shaped the mixture inside until she got the roundness of a bomb. Da, Frank, Bob, Noely Joseph, and myself patted the pudding. Ma sprinkled three drops of holy water on the pudding, then carefully put it into the pot of boiling water on the grate where it would simmer for eight hours. Smells of ginger, nutmeg and cinnamon filled the room, as the pudding sat simmering in the pot. Steam curtained our window, and Bob scrawled 'Happy Christmas' on the clouded window with his finger.

After the pudding was cooked, Ma said a prayer over it before she lifted it from the pot to cool on a plate. With heart in mouth she slowly pulled away the calico from the pudding, pleased as punch it didn't collapse in the process. 'Thanks be t' God,' she declared, showing off the pudding naked as a round arse. She stuck a twig of holly into the top of the pudding. We looked up to Ma as she put the pudding on the table as if she were a renowned genius.

On Christmas Eve, my brothers and I wrote our letters to Santa Claus asking for the toys we wanted him to leave us. We put our letters up the chimney hoping for the best. I outlined a map of Cullen's shop for Santa Claus 'X'ing where Nora stood in the window.

On Christmas morning, I received an orange, a tiny doll wrapped in cellophane, and a silver sixpence. Nora never showed up. Frank got a ball, an orange, and a silver sixpence. Bob got a story-book, an orange, and a silver sixpence, and Noel got lead soldiers, an orange, and a copper penny. Da said Father Christmas did his best, and we all knew it to be true. There wouldn't have been any point in spilling tears over the doll.

Ma outdid herself in making the Christmas dinner. She served up a roasted cow's heart stuffed with thyme, onion, breadcrumbs, and sage. She made golden roasted brown potatoes, a plate of green cabbage, yellow turnips and peas. Ma sang as she ladled out our grub. She sang, as if to Da,

Red is the rose that in yonder garden grows,
And fair is the lily of the valley.
Clear is the water that flows from the Boyne
But my love is fairer than ANY!

I swore I'd never get into an argument with her for the rest of my life as she piled my plate with food. Ma saved some of the pudding to hand out to the neighbours. The women in O'Brien's swapped slices of Christmas pudding with each other. They compared the texture, colour and taste of the slices, never saying a word about who made the best pudding.

Granny Martin hadn't a slice of pudding for Ma or anyone else in the lane. She told us what happened to her pudding, if you want to believe her: 'I'd me long black stockings hung over the mantel-piece to dry for Christmas Mass, and without me know'n it, the stocking fell into the pot and simmered with me puddin. The dye from me stocking soaked into the puddin while it simmered for hours. The puddin looked like a devil's head with eyes all over the place because of the currants.'

Ma, Mrs Bray and the others told Granny Martin not to fret over her pudding. She soon perked up and invited Ma, Mrs Bray, Polly, Granny Murphy and Sadie into her room to have a Christmas gargle. She also beckoned Fanny, Angie, and myself to join in the celebration. After a few drops of whiskey, Granny Murphy began a sing song by singing,

When your hair has turned to silver,
I will love you just the same.
I will always call you sweetheart,
That will always be your name.

Then tenderly, Granny Martin warbled;

We'll build a sweet little nest,

Somewhere in the west,
There beneath a starry sky
We'll find a place that's known to God, alone,
Just a spot to call our own.
We'll find perfect peace,
Where joy will never cease,
And LET THE REST OF THE WORLD GO BY!

The get-together ended with us singing our lungs out with

Bless 'em all! Bless 'em all!
The long and the short and the tall.
Bless de Valera, and Seán McEntee,
For giving us brown bread and a half-ounce a tea.
We're saying goodbye to'em all,
The long and the short and the tall.
They'll get no promotion this side of the ocean,
So cheer-up me boys, bless 'em all.

Ma told everyone always to remember the old neighbours in O'Brien's and our Christmas together. We nodded in agreement. Before heading across to her room, Granny asked Ma what she had done with the one roll of Rolo's, and copy of *The Little Messenger of the Sacred Heart,* that the Saint Vincent de Paul gave to our family for Christmas. 'Jaysus break their heart for their generosity,' said Granny Martin at the thought of the well-heeled Christian charity having the nerve to offer one roll of sweets and a religious magazine to a poor family of six in a stinking room for Christmas. 'What did ye do with the copy of the *Messenger,* Mary?' 'Rolled it up tight and lit the fire with it,' answered Ma, truthfully. 'Fair game to ye,' said Granny, letting a dribble of whiskey spill down her chin for effect.

A day out

At the end of one summer some of the women in O'Brien's thought it would be great to leave the laneway for a bus excursion to the countryside. Day out became a popular idea, and the neighbours sprang to get it going. The women in the laneway agreed to cut back on buying something, and put the extra pennies in a pot to pay the bus fare for all who wanted to go on a day out.

Someone in O'Brien's heard that it cost little to get into Lord Lucan's estate on the outskirts of Dublin city. Lord Lucan's estate, it was noted, at one time belonged to the great Irish hero, Patrick Sarsfield, the Earl of Lucan. The estate opened to the public for day picnics for a small entrance fee: a shilling for an adult and sixpence for a child.

The day out took place in late August, the ripe part of the year as far as the outdoor facilities were concerned. Mammies made sandwiches of bread and jam, and wrapped-up bottles of milk and lemonade to take along. Mammies also took teapots, loose tea and sugar to make daddies tea in the afternoon. All the picnic supplies were stuffed into shopping bags, and what couldn't be stuffed into the shopping bags was carried by the kids.

Only two fathers joined the mammies and the kids as they headed to Northumberland Road to take the double-decker bus into O'Connell Street to get another bus for Lucan. The bus conductor good-naturedly helped the mammies with their loads and helped the little kids get into the bus. As soon as everyone filled the bus, and all the stuff had been put in a niche, the kids burst out in song.

The same scene was repeated on the doubledecker to Sarsfield's Castle in Lucan. The bus soon left the city behind, and the scene shifted to a lovely green and gorse yellow landscape of hills and dales where hundreds of fluffy white sheep studded the green hills like snowballs.

The doubledecker stopped outside Sarsfield's demesne where we all disembarked, retrieved bundles, bags, teapots and kindling, and marched in a line to the entrance of the estate. The adults paid our way into the magical place. We walked towards a green meadow and set all our stuff down. A beautiful river edged the green meadow. Small low-flying planes, like dragon-flies, buzzed overhead heading for the runway across the river.

Mammies told us where to lay the blankets down in the grass, and all the kids wanted to eat right away. Sandwiches were unpacked, bags of fig roll biscuits were passed around. Bottles of lemonade were shared. The two daddies made a twig fire in order to heat water for their tea, and in the meanwhile they contented themselves with bottles of Guinness.

After all the gluttons were full, the older kids organised games, hiking excursions in the woods, and blackberry picking. Ma had advised us to take a couple of empty tins in case we ran across some blackberry bushes. We filled our tins in less than an hour with luscious plump purple blackberries that everyone grabbed into.

The river flowed slowly through the estate, a deep river of emerald green. A pair of cream-coloured swans glided on the emerald water like scoops of cream. The day out ended too soon. Mammies and kids, not used to having all day to bake in the sun, began to turn as red as roses. The moaning and groaning from the kids about having to pick up all the leftovers from the picnic before heading home caused the two daddies to turn very narky. Everyone headed for the entrance gate, and then for the doubledecker to take them back to the city, and then the bus back to Northumberland Road, and the walk to O'Brien's.

The day out provided stories for all the winter—the winter I came down with pneumonia.

Baggot Street Hospital

I came down with double pneumonia shortly after my eighth birthday. It wasn't the first time I had got sick, but this time Ma got scared because I had a hard time breathing. Ma bundled me up and took me to Baggot Street Hospital. We sat on one of the wooden benches in the dispensary room reserved for the poor and waited for a doctor to see me. The nurse wrote down my name in a big ledger.

Everyone who came to see a doctor had to have their name written in the ledger. A nurse came over and told Ma to take me into a small curtained cubicle where, after a long time, a doctor came and examined my chest with a stethoscope. He told Ma I needed to be admitted into the hospital. I told Ma I wanted to go home, but the doctor insisted that I be admitted. He wrapped me in a red blanket and carried me himself in his arms to the hospital lift.

After getting out of the lift, he took me into a ward. The only light in the ward sat on the nurse's desk. The nurse told the doctor to put me in a bed. The doctor left, and the nurse told Ma she had to leave. I begged Ma not to leave but the nurse insisted. I did not see any of the other patients because of the dim light.

The nurse told Ma that parents were only allowed to visit on Tuesday and Thursday. I went into the hospital on a Sunday night. It would be four days before Ma could get in to see me. Before she left, Ma undid my plaits and said she and Da would be up to see me as soon as they were allowed. She kissed me and told me to go to sleep.

As the morning light entered the ward, I saw other beds. I heard someone in the cot next to mine. I waited, then opened my eyes. I looked at the child in the bed next to me. She didn't look like any child I had ever seen before. She stood up in the bed and shook the rails. She grunted like an animal and I smelled a terrible smell. I looked at her in disbelief. Her eyes were round as saucers and her tongue stuck out. Her mouth, hands and nightdress were smeared with faeces.

I thought that I had died and woken in hell. I couldn't move my eyes away from her and I felt my mouth going numb. As the ward got brighter from the morning light, I saw the other children. They all looked like her. There were no children who looked like me. Shock set in and I remember a strange numbness began to spread over my face.

I struggled to keep from sticking my tongue out like the other children. My tongue kept wanting to push out from between my closed lips. I didn't know what to do or where to turn. Everything appeared so strange. The faces before me were like pictures of gargoyles in a book. I had died and gone to hell. Terror made me feel sick.

Then a nurse came into the ward, checked on everyone, and acted as if everything was normal. I couldn't make sense out of anything or understand what had happened to me. If I weren't dead, then the children had escaped from hell and I had to be with them. The nurse must not be able to see the children, I reasoned, or she would have said something to me.

The nurse came over to my bed and said nothing. She turned to the monster child in the bed next to mine, still covered with faeces, and shouted, 'Ann Mullen', which must have been the child's name. I didn't know if I were real any more.

Another person came in with food on a tray for me to eat. She said she was the wardsmaid, and that I was to eat the bowl of porridge and drink the glass of milk before she got back. I took the spoon in my hand and tried to eat some porridge. My mouth would not open. It felt as if someone had caged it closed. The wardsmaid took away the tray and told me I had wasted the food.

I lay in the bed unable to move or open my mouth. Then another nurse came in holding a washbasin and a pair of long scissors. She told me to sit up in the bed. She took the scissors and began to cut off chunks of hair. She cut and cut until all my hair lay in the washbasin like straw. After she went away with the basin of hair, I reached my hands to my head and drew them back in anguish, feeling the stiff, clipped hair on my head, no longer now than a boy's.

The woman returned again with the basin, and without a word began to wash my body. She must have thought I was invisible. When she got to my feet, she stopped and scolded me about being a big girl—a girl eight years old—with dirty feet. Her words cloaked me in shame. If I could have opened my mouth to speak I would have told her that I didn't have any shoes to wear to keep my feet off the ground. By now I felt so tired I could hardly keep from falling asleep as she washed away and complained about scruffy dirty Dublin children.

The wardsmaid came back with more food on the tray and demanded that I eat it. I tried to unlock my jaws but they would not open. I couldn't open my mouth! The wardsmaid grabbed my head and pushed it back and tried to force a spoonful of mashed potatoes into my mouth and I choked. I couldn't swallow. I kept gagging and choking at her insistence. With great annoyance, she dropped my head back on the pillow and left again with the tray of food. The only place I felt safe looking at was the ceiling overhead. I had a terrible fear of looking at the strange children who grunted and let their tongues fall out.

Then, I recall, a group of doctors dressed in white coats formed around my bed. An older man in a long white coat did all the talking. He told the others I was admitted with 'double pneumonia'. A voice in my head tried to say something to one of the men but I could not speak. I wanted them to tell me what had happened to me since my mother left. Something terrible had happened because my face had no feeling and my mouth had closed shut.

'Please, help me,' I begged the doctors in my mind. One of the doctors pulled down the top of the blanket and pushed up my shift. He held a stethoscope to my chest and told me to say out loud 99. 'Say 99. Say 99!' he demanded. Only my eyes could answer.

My mind asked God where he was in this place. I pleaded for God to help me. I pleaded for God to take me out of the terrible place. But he never answered or came. He wouldn't come. I began to realise that if God existed he would never let me stay in the horrible place with all the gargoyle children. When God did not come to rescue me I knew there was no God. There wasn't any God. God did not exist. Someone had made it all up about God. They had all lied.

It must have been the next day when two doctors came to examine me again. One of the doctors told me he was going to listen to my chest. He smiled at me. Then he turned to the other doctor and said, 'The cat must have her tongue. Such blue eyes she has, too,' he added. Then as if to get me to respond to something, he picked up my wrist, took a ballpoint pen from his pocket and wrote something down on my arm in ink. He lifted my wrist to show me what he had written down. 'See? F. A. W. F. A. W. are my initials. They stand for Frank Anderson Walker.'

When Ma came to see me, she sat on a chair next to the bed. She acted and talked as if nothing had happened and nothing appeared out of the ordinary. She looked around the ward, then at the child in the bed next to mine, and made the sign of the cross.

When Ma talked to me, I never answered any of her questions. I wasn't able to tell her about not being able to open my mouth or talk any more. I couldn't tell her about my face being numb. I couldn't explain anything. Looking out from my eyes, she seemed to be in a fog and unreal. Ma complained that the nurse had told her I would not eat any food. Ma said, 'You have to eat, love.'

I wanted her to go away and leave me alone. I wanted to fade away. But Ma bent over my ear and sang.

Hey, little hen, when, when, when,
When will you lay me an egg for my tea?
Jump into your nest, and do your very best
And lay me an egg for my tea.

And she sang again,

She was sweet sixteen, little Angeline
Always dancing on the village green,
As the boys passed by, you could hear them sigh,
'There's little Angeline!'

Ma kissed me before she left.

The nurses kept trying to make me eat, and I kept choking on the food. I found it impossible to swallow. Some voice appeared in my mind and told me to make my 'real self' go away—told me to 'fade away'; said the 'me' in colours had gone away forever and that only the 'me' in grey could live. It said, 'Angeline in colour wants to die. Send her away. Make her go away! If you don't make Angeline in colour disappear, you won't be able to live.'

In order to stop the voice in my head, I began to say all my prayers backwards, count all my numbers backwards and recite all my stories and songs backwards; if I didn't do that the demanding voice came back and told me things. I wanted to drift away, to die, to become as invisible as air. I could feel my body getting lighter because of not eating any food.

My lips were chapped from people trying to force food into my mouth. And my head hurt from people telling me how bad and wilful I was for not eating my food. The nurses and wardsmaids stopped bringing me trays and left me alone.

One night, someone woke me up and lifted me up in the bed. A young nurse held me in her arms. She rocked me back and forth. 'You must eat some food,' she told me. And she said, 'I'm going to stay with you until you can eat something. I want to take care of you. You have to eat. Otherwise, in the morning the doctor is going to put a rubber tube down your throat and it will hurt you. Please, for my sake, eat.'

I wanted to tell her that I wasn't hungry and for people to stop worrying about me having some food. I wasn't trying to be bad I only wanted to fade. I didn't need any food. I was getting lighter, even now . . .

She tried to put a spoon of food into my mouth. I couldn't feel my mouth. I started to vomit up salty water. She cleaned off my face. She whispered she'd be back and to rest. She came back, and this time she whispered my name. She lifted me up and held me again in her arms. She said, 'You're a lovely child. Do you know you are a lovely child?'

She continued saying things to me. Then she whispered in my ear. 'I went to one of the private wards and stole some lovely food for you. Let me feed you with my fingers.' She pried apart my sore lips and inserted tiny pieces of chicken with her fingers. I tried to swallow the food but could not. I vomited. She cleaned out my mouth with her fingers. She tried again, and I vomited more salty water. Then she told me to rest. She picked me up again and held me. She used her fingers to pry my lips apart again, then she squashed a sweet raspberry inside my mouth and the juice began to trickle down the back of my throat. I tasted something sweet and I began to swallow. She put in another squashed berry and another.

She let me rest for a little while. Then she picked-me up in her arms again. She put a tiny taste of the chicken meat in my mouth, and I started to chew it, and I started to feel hungry. I felt like eating a horse. The nurse kept telling me, 'Oh, good! Oh. good!'

She continued to hold me in her arms. She told me that I had been so good because she said when a person hadn't eaten for days, it was the hardest thing. She brushed my shaved head with her hand, and told me to sleep. She whispered that she'd tell the doctor I had eaten food, at last.

When I got out of bed, I remember walking around the ward. I saw a nurse letting some of the kids out to play on the balcony outside the ward. I went onto the balcony, and the world outside seemed so beautiful. The sky was blue as clover. The colours seemed astonishing. The wrought-iron balcony reached above my head. I looked through the railings down to the street to where people were passing by. From the height of the balcony, the people looked like toys. And none of the trees growing in front of the hospital entrance reached as high as the balcony.

As I stood looking out through the space in the railings, I could see birds flying back and forth. I wanted to get away from the hospital. I started to talk to the birds in my head. One bird flew towards me and landed on the balcony. I asked the bird to carry me away. It said that I was too heavy, I had to stay where I was. The voice in my head told me to climb over the balcony and jump. 'It won't hurt,' said the voice. The voice got stern, and ordered me to 'Jump over!' I started to climb up the railing in my bare feet. The iron grillework stuck into my feet. I tried to climb, but the grillework dug into my feet and prevented me from climbing over the rail.

I heard one of the nurses calling me back inside. I began to rage for not having been able to climb to the top of the balcony and jump off. I looked out again through the grillework and told myself the world outside, because it was so beautiful, had to vanish. I hated it! I hated all the colours. I never wanted to see the world in blue again for as long as I lived!

The voice returned, sounding more reasonable. It told me I could never live in colour again, only in grey. The voice said I had to make the colours fade out! 'Because,' the voice reasoned, 'Angeline who loves colours can't live any more. She has to be sent away.' The voice warned again and again, 'If Angeline in colour is not sent away, the "Angeline" in grey won't be able to hold on anymore.'

I don't remember leaving the hospital.

I recall being in O'Brien's watching some birds pecking something in the laneway. They were all grey birds and their beaks and wings were all broken. They kept trying to fly up into the air, but they kept falling back down. I told them, in my mind, they were stupid little birds with broken beaks and broken wings, and that I hated them and would never give them any more breadcrumbs. One of the birds answered me back, in my mind, and said, 'We're just like you. We're just like you.'

I raved at the birds in my mind. I screamed that I never wanted to see another bird of any kind for as long as I lived.

I leaned my face against the whitewashed wall and inched myself all along the wall until I got home.

Even when back in our room, the greyness of the world inside and out seemed unbearable, but it had to be grey, went reason, otherwise madness. It took desperation to try to keep whole no matter what Ma and Da tried to do for me. Reason told me to make a file in my mind in which to put all the memories of the hospital and of the broken birds in O'Brien's and to seal the terrible memories away for ever. The file could never be opened. Never.

Sleep held me in its clutches. One eye could not hold the other eye open. I sat by the fire to keep warm and gazed into the flames. I remember Ma arguing with me for not responding or talking to her or Da. She'd say, over and over, 'What's happened to our gabbygut?' But only drowsiness prevailed.

Poor Da sat by and made up songs and stories to sing or tell me to make contact with me. Finally, it was his lovely stories and singsongs that drew back the grey curtain and let a few blue sparks enter.

Da's yarns

Da made up stories and told me rhymes and riddles he'd known since he was a child. I remember them yet.

> As I went down a guttery-gap,
> I met an old man in a red hat.
> He'd a stick in his hand and a stone in his belly.
> Riddle me that and I'll give you a penny.

He made me laugh with this song:

> Paddy McGinty, an Irish man of note,
> Fell into a fortune, and bought himself a goat.
> 'Goat's milk,' said Paddy, 'I mean to have me fill,'
> But when he brought his nanny home,
> He found it was a bill.

And he sang,

> And, up he spoke the little thrush,
> And he kept whistling in the bush.
> O! I lost my mate in the last big snow,
> And I'm wondering since where she ever did go.

Another of Da's stories went like this:

Once upon a time in the backwoods of Australia, lived a little girl by the name of Hanna Banana. One day her mother carried her in a basket on her back to work in the fields. Her mother told Hanna Banana not to wander off while she worked, because there were big eagles living around. Hanna Banana didn't listen to her mother, and she wandered off on her own.

A great big eagle flew down and picked her up in his claws and carried her to his nest in a great tall tree. The eagle put Hanna Banana into its nest that was filled with baby eaglets.

Hanna was frightened. Meanwhile, her mother noticed that the little girl was being too quiet; she wondered why Hanna Banana wasn't making any noise. The mother got worried about her daughter, and started to call out her name: "Hanna, Hanna-Banana! Where are you?' She was nowhere in sight! She was gone!

Just then, Hanna's mother looked up into the sky and saw a great huge eagle circling above her. She watched the eagle and wondered . . . Then the mother saw the eagle's big nest in the tree, and she heard Hanna Banana cry out, 'Save me from the big eagle! The eagle has me in his nest. Save me!'

Hanna Banana's mother ran home as fast as her two legs could carry her, and she got a ladder so she could climb up the tree and rescue Hanna.

The mother ran back to the tree where her daughter was, as fast as her two legs could carry her. She could see the big nest in the branches where Hanna was with the young eaglets. The mother put the ladder against the tree, then she tied the rope around the tree and inched herself towards the top of the branches.

Just then the big eagle saw Hanna Banana's mother and flew towards her head; he flapped his large wings at her to make her go away. She still kept climbing towards the nest. When she finally got to the nest, the eagle flew at her again! She fought with the eagle. Then the eagle covered the nest over with his great big wings, and Hanna Banana was covered up.

Then the mother took a stone from her pocket and she stuffed it into the eagle's ear. The eagle had to fold back his wings in order to rub his ear, so just then, Hanna Banana's mother grasped her daughter and climbed down the rope to the ladder, and the two of them ran home. And from that day on, Hanna Banana never went off into the wilds of Australia by herself to get captured by another giant eagle.

Another favourite was about the witch in Castleblayney:

In Castleblayney the cattle stopped giving milk, crops withered, and the drinking water reeked. The people in the town wondered what was happening. Farmers said, 'This is the first time that our cattle have all gone dry,' and their fields were failing to grow barley, wheat and hay. They sought advice from various authorities to find out what was happening to their cattle and crops. No one seemed to have an answer. Then the farmers went to the parish priest for advice. He asked them if anyone had noticed anything unusual in the village or round about.

Some men then remembered that they had seen a black-clad figure of a woman sitting and singing by the edge of the Black Lake. The woman had hailed the men with laughter and verse! In return, they had cursed and thrown stones at her and ordered her to leave the lakeside, but she had refused to go.

The parish priest wanted to know all about the gangly woman they described from near the water. The priest said that in light of what was happening to the cattle, crops, and drinking water, it seemed to him that the woman by the lake must be a witch, and it was surely she who was to blame for the mischief to the cattle and crops. The priest and the farmers went to the lake, and they saw the willowy woman enjoying herself by the edge of the lake. She shouted out strange verse to invisible ears. The priest took this as a sign of witchcraft. He approached her in trepidation, fingered his cross, and told her to take her evil away from the Black Lake. She laughed in his face and told him he looked like a raven. She refused to leave her home by the lake.

For days and months, the priest and farmers went to the Black Lake and demanded that the witch go, and she continued to defy them. She told the men that she had not put a curse on the crops, cattle, or water, but they refused to believe her. They threw rocks and sticks at her. She got angry, and told the priest that she was indestructible to every force but one, but she didn't tell him what force that was.

Giving up attempting to banish the witch from the lake, the priest and farmers turned to the women of the town for help to rid the town of the witch. The women sent out word around the town that they were having a party, and that every woman in the town and the countryside was invited to come.

The witch by the Black Lake got word of what the women were planning. She often got lonely for the company of other women, so when the women met in one of the small cottages, stoked-up a big red fire in the grate, covered the kitchen table with a starched white table-cloth, and sat by the table hoping that the witch would come, the witch was happy to drop in. When the witch appeared in their company, the women made a fuss of her, and told her how glad they were to see her and all.

The women pretended to talk about things in their normal fashion, in order not to make the witch suspicious of anything unusual. One woman brought up the question to another in the room, 'Can anyone here change their appearance if they want to? Can anyone here turn into anything that might be imagined?'

Another asked, 'Does anyone know what the strongest thing in the world is?'

The quiet was broken when the witch informed the women that she could turn herself into anything she wanted to in the world! At this moment, another woman piped up, 'Can you turn yourself into the softest and strongest single thing in the world?'

'And what is that?' asked the witch. The woman answered her: 'The softest and the strongest single thing in the world is a hair from a woman's head.' The room grew silent. The silence in the room roared. The women sat around the table and waited in silence. They sat watching the white cloth on the table. Something started to move on the white cloth. The women saw a long strong coal black hair move on the white tablecloth. It was easy to see against the whiteness. Then they noticed that the witch no longer sat in her chair. The women stared in wonder at the long hair moving on the table, soft and strong.

The woman nearest to the table stepped forward, lifted the hair from the table with her fingers, ran to the fireplace, and dropped the single hair into the red roaring coals. A screech pierced the room.

Later, the priest and the men were overheard to say that only another woman could have fooled the witch like that. Men had been trying for years and years to destroy the witch of the Black Lake, they said, without success. The witch of the Black Lake had got herself caught in the tangle of a woman's crowning glory.

Da's yarns lifted me out of an abyss. He must have got blue in the face from singing so many songs and telling so many stories. I held onto every word. After a while, my desolation waned.

Granny Martin also lifted my spirits when she told Ma to tell me she wanted to teach me how to knit socks and learn how to turn a well-shaped heel of a sock. Granny Lynch had her niece Kathy come over to our room with a fresh egg for me twice a week. Kathy would tell Ma in the doorway, 'The egg just dropped out iv the hen's backside.'

Bob let me read his comics, the *Beano* and the *Dandy* from page to page. Comic characters like Keyhole Kate, Desperate Dan, and Korky the Cat made me laugh. Ma cut out paper dolls with me from old newspapers and pasted them into copy books. My brother Frank bought me a fairy cake now and then. Noely Joseph, surprised by my silence, continued to slobber me with jam-tasting kisses. With time and care, the world opened up again, but would it ever be blue again?

Graveyards

Dolores lived with her aunt and uncle and three cousins in the same room. She had lived with her three sisters, her brother and their parents in a room in O'Brien's until tragedy struck the family. Her father served in the British army in World War II. Soon after he returned to Dublin, he was killed in a motor accident. Dolores knew what had happened and told me the story. Her father had hitched a ride in the back of an army lorry that drove under Boland's Bridge and he forgot to duck down in the back of the lorry as it went under the low bridge. He got his head bashed and died. A year later her mother died of consumption. Her mother had been my godmother.

Dolores went to live with her aunt and uncle and three nieces in the tenement next to ours. Her sisters and her brother went to live with other relatives scattered along O'Brien's.

Everyone talked about how generous the English government acted towards Dolores's family. They paid for the father's burial and a gravesite in Dean's Grange cemetery, on the outskirts of Dublin because of his service to the crown. When Dolores' mother died she was buried with her husband in Dean's Grange.

In springtime, Dolores got an urge to visit her parents' grave. She asked me to walk out to the graveyard with her. It took us all morning and half the afternoon before we arrived at the place. When we found the grave, Dolores began to tidy it up. Since nobody was around, Dolores hopscotched from one grave to another and collected flowers that she brought back and placed on her parents' grave.

Then we circled the grounds to collect white pebbles which we carried scooped in the front of our frocks. Dolores pressed the white pebbles onto her parent's grave mound in the shape of a cross.

The graveyard seemed so peaceful compared to our cramped rooms in O'Brien's. If we had had our way, both of us would have camped out in the serene setting. After she moved in with her relatives, Dolores worked like a child in a Victorian novel from morning 'til night. Every time I saw her, she was either on her knees washing the floor or swirling soot with a dustrag from the window. When she could get away, we both loved to go to the graveyard and absorb ourselves in its peace.

Because of the generosity of the British government in buying a gravesite for her father, Dolores knew where both of her parents were buried, unlike the relatives of the dead who were put in unmarked graves. For them, it was altogether a different kettle of fish.

When Granda O'Connor died, a little after my ninth birthday, Ma had no money to bury him. He went into another pauper's pit.

Ma's father, Joseph O'Connor, enlisted in 1915 in the Royal Dublin Fusiliers to fight for England in World War I. The O'Connors included Ma, her brother, Robert, her father and mother. The four of them lived in a rented room in 1 Leitrim Place, Grand Canal Street, Dublin. Granda, like other Irish men, had joined the British army for a job.

Ma showed me the small leather soldier's identification book he had kept with him through the war. He enlisted on 10 June 1915, and left from Cobh, County Cork, for France on 5 October 1916. In the midst of warfare, he wrote down a recipe for Fruit Ball candy in his identification book for his two children back in Ireland.

After three years of war, Joseph O'Connor received an honourable army discharge. His army record bears the following information on Granda: 'A sober and willing man. Disability aggravated by Active Dementia.' When he returned to Leitrim Place after fighting with the British forces, Joseph O'Connor still had poison gas in his system, had lost half an index finger, could no longer completely shut his eyelids for the rest of his life, and remained shellshocked.

Ma recalled that her father had no idea how he got home to Ireland, that he had to be reacquainted with his wife, wondered who she and her brother belonged to and insisted on sleeping under the bed. And, she recalled, if a pin dropped, her father trembled like a hosed dog. It took a while for Granda to come out of his fog, but he never got over life in the trenches.

Besides taking care of her shellshocked husband, Granny O'Connor had to find outside work, Ma had to leave school and work as a child's maid, and Robert O'Connor did any job available, until he got old enough to emigrate to England to find work, and send money back home.

Ma said that when I was born her mother ran up and down O'Brien's calling out to the neighbours that her daughter, Mary, had given birth to a baby girl. Ma said Granny O'Connor rocked me on her lap 'til I nodded off like a spinning-top. Ma also explained that Granny pointed out to her the difference between having sons and daughters: A girl is a daughter all of her life, but a son is a son 'til he gets a wife.

Granny O'Connor died of a stroke after I reached the age of two. Ma said the stroke had been brought on by worry about taking care of Granda, paying the rent and finding money for food, and her without a shilling to her name.

When Granny died there was no money to buy her a gravesite. She had to be buried in a pauper's grave, an unmarked pit. It tore Ma that she had no money to buy a burial plot for her mother. Granny O'Connor and Ma's firstborn were now both buried fields apart in paupers' mounds. Da wrote a letter to the British army council letting them know of Granda's death. Da thought that the British government might foot the bill for a gravesite for one of their honourable veterans of World War l, but Da was wrong.

Da respected Joseph O'Connor and often invited him over to spend an evening with us in O'Brien's. Granda would plant himself on the chair in front of the fire, take out his tobacco pouch, and filled his pipe. He stuffed the tobacco down in the bowl of the pipe with the remaining joint of his index finger, the first two joints having been lost to the war.

Da encouraged Granda to talk about the war. Granda had fought in France. He talked of fighting side by side with other men from Ireland by the names of Louis Nolan, Frank Kavanagh, Tom Murray, the chap O'Dowd, Paddy Doyle and a chap with the last name Wall. My two older brothers glued their ears to Granda's recollections of the war.

He told them when he got on the battlefield for the first time, he heard a terrible roar the likes of which he had never heard before. The roar came from a horse hit by shards from a bomb. The animal roared out with pain. The horse had been used, like hundreds of other horses in the battles, to haul wagons outfitted with machine guns. The horse's roar still roared in Granda's head. He heard it in dreams at night and before he opened his eyes in the morning light. The dying horse, screaming out in mortal agony, became the most vivid image of the war for Granda.

He also told how the soldiers constantly gave attention to their leg wrappings to make sure they didn't become undone and trip up their feet. There had been cases where a soldier's leg wrapping became undone and caused him to trip and fall, making it easy for the enemy to pick him off with a bullet. Granda rolled off the serial number of his rifle and bayonet: 2969.

One of the worse parts of Granda's war story had to do with women. Some German women stayed in the trenches with their husbands or sweethearts or whatever. When the trenches were charged, the women ripped open the top part of whatever they wore to bare their breasts to the fighters to show them they were women and not men, hoping the soldiers would not use a bayonet or rifle on a woman.

Da asked Granda if he, himself, ever saw such a thing, but Granda remained mum. When it got time for Granda to go home, Ma took out a tin can, scooped a couple of red smouldering sods of turf from out of the grate and dropped them into the can. She handed the can to her father so he could use the embers to start a fire in his own grate when he got home.

Now Granda's coffin sat on the soggy grass, along with others, until the priest came to say a prayer over the dead. The gaped maw of black earth already held an armful of decomposing caskets with room for more. Today's supply of caskets would fill up the maw and the gravediggers would shovel back the black clods of wet earth and fill the pit in for the last time. Wild grasses and ferns would soon cover the lot and leave no trace of occupancy.

The Dublin agency in charge of burying the dispossessed, insisted that no marker be placed upon their mound: 'out of sight out of mind' was their motto.

While we waited in the pouring rain for the priest to come, Da remarked that the poor, whether alive or dead, are sent to oblivion. 'We're not within an ass's roar of being the country I pledged to die for,' he said. Then, I remember his voice as he hissed, 'Damn the winter cold.'

Ma, herself drenched by the bleak rain, tried to keep her father's coffin dry, wiping it off with the edge of her coat while Noely and Bob fought to keep dry by ducking under the back of her coat.

'This God blasted rain c'd be cut in two with a knife,' hissed Da as he took Ma's arm to link in his. The priest finally came and started to mumble over the coffins glossy with rain. I blotted out the mumbling of the raincoated priest from my mind and repeated silly words in my head that went: soggy, woggy, boggy, loggy, sloch, shite, shite and cauliflowers. And, why do Ma and Da not have a raincoat nor an umbrella like the priest to keep them dry from the soaking rain?

The priest glued his eyes on Ma as he gurgled. He seemed taken by the blue of her eyes, the absolute colour of violets. As I watched

Ma by the graveside, the rain oozing from holes in her rat-nibbled shoes, I recalled Ma's story about some gunmen they encountered.

Before her father shipped off to serve in the British army, he took her out for some ice-cream. He wore his British army uniform. As they crossed over O'Connell Bridge, Granda holding Ma's hand, they were set upon by a group of men who had spotted Granda in his uniform. One of them pulled out a gun and told Granda to get against the wall to be shot as a traitor. It was at this moment, said Ma, that another one looked at her frightened face and told his comrades to put their guns away, for the sake of the child.

Granda said that if Ma had not been with her, he'd have been shot dead. After I thought about the incident, I prayed that the light of Jesus would beam upon Granda's soul and beam him to heaven, where there was no bitter want nor hatred.

The gravediggers might have been stone gargoyles as they shovelled the thick black mud over the coffins, never lifting up an eye from their task or uttering the sound of a word. After the coffin got slid onto the others, the priest went over to the gravediggers and told them (for us to hear) not to take any money from the poor woman. The six of us headed off for the long walk back to O'Brien's. The pauper's pit housed the dispossessed in death, just as O'Brien's housed the disadvantaged in life. So Ma's first baby, Granny, and Granda O'Connor and all the others without a fag to their name, were bedded down with unknown companions.

Pedlars

Mr Ferguson came around to O'Brien's every Monday night to collect the rents. His grey mackintosh coat lapped at the bottom of his black boots, he wore a bowler hat which came down to meet his pleated forehead, woolly gloves covered over the chilblains on his encrusted hands, and he carried a knockabout valise, in which he kept his rent ledgers. After Mr Ferguson collected the rents, he put the coins into a drawstring cloth bag, which he pulled tight with his teeth. He kept his small snuffbox in his trouser pocket. He'd take a rest from collecting money, and reach into his trouser pocket for his snuffbox. A nice smell, a little like fresh horse shite, came from the little box when Mr Ferguson pinched a sniff of snuff from the box with his forefinger and thumb. He put the snuff into each side of his nose, sniffed then snorted and offered a pinch of the snuff to Granny Martin and Ma. I asked him for a try once, and nearly choked as a result.

Some of the neighbours called the rent collector names behind his back. It wasn't out of the ordinary for someone to call Mr Ferguson 'an auld whore's melt' for expecting people to pay rent for the dives he collected on. Ma asked him one night who he collected the rents for. He told her that the places were owned by very well-known men in the city, whom he wasn't at liberty to name. The landlords who owned the ten tenement buildings never showed their kissers on the street. No upkeep of any kind was ever done on the dumps.

Mr Erwin, the milkman, galloped into O'Brien's in a horse-drawn milk cart. He sat in the chariot type contraption like a Roman emperor. Two large steel milk vats were secured to the floor of the chariot. Everyone heard the hooves of the horse's feet clattering over the cobblestone street, at precisely the same time every afternoon. The milkman stopped the cart in the middle of the street, and banged on one of the metal vats with a measuring cup.

Mr Erwin wore a long white coat over his street clothes. He carried three sizes of measuring jugs in the cart and used each to measure out a specific amount of milk for a customer. The women came out of the buildings to buy milk. Some carried small metal milk cans, others had delft milk jugs, jamjars, or milk bottles, and the poorest ones of all would carry a tin cup. The usual amount of milk purchased was a pint, though it went all the way down to a penny's worth.

Granny Legg hobbled out first at the sound of the horse's feet hitting the cobblestones. She had two gripes that she constantly confronted the milkman with. She went on and on about how terrible it was that the government now pasteurised the milk sold to people. Mr Erwin had to listen to her repeated recording about pasteurisation. 'It's like taking the blue out of ink. How can ye take the blue out of ink and it still be ink?' Then she was off about the horse. 'That horse is naked. The children can see everything it's got. Have ye seen them down on their knees looking under its belly? Throw a blanket over the beast!'

Mr Erwin's horse, Chestnut, pissed and shat in O'Brien's every time he was there. Ma thought the animal's running on the cobblestones loosened-up its bowels, and it couldn't help but drop its load. The poor thing wasn't doing it on purpose.

The sight of the big animal doing its number one—and number two—with the steam and everything on a frosty day drew gawkers by the bunch. Seeing the physical change the horse was capable of performing mesmerised us. Had old Legg got her way, the show would have come to an end.

Paddy the coalman seemed the complete opposite of Mr Erwin who never showed a speck of dirt on his body. Paddy was covered with coal dust from top to bottom. He dressed in old clothes and wore a gunnysack tied around his shoulders that met under his chin and was fastened with a safety pin. He sat on an old wooden crate on the cart in front of a big grey horse, reins held in his hands. The horse pulled a long flat wooden cart piled with sacks of coal. Coalmen like Paddy, had young helpers, young boys, to help open the sack of coal, weigh out the coal for customers, and deliver the coal. The boys looked like their hearts were going to burst from having to handle the dirty, dusty coal all day long.

Granny Martin usually had the money to buy a sack of coal, but most of the other women had money only for a bucketful. Paddy, to his credit, let some of the women buy the coal on tick. He'd wait until they were able to come up with some money, and not let their family go cold.

The pedlars who traded in O'Brien's were all men, except for Nanny-the-fish and the fishmonger. Nanny-the-fish owned her own horse and cart. She came down the cobblestones on a Monday and Friday, her cart loaded with cabbages, turnips, parsnips, onions, scallions, green apples, red apples, and sacks of potatoes. Neighbours thought that Nanny had a hard nature. She muffled herself up in a secondhand army topcoat, wore a pair of men's trousers and a turban wrapped around her head. She smoked and coughed like a chimney on fire.

Nanny-the-fish took no chances. Before she handed anything over on credit, she made sure whose husband had a job and whose husband was idle. She took down the creditor's room number, how many kids they had, and where their husbands worked. She charged interest on the food she sold on credit. I see her complaining to Ma, eyeing her up and down, 'If ye didn't keep particulars on giving out credit, people would take the eye out of yer head and come back for the lashes.' We nodded in agreement, as Nanny listed the credit given to us.

Mrs Daly the fishmonger showed up on the street only on Friday mornings or on fast days when Catholics couldn't eat meat. She pushed an old baby's pram loaded down with wooden trays filled with fish. She parked the pram in the middle of the street and began to sing out, 'Nice Howth herrin', nice fresh mackerel, plaice and CODFISH!'

The ragman came to O'Brien's about twice a year to collect glass bottles and old clothing. He pushed a wooden pushcart. He shouted out, 'Any rags, any rags for sale? Money for rags. Any rags to sell. Any glass bottles to sell? Any glass bottles to sell?' He'd offer kids money to go around and knock on the neighbours' doors to get him rags and bottles. Those who had any rags to sell, other than the wornout clothing they wore on their bodies, were few and far between.

The ragman paid sixpence an armful for old clothes and a penny for four glass bottles. 'He'll get sweet fuck-all around here,' laughed a gurrier within earshot of the ragman.

The most talked-about pedlar to sweep into O'Brien's drove in a motorcar. The woman came to be called the 'Jewess' or the 'film star' by some. She set up business in Bridie R's room. Bridie decided who got to meet the film star and try for a loan.

The film star was a dead ringer for Shelley Winters. Ma and the other women were glad to be able to borrow money from her because no Irish bank would lend anyone in O'Brien's a farthing. Banks would not even allow a poor person to enter their doors, sending their doorman to shoo them away like flies. To be able to borrow a little money from someone other than the Panther seemed a blessing.

The film star showed-up on Monday afternoons. She had the run of Bridie's room. She sat on a chair in front of the kitchen table, and interviewed the women Bridie lined up for her. The film star had similar set-ups around various parts of Dublin. The glamorous woman wrapped herself in a cuddly butterscotch teddybear fur coat. She wore make-up and had blond curly hair. Her perfume drifted like the smell of roses. She asked borrowers a set of questions, looked in Bridie's direction, got a nod from Bridie, and gave out the loan.

The borrowers were expected to pay interest back on the loans, and Bridie expected a payoff for recommending them for the loans. When some of the women failed or were late in paying back the loans, Bridie, not the film star, came around and ate their faces off.

Men in O'Brien's resented the moneylender, not because she had money to loan, or because she drove a motorcar, or because she made their women seem faded, but, they said, because she was Jewish. As far as Ma, and other women were concerned, The Panther still stood alone as the highway robber.

Like her son, Granny Martin kept an eye open to find ways to bring in a few bob. I remember how once she came up with a harebrained scheme that still makes me crimson in the face.

Amateur night at the Queen's

Granny Martin came by her idea to get some kids in O'Brien's into show business from seeing a talent show at the Queen's Theatre in Pearse Street, Dublin. Every Sunday night the Queen's held an amateur talent show, and the winners received prize money. The weekly show attracted contestants from all over the city. It was divided into two sections: the early show for kids up to the age of fourteen, and the second part for adults. Working-class people flocked to the weekly shows at the Queen's.

Granny Martin went every chance she got. She convinced Ma and other mothers to enter their daughters in the amateur show to win some money, or maybe get a chance to become another Gloria Green. Granny had heard us singing sitting on the stairs.

The Queen's and Gloria Green went hand-in-hand like Maureen Potter with the Gaiety Theatre. Gloria always played the part of Prince Charming in the Christmas pantos every year. The possibility of becoming another Gloria Green held appeal.

Granny Martin stood over Da's shoulder as he wrote to the people in charge of Amateur Night at the Queen's. Every participant had to send in a letter before he or she would be allowed on the show. Da wrote down every word Granny Martin told him to no matter how much he shook his head in disbelief.

Weeks passed before the postman delivered a letter from the Queen's. Gracie, Bernadette, Patricia and myself were all invited to be on the amateur show. We had two weeks to get ready, though none of us yet knew the complete words to a whole song. Word spread throughout O'Brien's we were going on the Queen's. As soon as old Legg got wind of it, she came round to say to all, 'If ye're going to sing a song, sing an Irish song, and not common love things.' Legg got Da's attention.

'Titch! Sing the great old Fenian Song, "Down by the Glenside". Or the "Song of Fionnuala", the lament for King Lir's three children who were turned to swans. Or "The Bard of Armagh".' But Da's suggestions were unacceptable.

'I'm only going to sing catchy songs. The kinds on Sadie's wireless set. "The Alphabet Song" or "Wheel of Fortune" or "There's a Pawnshop Round the Corner in Pittsburgh, Pennsylvania",' I shouted at Da.

'I never heard of such songs,' he said.

'That's because we haven't a wireless set,' I retorted.

'Well, sing me a few bars of a catchy song, as you call such songs', said Da, pretending to be all ears.

I stood in front of him, flared the end of my skirt, pointed a toe, and began to sing.

'A, you're adorable, B, you're so beautiful, C, you're a bundle full of charms.

D, you're desirable, E you're exciting, and F, you're a feather in me arms.'

'Holy smoke! Go no further. God save us! Is that what's coming over the airwaves into Ireland from England and America, and falling into young ears. I want you to sing "Down by the Glenside" and not some disgraceful song like you've just sung,' Da pouted.

'All right, I'll sing yer song, "Down by the Glenside", if it means that much to ye.'

Da didn't know the original words to the first verse, never mind all five, but he didn't let that get in the way. When he drew a blank he added his own words.

'How can I learn a hundred and fifty versions of "Down by the Glenside"?' I asked him. 'Every time you sing it, it's a different version,' I screamed in exasperation. He finally, agreed to write down his latest version of 'Down by the Glenside', in a penny notebook.

Meanwhile, Bernadette, Patricia and Gracie had their ears glued to Sadie's wireless set, day and night, learning catchy songs. Each one of us practised our songs until showtime. Our mothers were hard at work too. They borrowed money to buy us new dresses and shoes and to pay to get themselves into the Queen's to see us perform.

On the night of the performance, our mammies took us backstage and made us up. They unrolled the pipe-cleaners they had used as curlers in our hair, leaving us with frizzy mops, plastered tan leg-polish over our faces, buffed our cheeks with red rouge, and lipsticked mouths to cupid bows. The make-up had been Granny Martin's idea. She knew on the gospel about such things.

The master of ceremonies for the amateur show came backstage to introduce himself; His name was Frankie. He'd a big booming voice, and a mouth packed with teeth. 'You're the first on the programme tonight,' he told me. He said that as soon as I heard Mr Gill, the piano player, ending the show's signature song I was to walk on stage. We could hear all the people getting into their seats, the yells coming down from the gods, and everyone arguing back and forth.

I'd never stepped on a stage before. Ma noticed the dribble of pee slowly sliding down my leg, and wiped it with her hankie. The fright of going on to the stage, with all the roaring people—you could hear the noise a mile away—nearly caused me to faint. Mr Gill began to play the signature song and it ended in an instant.

'Ladies and gentlemen,' roared the announcer over the noise, 'Our first contestant tonight is a little lady from O'Brien's Place by the name of . . .' and someone shoved me onto the stage.

The size of the stage, the noise, the blinding lights, the spotlight, the sounds of the audience, and the announcer's booming voice shook me like a wave. The MC gently led me to the microphone, and told me I'd better do something. Mr Gill began to play a few bars of 'Down by the Glenside' and nodded for me to begin singing the song. Frightened as an animal, I could not remember the words to any of Da's 150 different versions of 'Down by the Glenside', so I made up a new one. Frankie led me off the stage after Mr Gill went into a loud crescendo on the piano.

Bernadette sang the song, 'Your Cheating Heart', and got some applause when she finished. Gracie sang her mother's favourite song, 'Red River Valley', and got applause, and Patricia sang 'The Wheel of Fortune', with a sobbing edge and she got a better response from the audience than all of us put together from O'Brien's.

Then on came the other contestants one by one. A girl from the Iveagh Flats, dressed in red organdy, head a mass of curls and dimples everywhere, sang and danced 'The Hop Scotch Polka' to thunderous applause. After the ten contestants were finished, we filed back on stage and formed a line facing the audience. Frankie reminded the audience that they voted for the winner by their applause. He held a ruler over my head and the audience responded with a few claps, then on to Bernadette, louder for her; Patricia about the same loudness. Gracie did better. When he held the paper over the head of the girl who sang 'The Hop Scotch Polka', all hell broke loose, and she walked off with the first prize.

After word got out in the lane that neither Bernadette, Patricia, Gracie nor I had been placed in the talent competition, we were treated like stink bombs, especially by the other kids.

Da said that the Irish were losing their love of the great ancient songs of their forefathers, and that's why I hadn't been placed in the competition. Ma said not to worry, tomorrow is another day. And Granny Martin the instigator of the harebrained scheme, behaved as if she had never clapped eyes on me. She acted as if I had lost the contest on purpose. It took a week for her to come around and admit that I had done the best I could.

Soon O'Brien's Place had more important things on its mind than a talent competition at the Queen's. The Irish government sent a woman to O'Brien's to spy on the families who lived there. The spy came to be known as the 'sanitary lady inspector'. She called herself a 'social worker'.

Sanitary lady inspector

Word got around in O'Brien's that the government had sent a spy to the neighbourhood. I saw her get out of her motor car. She looked to be Ma's age, only healthier. She wore a tweed uniform and carried a briefcase. She told Ma and the other women that she had come to inspect the living conditions of every household. She warned the women that she had the right to come into their homes and inspect them, and furthermore, she would come unannounced, and anyone who refused to let her in would be written-up about.

She told Ma and others that if they neglected their children, she had the power of authority from the Irish government to take the children away. The children would be put into a boarding school until they reached the age of sixteen. Her threats mortified Ma and the other mammies.

The families in O'Brien's struggled every day to survive and did the best they could to raise their children in the rented pigsties. One of the neighbours, Mrs Walsh, let the spy know that the landlords who owned the places never set a foot in the lane nor did they care if every man, woman, and child got typhoid from using the filthy swills in the backyards.

The threat of taking children away from their mothers caused great anxiety not only for our mammies, but also for us kids. The sight of the woman in tweed began to sicken our stomachs.

'Did she get her orders to spy on us from the British Crown or the Irish Free State?' inquired Master John on the street corner.

'So, the day is here when people like her can tell Dublin people like us how to manage our lives?' lipped Peter back to Master John.

We knew that no amount of soap and water could wash away the stench of poverty or patch the unpatchable. Nevertheless, all the mammies got out their scrubbing brushes and pails of water and went to work. They scrubbed stairs, walls, windows, doorframes and hallways, but after everything dried out, it all looked the same. It was the hardheartness and stinginess of the poxy landlords, and the government who let them operate the dives that bothered Da the most.

Mrs Bray told the spy how hard it was to keep her family healthy in such conditions. Ma said to nobody in particular, 'Christ i' th' night it makes me legs boil standing here waiting to see if she is making the rounds.' Mrs C., with six children under the age of ten years old, and an out-of-work husband, vowed to cook the spy in oil if she dared knock on her door.

There wasn't a family in the lane who looked healthy and well-fed. There wasn't a soul in the lane who had an extra pound of flesh on their body or who had a healthy set of teeth in their head, and that included all the children in O'Brien's. What would the sanitary lady inspector have to say about that? Blame the mammies and daddies?

After days of intimidation from the spy, husbands told their wives to ignore her and not let the shagger or any shagger from the government enter their rooms.

The spy, frustrated with not being allowed into the rented rooms, turned her attention to the children in the lane. She questioned kids about what they ate, how many hot baths they had a week, if their daddies drank at the pub, what their mothers did during the day, if their beds were changed once a week, and if they had lice in their hair. I expected the spy to pick on me any time.

One day, Da gave me a penny and told me to take Noely Joseph out for a walk and buy some sweets. He told me not to hurry back as he and Ma had things to talk over. I took Noely for a walk and then we went to the shop for a penny's worth of hard toffees. Noely started to get cranky and wanted to go home to his mammy. We were baby-footing it back to the room when the sanitary lady inspector beckoned us to stop. She asked us our names, our ages, what we had for dinner, if we had a bath every week, if our daddy went to the pub, what our mammy was doing, and if we had lice in our hair.

Noely just looked at her. He had a wad of toffee stuck in his mouth, and could only make a face. I knew about the spy. I knew she had the power to take Noely and me away from Ma. I was afraid to lie to her. I told her my name, age, and what we had for dinner on a good day: Dublin Coddle made out of water, sausages, and potatoes. I told her that we hadn't a bath or hot water to wash in. I wouldn't take a bath anyway in our room, I let her know, because my brothers would be sure to gawk at me naked.

I told the sanitary lady six of us slept in one bed because there wasn't another place to sleep. I informed her that Ma dusted our heads with DDT powder killing all the lice on our heads, and now Noely Joseph and me had nothing to play with.

'Tell me what you mean,' she said. 'About making playthings out of anything so horrid as lice.'

'I capture them out of Noely's hair and he captures them out of mine. We put them in matchstick boxes to play with them. Noely always wants the big ones, the bruisers. He puts the bruisers in his matchbox and pretends they are his army men. He plays war games with the lice all day.' I told her that I separated my lice in the matchbox into baby ones, big brother ones, sister ones, mammy ones and daddy ones, and that I kept them all separate from each other with blades of grass. I told the biddy that sometimes I captured fleas out of my friend Georgina's red hair because the fleas in her head were red just like the colour of her hair, and that Noely and I liked the red fleas better than the brown ones that bit our heads off.

When Noely got tired of playing war with his lice, he'd slap a fly off our wall and put it into the matchbox with the fleas. 'They go mad over the fly and jump all over its back looking for a ride. Sometimes we take a sewing needle and hold it over a lighted candle 'til the tip glows red. We stick the hot point into the lice's bellies and watch as they scatter like mad and try to climb up the walls of the matchbox. Didn't we do that, Noely? Isn't that right, Noely?' I wanted to include Noely in my conversation with the spy because I didn't want to be the only one caught in her net.

The wad of toffee still held Noely lockjawed, so I continued, 'Ma hates lice. She says they're always humping.'

The sanitary lady inspector took in everything I said. 'Take me back to your room,' she ordered. When we got into our hallway, she said that she had already knocked on our door but had got no answer. She said she knew someone was in there but would not open the door.

'Who is inside?' she bellowed. 'Tell me this moment and don't lie!' Noely grabbed onto the hem of my frock and tried to cover his head. Trembling, I told her Ma was home.

'Knock on the door,' she ordered. 'Knock on the door.' No answer came back. Then she demanded, 'Call out to your mother that you need to get in.'

'Ma, it's me and Noely back from buying the sweets,' I called out.

'Push the door in. It's open,' Ma called out. With that the sanitary lady inspector thrust Noely and me aside and marched into the room. She found Ma and Da in bed in the middle of the afternoon.

'Who let you into this room?' demanded Da as he sprang out of the bed as naked as a bluejay, and roaring like a lion. The spy looked away from Da, her face as red as a beetroot. Da covered himself with the bedspread. The spy looked at Da with a downcast, painful glance and told him how sorry she was for intruding. She told Da that she had told me to call out to Ma to let Noely and me in and that we were not to blame for the embarrassing situation.

She told Ma that Noely and I were good children and that she apologised for their living conditions and for the living conditions of all who lived in O'Brien's. She told them that she'd put our names on top of the list for the new public housing the government was starting to build. She said O'Brien's was unfit for human habitation and she intended to put that in her report. And she told them that she was sorry for coming on like a tug-boat.

We all breathed a sigh of relief when the spy stopped coming into the lane. The living conditions and the poverty remained, but we weren't going to fade away. Frank found a job selling fresh brown country eggs door to door for a shopkeeper in Powerscourt, for a few shilling a week. Bob chopped wood into kindling and bound the kindling into small bundles to sell for two-pence a bundle. He carved tiny Irish cottages from sods of hard turf. He penknifed two windows and a door out of the sod, pared a corner off each end of the turf to fashion a sloping roof, and dusted the roof with flour to give the miniatures a picturesque touch. He sold the art on Haddington Road for sixpence a sod.

Not to be outdone by my brothers, I found a way to make some money as if by magic. I'd go up to the corner of Haddington Road and wait for people to get on or off the trams. I'd run up one of the departing passengers, always a man, and ask if he had a penny to exchange with me for half-pennies because Ma needed a penny for the gas meter. The gas meter would not take half-pennies.

The man would root into his pocket to find change, pick out a penny and thrust it towards me. With a heartfelt look and a projected cough, I'd offer up the two half-pennies. 'Ah! keep the two ha'pennies for yourself,' most of the men said. On a good day, I came home with a shilling in change. Da didn't like the scam. Ma looked gratefully at the handful of change I placed in her hand; she lashed at Da for being ungrateful for my enterprising spirit, letting him know it wasn't a turnip I had for a head. Da asked that a few cigarettes be bought out of my earrnings.

My Jewish friends

Da found a job working as a petrol pump attendant in a garage on the corner of Orwell Road in Rathgar, a posh area of Dublin. Sometimes I took a sandwich up to Da's workplace for him. He looked like a medical doctor in his white uniform. Few motor cars came to the station, as there were few cars in the whole of the city. Once in a while a motorist tipped Da a sixpence for pumping the petrol and cleaning the windows of the motor car. Da took a dim view of the small tips he got. 'Not enough to bless myself with,' he moaned.

Mr Resnick became a regular customer, and Da got to know him. The Resnick family lived on Orwell Road, and were as posh as could be, noted Da. The family were recent immigrants to Ireland from somewhere in Europe. Mr Resnick noticed me at the petrol station talking to Da or pulling on his arm for a penny for an ice-cream cone. The man told Da that his daughter Cynthia had no one to play with, and asked if I'd like to go to their house and play with her. The auld fella told him I'd be delighted to. Da told Ma about me being invited to play with a toff's kid. Ma said I'd get a gawk into a different world than the one we lived in, and that it was up to me to decide if I wanted to play with the girl or not. Mr Resnick wrote down the house number on a slip of paper for me. I told Da that I'd love to play with a girl like that. A girl who lived in a big house.

I'd no trouble finding the big house on Orwell Road. I unlatched the front gate and walked up to the door. Before I even had time to press on the doorbell, the door was opened wide by a beautiful woman, and she invited me to step inside. 'You are the daughter of the man who pumps the petrol,' she said with a greeting. 'I'm very glad to see you.' She called out, 'Cynthia, Cynthia, my dear, Angeline is here to play with you.' She surprised me by knowing my name.

The daughter acted shy as she came over to say Hello. Her mother took Cynthia by one hand and me by the other and led us into a lovely carpeted room and invited me to sit down on a huge sofa. Cynthia's mother looked so young, like a girl, unlike Ma who always looked weatherbeaten. Mrs Resnick had on stylish clothes and wore cosmetics. She had great big brown eyes and a head of bouncy black curls lit with amber. She had beautiful white, even teeth, and her body smelled of perfume.

Cynthia looked like an exact copy of her mother, dressed in the latest fashion, with bouncy hair, big brown eyes and the most beautiful tiny white teeth in the world. This day she wore a plaid red and black pleated skirt, a red jumper with long sleeves, white ankle socks and buckled black shoes. I felt like a lump of coal looking up at the two of them. I tried not to smile so that they could not see my front tooth that I knew looked like the beginnings of a 'z' due to decay.

Mrs Resnick seemed to be able to read my mind about feeling like a lump of coal. She asked me about where I lived, about my mother, and if I had brothers and sisters. I could understand every word she said, but she spoke with a different style than any I'd heard before. She didn't sound like someone from Cork or Limerick or from Kerry nor did she sound like anyone I noticed in a Hollywood film.

I told her where I lived, about Ma and my three brothers, and how I had always wished for a sister. Cynthia took everything in but didn't say a word. Mrs Resnick asked me if I would like some 're-freshments'. I told her I didn't know what that was. 'Tea and cakes,' she said with a bounce in her voice.

Cynthia took me by the elbow. 'Mommy serves tea in the sitting room, right this way through the French doors.' I figured a person would need a map to find their way around in the big house, not like our room where everyone knocked into each other. The room looked like a film set: high white embossed ceiling, beautiful brass light fixtures handing from the centre. The walls were also wallpapered white, and all the windows faced into a lovely garden teeming with rose bushes. The carpet felt like a sponge under the feet. It had scrolls and roses all over it. Two pink love seats and a green sofa sat on the carpet. A low kidney shaped table sat in the middle of the floor. A clear glass vase held cut flowers on the centre of the table.

Mrs Resnick invited me to sit on one of the love seats, and Cynthia cuddled with her mother on the other love seat. Mrs Resnick asked me if I liked to read storybooks. I told her I only liked to read comic books, the *Beano* and the *Dandy*. Cynthia and I looked at the books while her mother made the tea. She asked me if I could read the comic books by myself. I told her that my brother, Bob, taught me how to read the *Beano* and the *Dandy*. Mrs Resnick asked her daughter and me if we would like her to read a story while the water boiled for the tea. She mentioned that the girl had the day off, and she was making the tea herself.

Cynthia cooed out, 'Mommy, Mommy read *Winnie the Pooh*. I want to hear about Christopher Robin and Pooh Bear.' Mrs Resnick began 'The adventures of Christopher Robin and Pooh Bear'. It seemed like a stupid story to me. I didn't know boys like Christopher Robin nor did I know anyone in O'Brien's who had a nanny. At first I thought Mrs Resnick read that Christopher Robin had a nannygoat. I knew about nannygoats and how they loved to bunt everyone in the arse.

We listened to the adventures of the sissy boy until Mrs Resnick jumped up to make tea. By that time my jaws were getting stiff from yawning. Cynthia came over to sit beside me and asked if I would like to go on an adventure with Christopher Robin. I told her I liked boys who played cowboys and Indians or cops and robbers better. She asked me to show her the comic book I had in my pocket.

Her mother came back into the sitting room with a loaded tray and put it down on the table. She poured tea into a lovely cup and passed it to me with a matching saucer. She did the same for Cynthia, and filled one for herself. She passed around a small milk jug that matched the cup and saucer. She handed me a thingamajig to pick up lumps of sugar from the sugar bowl. She called it a sugar tongs. Then she passed around some small plates and then small iced cakes and fancy biscuits.

Cynthia and her mother took tiny bites out of the cakes and nibbled on the biscuits like beautiful bunnies. I copied how they ate and how they drank their tea. I lifted my little finger into the air as I raised the cup to my lips like they did.

After tea, Cynthia and I went out to play in the back garden. She had a swing set, a tennis set, a scooter, skates and a miniature motor car. We played with all the toys. Then we walked to the beautiful pond behind the houses. Swans paddled in the water, and some boys were sailing toy boats in the pond. When the afternoon began to fade, Mrs Resnick came to the pond to find us and bring us back into the house. She made sure that I got on the right bus for home, and always gave me the money for my bus fare.

That summer, I spent more time with the Resnick family than with my own. Ma said roses were blooming on my cheeks from the good food and fresh air that the family gave me. Ma especially seemed glad that I had a chance to get away from our room, away from the stinking lavatories, and the ever grinding poverty.

When Cynthia's father came home, he greeted and spoke to his daughter and wife in another language. Then he would ask me how I was doing and how Da was doing at the petrol station. When Mr Resnick spoke in English all he talked about was a Morris Minor. He asked me if I knew anything about a Morris Minor, and I told him I'd never heard of that fella. 'No! No! my motor car is called a Morris Minor.' We all laughed. I thought he might be a bit mad, the way he laughed so much. I felt a bit strange eating a meal with Mr Resnick at the table with us. He kept passing me plates of sliced cucumbers, pickled herring, marinated kippers, sliced pickles, pieces of flat hard bread.

I watch how the family handled their knives and forks, how they dabbed at the corners of their mouths with a cloth napkin, took sips of water after every bite, and how softly they chewed their food.

Cynthia invited me to her birthday party. Her mother and father insisted that I come and meet their other relatives who were also coming to the party. I told Cynthia that I would knit her a pair of mittens for her birthday, but maybe it would be Christmas before they were made. I'd never been to a birthday party. No kid in O'Brien's Place ever had a birthday party.

Mrs Resnick had the house decorated with coloured streamers and balloons. All the kids were given a birthday paper hat to wear. There were men, women and children at the party. They all spoke together in a different language. They never stopped talking and hugging each other. They wanted to know who I was and they patted me on the back and shook my hand.

Some of the people could not speak English, but they all brought presents for Cynthia. We all ate birthday cake, ice cream, and fancy biscuits. None of the men drank any porter. Instead the adults drank wine out of lovely, long stemmed glasses, stopping every minute to tip each other's glass. To my astonishment some of the grown-ups burst into tears as if their hearts would break. Mr and Mrs Resnick rushed to them and put their arms around them and cooed as if to the broken-hearted, words sounding like 'shalom, shalom'.

Someone began to sing in a foreign language, and then everyone joined in a circle, clapping and stomping their feet. A hand grabbed me into the circle. They sang and sang without using a word of English. I told Ma and Da that Cynthia's birthday turned into a great hooley. A real smasher!

Later in the month, Da told me that Mr Resnick had been to see him. He told Da that his wife had made an appointment with her brother, a Dr Shankmann, to take a look at my front tooth. Dr Shankmann had a private dental practice in Dublin city. Da would only have to pay a few shillings whenever he had it to have my front tooth filled.

Ma and Da were delighted to know that my front teeth would be saved. I went to see Dr Shankmann and he drilled and filled my front tooth. He seemed crotchety. After he filled the tooth, he warned me to drink plenty of milk, eat lots of cheese and consume quantities of fresh fruit. I was overjoyed with the work he did on my tooth. It looked brand new. I stopped putting my hand over my mouth when I smiled. I don't know if Da ever paid him off, but I still have the filling. Mrs Resnick seemed delighted with my newly restored front tooth and told me never to hide my smile again.

One afternoon as I headed for Cynthia's house, the next door neighbour jumped out her gate and grabbing me by the arm tugged me into her front garden. She then directed me to the side door of the house where she pushed me through the kitchen door.

'I'm Mrs O'Farrell. I have been watching you go into the house next door to play with the girl there. This is my daughter Margaret and my daughter Ellen and they noticed you playing with the girl. I will not let them play with her because she is a Jew. I have something very important to discuss with you,' she said. 'My husband has been greatly disturbed about you going over to visit the Resnicks. You're the daughter of the petrol pump attendant up the street. I'm sure you are a Catholic and a Christian.'

I nodded, Yes.

'It is my Christian duty to tell you about the Jews. The Jews are to blame for the death of Christ. They got him nailed to a cross, scourged by the Romans, and crowned with a crown of thorns. Christians must have nothing to do with the murderers of Christ! And, now Jews live on Orwell Road, next door to us. And, more Jews are entering Ireland. We will not let our daughters play with a Jew, and we do not think that you should be playing with a Jew. Now that I have told you about Jews, you won't want to play or go near the Resnicks anymore. Remember the death of Jesus took place at their hands.'

I felt lightheaded and sick, and needed to sit down on the kitchen chair. I had never heard anyone talk like that before. Then Mr O'Farrell came into the kitchen and asked his wife if she had explained things to me about the Resnicks. He went over all the same things about what the Jews had done to the son of God. I couldn't bear to look at his face. I lowered my eyes and looked down at the carpet slippers he had on his feet, and prayed to get out of the house.

I could not say a word to either of them. Mr O'Farrell then pointed out that he and his wife were both teachers in the national schools. And, as a closing shot, he said that the Resnicks only invited me, a petrol pump attendant's daughter, to play with Cynthia because no God-fearing Christian child, who knew about Jews, would play with her. The couple led me to the side door, and told me to go home.

After I got outside, I felt like I'd been smashed to smithereens. I was too upset to go next door to play with Cynthia, so I ran all the way to the petrol station to talk to Da. He asked me what had upset me. I told him what the O'Farrells had said. Da listened and said he knew Mr Resnick was a Jew, and that the whole family and all their relatives were Jews. And what difference did that make? Then he remarked that Mrs Resnick was a cultured lady, and a beautiful looking woman. But, unfortunately, like all Jewesses, she'll fall into flesh by getting too fat after having a few children. I told the auld fella I had a devouring headache and needed to get the bus home to Ma.

After Ma, I loved Mrs Resnick and Cynthia. I needed the love they gave me, especially all the love and kindness that Mrs Resnick gave to me. I never discussed it with Ma for fear of upsetting her, but sometimes I felt all alone in a grey world. It seemed Mrs Resnick picked up on my sad feeling, and offered me love. And Mrs Resnick had got my front tooth fixed. How could the O'Farrell's say such hateful things about people like the Resnicks?

I was terrified the O'Farrells would destroy my friendship with the Resnick family. They acted as if they would kill me if I continued to play with Cynthia, or have anything to do with her family. They would report me to the parish priest for being a traitor, and have him condemn me to roast in hell for all eternity.

When I got back to O'Brien's Ma was surprised to see me home so soon. She wanted to know if I was feeling all right, and felt my forehead with her hand. I didn't feel like telling her what had happened, so I watched while she make a pot of lamb's head stew.

She put the lamb's skull into a pot of water along with a bunch of green onions, some carrots, lentils and spuds. Then she tossed in a good shake of salt and pepper to flavour the lot. She put the heavy potful on the grate to simmer over the coals. Then she turned to me and asked, 'What's the matter, love? You look feverish.'

As the lamb's stew simmered, I told Ma about the O'Farrells. Ma listened carefully. After I told her the story, she said the only thing she ever heard about Jewish people causing the death of Jesus came from nuns and priests. How could anybody know what happened to him, when it took place so far back. 'Dust off what the O'Farrells said about Jewish people. Dust it off.' And for added measure she said the likes of the O'Farrells would eat Jesus Christ alive without the benefit of salt or pepper if it were to their advantage. 'They think they're great Christians, but they wouldn't wet the lips of a dying child or give the smell of their pee to a dog.' Ma knew the ropes about people, unlike Da who went around in a bloody fog.

Ma always tried to stream kindness into the veins of my brothers and me. I knew that what the O'Farrells had said about the Resnicks would have no lingering effect upon me. I'd love Mrs Resnick and Cynthia forever. The next afternoon when I went to see Cynthia, Mrs Resnick seemed upset. She said that she had seen what had happened yesterday with the O'Farrells. She asked if they had frightened me away from playing with Cynthia.

'Certainly not!' I said.

When summer came to an end, school started up. Cynthia went to a swanky private school somewhere in the city. I went back to Saint Mary's. The winter looked like it would be a long one, and it would have been had it not been for Jenny Powell.

The Mount Street Club

Jenny Powell rapped on our door and asked me if I wanted to join a percussion band that a Protestant group had organised for poor

Catholic kids in the neighbourhood. Jenny's father worked for the Mount Street Club as an errand-boy. He was the only proddy-woddy in O'Brien's. He married a Catholic woman and they had six kids who were all Catholics. The family lived at the very end of O'Brien's. The neighbours knew Mr Powell was a Protestant but overlooked it because they believed that the man was soft in the head. Something missing between the ears, if you will.

No one in O'Brien's bothered to try to convert Mr Powell to Catholicism because of him being so harmless. They figured that God knew the poor man had no idea of the differences which existed between a Catholic and a Protestant and that it would take until doomsday for Mr Powell ever to get it through his head.

But in spite of him being seen as soft in the head, the family fared better than most in the laneway. The Mount Street Protestant Club hired Mr Powell to do odd jobs around the club and other odd jobs around the town. Mr Powell did all the deliveries for the club in an ass and cart. When he drove into O'Brien's on his lunchtime, all the kids screamed 'Giddie-up!' and wanted a ride in the cart. Sometimes Mr Powell barely skimmed away from the brick wall as he giddie-upped the small ass down the length of the lane.

Old grannies crossed themselves at the sight of Mr Powell acting as if he were driving in the American West. At least twenty times a week, he almost somersaulted the ass and cart as he drove it hellbent into O'Brien's, yelling 'Giddie-up, Roddie, giddie-up, Roddie!' acting more like a stagecoach driver for Wells Fargo than the Mount Street Protestant Club.

I told Ma that Jenny Powell had asked me to join a percussion band being formed at the Protestant club in Upper Mount Street for kids in the neighbourhoods. Ma asked Da if it was all right for me to join a Protestant band. He muttered something about all the ridiculous problems that religious rubbish caused. He told her to let Titch decide for herself. Dolores and me were the only kids in O'Brien's who joined. We went with Jenny and Maura Powell.

The organisers of the percussion band were Mr and Mrs Kitley, two unmistakable toffs who wanted to do something for poor kids in the neighbourhoods within walking distance of the Mount Street Club.

Mr Kitley did all the talking and his wife smiled and played the piano. He told us that it would be great for us all to learn about music and play an instrument. He never mentioned anything about religion. He told the bigger kids like Jenny Powell and Maura to stand in the back of the room and put smaller kids like Dolores and me in the front.

Mr Kitley passed out castanets, triangles, tambourines, bones, bells, drums and cymbals to the different kids. He gave Dolores a triangle to play and me a tambourine. Then he set out music stands. He put a music stand in front of each two kids. Some of the Protestant kids already knew how to read music and play an instrument. The four of us from O'Brien's didn't have a clue.

Mr Kitley said that the first piece of music we were going to learn how to play would be Brahms's 'Hungarian Rhapsody Number Two'. We were all shaking with anticipation and eagerness to play any kind of music and I could hardly wait to start banging and shaking the tambourine. Mr Kitley stood up in front with a music stand in front of him and a baton in his hand and told us to pay attention to his every gesture. Then he turned to Mrs Kitley seated at the piano and nodded for her to begin.

With a flick of the baton, Mr Kitley nodded for us all to play our instruments. I walloped the tambourine, Dolores clanged the triangle, Maura clicked castanets and Jenny beat the hell out of the drums. The others kids clashed cymbals and the Kitleys' son blasted away on the tuba. I had never heard such a racket. It seemed as if everyone went mad at once.

Mrs Kitley beamed towards us as she pounded the piano and Mr Kitley rocked back and forth on the heels of his shoes as he tapped the baton on the music stand.

We went every Monday night during the winter to practice for the band. Getting away from our room, and getting to be with all the kids making music seemed glorious. Walking with the kids from O'Brien's to the club also seemed grand. We could smell the coal smoke that belched from all the chimneys, and the smoke from some turf fires that ebbed out of some of the buildings.

Usually, the stars were about to brim the sky as we walked along the canal to the club on Mount Street. We never missed a meeting, even when the weather grew cold. On winter nights we tossed a gunnysack over our threadbare clothing for extra protection against the cold. Ma always worried about me getting my feet wet for fear that I'd get bronchitis.

When we got to the Mount Street Club, the caretaker, old Jim, beckoned for us to come closer to the blazing coal fire he had going in the fireplace. 'Come over and warm yer poor little selves,' he'd say, with the deepest of kindness in his voice. The people who ran the programme offered us hot cocoa, which Jim served us in tin mugs. After we were warmed-up, we headed into the music room. To our astonishment, the four of us from O'Brien's began to make sense of the lines and squiggles that noted the music. Mr and Mrs Kitley never got impatient with us as we struggled with notation.

During a practice, Mr Kitley told us we were going to play music for the club's children's Christmas party and that we were also going to be on a children's programme, on Radio Eireann. He told us that being on the radio would be a memorable experience in our life. And so it was!

We told everyone in O'Brien's Place that we were going to be on the wireless. Da wrote to his mother in Castleblayney, to tell her about me being on a band on Radio Eireann, and hoped that she would tune in to the radio for the occasion. Before we went on the radio, Mrs Kitley arranged for each one of us in the band to get a beautiful purple sash inscribed with the initials of the Mount Street Club Percussion Band, to wear across our chests.

A week before we were to perform on the wireless, Mr Kitley took us all on the bus to the Radio Eireann studio in Henry Street, to familiarise us with the studio. Everyone was excited about going on the wireless.

When the day came, Mr and Mrs Kitley told us to meet them at the club. They gave us the bus fare to Henry Street, and they took the musical instruments in their car to the radio station.

We all met at the front door of the station. Mr Kitley led the way upstairs to the studio, and we set up the stands and music sheets, and went through a practice of the Brahms's 'Hungarian Rhapsody Number Two'. Before the live performance, a few of the kids started to feel sick with stage fright. Mrs. Kitley gave them a peppermint bull's-eye to suck on.

Minutes before we were to go on the radio, a man came out and talked to us in a hushed voice about what was going to happen. He told us to look at two red lights and the one green light that were embedded in the wall. He pointed out when the red lights went out, the green light came on, and when the green light came on we were on the air.

He also pointed to a microphone which hung from the ceiling, and told us that the microphone would transmit our playing across the length and breath of Ireland. You could hear a pin drop in the studio when the announcer finished his talk. Mr Kitley kept looking at the lights, and then he'd look at the band. Mrs Kitley sat at the piano and turned to smile at us. Mr Kitley, to our great astonishment, seemed pale, and he started to sweat. His face steamed, as he waited for the green light to go on.

As soon as the green blinked, he put his finger over his lips, tapped his stand, sucked in his breath, gave the count, and we were off with a smash from Jenny Powell's cymbals.

My family, along with others on the street, tuned in to hear the band on Sadie Sullivan's wireless set. Later Ma said she couldn't hear me play the tambourine with the noise the others were making in the band.

Upped Granny Martin to me, 'I could see that big lump of the Powells, the one a banging the drum—there wasn't any missing her—on Sadie's wireless.'

As my brothers roared at me in one voice that the Mount Street Club Percussion Band was desperate, Da in his dramatic way declared, 'That band could wake the dead from past generations,' and it probably could have.

Mr and Mrs Kitley were delighted with us, they said. Furthermore, Mr Kitley told the band that we were going to play for the Mount Street Club's Christmas party. 'And,' said Mr Kitley, with a gulp, 'the Lord Mayor of Dublin, the Honourable Alfred Byrne, is going to be there.'

We all enjoyed being in the band, and the people in the club, like the Kitleys and old Jim, made us feel cared about. Also, after we rehearsed our music, we were given a biscuit and a half cup of fizzy lemonade served in a tin mug for a treat. Getting to play for the Christmas party seemed like a gift in itself.

Mr Kitley told me that he wanted me to sing two solos with the band for the concert. He gave me the words to 'Away in a Manger', and 'My Old Kentucky Home, Good Night'. Mr Kitley said he loved the songs of Stephen Foster and that we were going to be singing and playing some of his songs for the Christmas concert. We learned the words to 'Oh! Susanna', 'Old Folks At Home', 'Camptown Races' and 'Old Black Joe'. The Kitleys told us to invite all the members of our families to the Christmas party.

The concert was performed on the stage in the back hall of the club. Ma, Bob and Noely came to hear me sing and see me play the tambourine. The hall was packed with poor women and children from around the neighbourhoods. The Lord Mayor of Dublin, Alfie Byrne, a short grandda of a man, was the guest of honour. He sat up in the front on one of the long wooden benches, waiting for the concert to begin.

Mr Kitley walked up to the front of the stage and talked about the band. Then we started to play. Mr Kitley nodded at me to come up and do my solo of 'My Old Kentucky Home, Good Night'. The band started to play the melody softly, and I started to sing to my shoes,

The head must bow and the back will have to bend,
Wherever the darky may go:
A few more days, and the trouble all will end

In a field where the sugar canes grow.
A few more days for to tote the weary load,
No matter 'twill never be light,
A few more days 'til we totter on the road,
Then my old Kentucky Home, good-night!

Before I finished the first verse, the others in the band stopped their playing and roared up to Mr Kitley, 'She's singing the wrong verse. She's supposed to sing the first verse first, and she started the last verse first and now we're all off our mark.'

We ended the concert with 'The Camptown Races'. The kids in the band roared out the song and banged the bejaysus out of every cymbal, triangle, bone, drum, tambourine, clickers and tuba. They lifted the roof off:

De Camptown ladies sing dis song,
Doo-dah! Doo-dah!
De Camptown race-track five miles long,
Oh! doo-dah, doo-dah day!
I come down dah wit my hat caved in,
Doo-dah! Doo-dah!
I go back home wid a pocket full of tin,
Oh! doo-dah, doo-dah DAY!

The Honourable Alfie Byrne came up to shake hands with all the kids in the band. He wore a pinstriped suit and a bowler hat. He had a grey moustache and he didn't seem very big. He took my hands in his (I still remember that his hands were warm and soft). He whispered in my ear that he had got a few things 'backwards' himself in his time.

Mr and Mrs Kitley came around and wished everyone in the band a happy holiday. All the kids in the audience, along with all the members of the band, got glasses of lemonade to drink and frosted biscuits to eat. Mammies all got a cup of tea and a slice of cake.

After the great concert and party, I reasoned that if the Kitleys were Protestants, and the people who made the tea and cakes were Protestants, then why did anyone in Ireland make a stink about

126

them? I thought about converting after my experiences with the Mount Street Club. Maybe when I got older, I'd marry a man just like Mr Kitley, and have a basket of Protestant babies.

Washing the babby

Ma and other women in O'Brien's were often involved in 'lying-in': they took turns in caring for a new mother and her infant. Most of the mothers in the laneway already had a roomful of children to care for, so any little bit of help offered to them during childbirth and afterwards, seemed a blessing. The arrival of newborns in the laneway gladdened the hearts of some and added an extra burden for others.

Ma took me with her to show me the ins and outs of caring for a new mother and her child. I figured everyone knew the ABCs of taking care of a baby: it meant shoving food in one end and cleaning up the other, or so I thought. I knew by the look on Ma's face, I had to tarry along and leave my scribbling on the table. Ma's words still sound in the ear.

'Cailin og put aside the pencil and paper, we're going to Lally's place to take care of her and the new babby.' Ma liked to pepper her conversations with bits and pieces of Gaelic she'd had in the head from girlhood, especially when wanting me to eat out of her hand. Lally O'Toole, three doors down, had had her first-born two days before. Lally's husband, Pat, unable to find a scrap of work in Dublin had taken off for Liverpool earlier to try to find work on a building site. He intended to send his earnings home to Lally to care for herself and their offspring. Ma felt sorry for Lally having to go through the wringer with her mister in a foreign land.

We climbed up the two flights of rickety stairs to Lally's room. We rapped on the door and got a 'Come in, it's unlatched', from a voice inside. Lally's dismal room replicated the rest of the pigeon coops we all lived in.

Thin fingers of light shone in from the narrow window in the direction of the cast-iron bed where Lally lay under an assortment of old coats and covers. Her mop of ginger hair fanned over the pillow. Her pale oval face, looked as transparent as a communion wafer, and her hazel eyes squinted at the sight of Ma and me standing at the foot of the bed. I thought Lally needed eye glasses in a desperate way or else she had a splitting headache.

Ma bent down and ruffled Lally's head of hair playfully, then whispered a series of questions into her ear, questions not meant for the ears of a ten-year-old girl standing by, but fortunately I'd the ears of a donkey. Whispered Ma, in all seriousness into Lally's cocked ear: 'Is yer flow heavy or light? A dark red or a pinkish red? How bad are the cramps? Are the breasts tender, hard or supple? Did the little duck latch on yet?'

Lally answered the questions with a louder voice than Ma used and between their going back and forth, I wondered if Lally had delivered a ton of bricks instead of a baby, and where had she hid it? Seemingly, Ma detected an uneasiness in Lally about being a mother for the first time and tried to reassure her by coming up with an old adage. '*Tá Dia láidir agus tá máthair mhaith aige.*' 'What does that mean?' we both asked, not being fluent in Irish. 'Remember God is strong and has a good mother,' answered Ma. After savouring the morsel, Lally bucked up. She tossed aside the bedcovers and showed the tiny baby lying across her bosom like a quivering arrow. The sight of the elfin creature both dumbfounded and delighted, and I sought Ma's eyes. She caught my drift. Then Ma started giving me orders for the morning:

'*Cailín óg*, take the kettle in yer hands and go down to the backyard and fill it to the brim. We need water to make Lally a strong cup of tea, and the rest of the water will be used for the babby's bath. For God's sake, don't trip up on the rickety stairway.'

Before heading out the door with the awkward kettle, I stood to watch Ma start a fire in the fireplace. She tore newspaper into strips and laid the strips in the grate. Then she arranged kindling in a crisscross way over the newspaper, crumbled a sod of turf into bits and put the bits on top of the sticks, flung a fistful of sugar over the lot in the grate, tossed in a lighted match, and Bingo!

I went down to the backyard and filled the kettle to the brim at the outdoor communal tap, a spit away from the shithouses. I inched my way back up the two flights of stairs with the heavy kettle, fearful of spilling water from the spout or tumbling backwards down the dark stairs. By the time I had hauled the kettle back to Lally's, time had tripped away. 'In the name of the Blessed Mother, we thought ye had gone to the River Shannon to fill the kettle.' I didn't realise the amount of time I had taken with daydreaming and letting the kettle tip over for the pleasure of seeing the brackish liquid spill down the drain and gurgle into the gutter, causing cockroaches to scatter in all directions. Ma took the heavy container from my numbed hands and sat it down on the coals in the fireplace where it looked like an old sitting hen hunched over a shimmering nest.

Ma scooted the wooden kitchen table closer to the fireplace, and told me to gather together the necessities for the baby's bath. I rounded-up a speckled blue metal basin, a brown milk jug and a towel. I placed them on the kitchen table. Then Ma gave orders:

'Pull the chair in front of the fire, sit down on the chair and spread the towel across yer lap to warm to wrap the babby in after its wash. Don't scorch it or it'll scald the flesh off the child.'

After the kettle hissed to a boil, Ma lifted it off the coals and poured some of the water into the teapot, tossed a few fingerfuls of tea leaves into the teapot, gave the pot a swirl, set in down on kitchen table, and returned the kettle to the hearthstone.

While we waited for the remainder of the water in the kettle to cool down, Ma, Lally and I sipped our mugs of strong black tea with as much reverence as drunkards applied to sipping their pints of black porter in the pub round the corner.

Ma continued to add sods of turf to the fire. The peat gave off perfumed smoke as fragrant as incense swirling round the loftiest cathedral. The scent made the dank room smell like heaven as it clouded the room before getting sucked back up the chimney by the pull of the draught coming from the fireplace.

When the water cooled in the kettle, Ma took the kettle over to the kitchen table and filled the washbasin half-full leaving some water over to pour into the milk jug.

Lally beckoned me to the bedside with the crook of a little finger. She extended one of her long thin milkwhite arms in front of her face, gawked at the outstretched arm, then folded finger and thumb to shape a beak. She darted the beak underneath her pillow and rummaged around. Upon finding what she rummaged for, Lally pulled out the beak now grasping a small pack which she pitched into my face and, as excited as a duck in a puddle, she exclaimed:

'Unfold it. It's me weddin' hankie and inside is a used bar of green, scenty-soap. They're souvenirs from me weddin'. Use the hankie for a washrag and wash the babby with the scenty-soap.'

The lace-edged handkerchief embellished with a stamped-on spray of green shamrocks in one corner, carried the message 'Greetings from Killarney'. The soap and hankie were given to Lally as a wedding gift from the woman she washed and ironed for. I put the hankie and soap on the kitchen table along with the other necessities for the baby's bath. '*Cailin og* are ye making sure the towel is ready for the *leanbh* when I beckon for it?' 'A course, Ma,' I replied, crossly.

Ma dipped the tip of her elbow into the washbasin to test the water before putting the baby in the basin. Seemingly satisfied, she scooted over to the bed and plucked the sleeping mite from its nest. It squealed like a pig at being plucked from its perch, and bawled even louder when Ma put it on top of the kitchen table to unwrap it. As she peeled away its clothing strip by strip, Ma cooed into its ear telling the baby what a lovely babby it was, what a beautiful young mammy it had, and how its daddy would come back to Dublin, please God, with a jingle in his pocket and on and on . . . The disagreeable imp stilled its quivering as it took in every word said into its ear. When Ma took the last stitch off the baby, the smell of soaked piss nearly blew our heads off, and baby shite had a smell all its own. Phew!

The smelly faeces held great interest for Ma. People who lived in O'Brien's were familiar with the dreaded words, 'green diarrohea'. The scourge stole the lives of infants and toddlers from the neighbourhood. Ma viewed 'green diarrohea' as a scourge of the poor coming not from an angry God, as the pious told us, but from woeful want. With hearts in our mouths, Lally and I watched the woman raking over the coals. 'Cler'ta God,' said Ma, after a meticulous going-over, 'its little stack is the colour and texture of new cut hay.' On hearing the good news, Lally made the bedsprings dance, and I gulped.

I turned back to watch the flames in the fireplace, towel spread over my lap like a map of the world, and let the flickering flames sweep me into flights of fancy that went well beyond the boundaries of O'Brien's Place.

I envisioned myself as a beautiful 'sunbonnet girl', neck upright and long, with apple-red cheeks and tossed golden-curls, dressed in calico blue and married to a lanky cowboy who sang and played the guitar all day. I'd make pots of mashed potatoes thickened with cream and butter, bake perfect round, golden-crusted apple and peach pies, placing the lot on a window ledge to cool, always mindful of rogue bears ambling in out of the wilderness drawn by the grand smell. What a wonderful life it would be living in the American West that I knew like the back of my hand from going to the picture shows. Out There, I'd never want; Out There I'd be a respectable looking girl dressed in blue instead of looking like a ragbag; Out There, I'd stuff myself with mounded plates of spuds mashed and mixed with cream and butter instead of dribbled water and coarse salt. My mouth moved back and forth as I imagined eating all the food, especially the homemade pies pregnant with fruit, and the thought of all the open space Out There caused my lungs and legs to stretch. Having lived now for ten years in a chicken-coop with three brothers, Ma and Da, all sharing the same bed, I had an urge to roam. In my childish imagination I'd have everything I yearned for Out Yonder, even my own bed to sleep in. I wouldn't have to put up with brothers shouting out, 'Don't stretch out yer long skinny legs. Keep`em up closer to yer chest. Ye nearly kicked me balls again.'

I did wonder about the strange urge in my body when I thought of being captured by a 'savage Indian' who flung me over the front of his black and white pony or brown and white pony and took me away from civilisation. We'd speed over the plains on the back of the beast and I'd feel the pony's jointed limbs outstretching to capacity as it raced to embrace the vast tundra.

The sound of Ma's voice, edged with irritation, hurled me back to reality as if she had shouted: 'Hands up!'

'Angeline Bridget, that towel nearly flew off yer lap and up the chimney while ye gawked into the flames. That mind of yers drifted off again into a bang-bang instead of it paying attention to what's needed,' Ma scolded. On occasion she could shrivel the lining in a pig's ear.

The gingerheaded baby lay naked on the kitchen table squawking and shaking with its spindly legs up in the air. Ma picked it up and held its head over the washbasin, scooped up a handful of water and washed the sleep from its face. Next she doused water on its head, and beckoned for me to pass the bar of soap. Ma lathered the baby's skull into a cap of glistening, green bubbles 'til it resembled a little gargoyle lodged in the crook of her arm or maybe it had transposed into a pooka out of Tir na nOg, or, God forbid, a changeling. Mercifully, it resumed the look of a Christian after Ma blew the bubbles away. She slid the infant, toes first, into the washbasin, letting the child's head lodge in the concave of her hand like a nut in a shell. From her perch in the bed, Lally observed every move Ma made. 'Pass me the hankie,' said Ma. I handed her the swatch of cotton, still stiff and smelling of newness, although a year old.

Lally yelped like a whippet starting out of the gate, as she saw elfin ears rubbed red with the hankie from Killarney. Every inch of the baby's body got a rub-down with the hankie caked with scented-soap. The baby ceased its bawling. I wondered if the irascible thing had swallowed a gobful of bubbles. 'Let me have the jug of clear water, love,' cooed Ma. I threaded her fingers into and over the jug's handle making sure she'd a firm grip on the container, then she raised the jug above the baby's shoulders and tipped the lip downwards.

The stream of water trickled over the soapy baby, and where it ran, skin showed as supple and pink as a Mexicalie rose. After rinsing, Ma let the baby loll in the washbasin, its head still locked in the palm of her hand. Obviously, the baby favoured this part of its bath. As it lay in the washbasin, its crinkled face became an oval. The squinty eyes opened to become a pair of blue willow saucers. It pushed arms outward from its sides, unclenched its fists into outstretched palms, then spread each of its matchstick fingers and thumbs (each capped with pearlescent half-moons) into the shape of stars, and its cap of ginger hair took on the shape and texture of a dandelion gone to seed.

'Pass the towel, daughter. Ye're a *cailin maith,* isn't she, Lal?' I liked it when Ma called me a good girl. I could tell Ma was relieved that Lally's bare towel had not got scorched or sucked into the fireplace.

The towel dry babe lay spreadeagled on the kitchen table. Ma rubbed a cup of cornflour all over its body from its feet to its chin. She invited me to toss an extra puff of cornflour on the rosy-red arse. The rascal rewarded my kindness with a petulant fart that shot a plume of white smoke from its sweet little arsehole. After its arse had been floured and diapered, the sight of the bundle reminded me of a Christmas pudding about to go into a pot.

Ma pointed out that now that the baby was two days old, it was old enough to be dressed like a real person instead of being swaddled like a mummy. She told me to pass over the baby's cloths that its mother had stored in a brown cardboard box.

I handed over the little white cotton vest which went easily over the kid's head. Next came the binder. The binder looked like it had been unwound from some Arab's head. It was about two feet long and eight inches wide and it got wound around the baby's midsection. I asked Ma to explain why the binder was used.

'It goes over the babby's umbilical cord to keep it dry and clean. It also keeps the babby's belly firm, and please God, when the child is older, the binder will keep it from getting a fallen belly later on in life.'

I looked over at Lally in the bed as if to say, 'Me mother's a druid?' After Ma wound the long strip of white cotton around the poor baby's belly, she used two large safety pins to keep the binder in place. It's a good thing the kid wouldn't be rambling around on its feet for a while or someone might have mistaken it for a war casualty or a lost mummy.

'Why are ye putting a dress on a boy baby?' I asked with indignation. Ma ran the question around in her head for a minute then came up with the answer:

'The British royal family dress all their little princes in dresses until they find their feet to walk on, that's why.' And Lally butted in, 'That's why the Irish dress their baby boys in dresses because the members of the royal family do it,' tit-tattled Lally.

'If it was me, I'd never put a girl's dress on a baby boy. It's old-fashioned and backward in this modern age,' I told the new mother.

'It's the way we do it and we're not about to change it now,' huffed Lally, keenly conscious of having saved hard to buy the little frock.

'Now now,' said Ma, restoring peace to our midst, 'let me have its first little frock to put over his head.'

The dainty, jonquil frock bedecked with bows and streamers, transformed Lally's boy into the picture of a primrose.

Te Deum, down to the last fig leaf.

While pregnant, Lally had knitted a miniature version of an a fisherman's jumper for her baby. She knitted the replica of Ireland's second most famous export in the tree of life pattern complete with a row of brown chestnut buttons down the front. The homespun garment, stiff as a shaft, made the baby scream as it resisted Ma's every effort to encase its small frame in Lally's woolly masterpiece. Had the kid the misfortune to topple into the raging Atlantic on a ship bound for Amerikay, the fisherman's jumper would have doubled as a lifejacket and saved the day.

Lally nodded to Ma to let me hold the baby, before passing him over for nursing, as a reward for all my work. Ma told me exactly what to do:

'Place yer hand firmly beneath the babby's wobbly head. Never let its head wobble. See that dent in the top of the skull heaving in and out with every breath it takes, that's the babby's soft spot. If ye accidentally hit the soft spot it could cause the babby to become paralyzed or get the jitterheads.' And she pointed out, 'The soft spot is also God's thumb print. It's the sign of the maker. Every babby comes with the mark of the maker dented into its head, whether in Ireland, China or America.'

I'd been looking forward to getting to hold the thing for all my trouble, but the information about the soft spot, the jitterheads and God's thumbprint put me off a mile. Swift as a swallow, Ma put the baby into the crook of my arm like a bouquet of flowers. Although in awe of the gorgeous child cradled in my arms, I fervently prayed it would spout a crop of hair as lush and thick as the mop that sprouted on the head of Moe in the Three Stooges, and the sooner the better.

'What are ye going to name him?' I asked Lally. 'Padraig, a course, after his daddy and Ireland's patron saint.' Lally used the Gaelic version of Patrick to impress Ma, and to show me that she knew a thing or two.

'Patrick's a drearysome name,' I hummed. 'Name him Roy or Kirk or Wayne or Montana or Cheyenne. Give the baby a modern name, an American name.' My suggestions were not taken as compliments by Lally. She propped up on her elbows in the bed, as if bitten in the arse by a flea, and slagged: 'Them names ye just mentioned are not Christian names. They are heathen names. Ye're seeing too many bang-bangs if ye ask me. If I were yer mammy, ye'd be going to more novenas to increase yer Catholic faith!'

The gobful nearly knocked me over, Ma seemed unaware of the shootout, being in a daydream of her own. I resisted the urge to stick my tongue out at Lally. I secretly wished the baby belonged to me and not to the gombeen of a mother it had, draped with Catholic solemnity in the squalid bed, hurling knuckledusters at me because I ate up cowboy and Indian picture shows.

I blocked my ears to the rest of the advice Lally had to offer me. I figured she had cramps or a headache from the turf smoke. The heated exchange lifted Ma out of her daydream, and she sent me a look to crimson my lips.

While Lally nursed her baby, she asked Ma to recall her own firstborn child. As far as I had known before that day, my brother Frank, an awful tease, had been the firstborn in our family.

Ma told Lally that her firstborn had been a little boy. She said she had named the baby 'Edward', after Da's grandfather in Castleblayney. 'How come I didn't know y'd another babby, Ma?' I asked with great indignation.

'I don't talk about it, but ye can hear the whole story now if ye want to. The babby died of green diarrhoea that led to pneumonia when it was two months old, didn't have the strength to rally it off. Its little rosy mouth is what's left sticking in me mind. I almost went with it. I got abscesses in both breasts after. Granny Martin made all kinds of poultices to cure the abscesses, but nothing worked. Granny Martin even went out and collected fresh horseshite in the lane to use as a poultice to place upon my breasts but it didn't do any good either. Someone sent over a dish of holy water and I rubbed it over my breasts. After some days my breasts went from feeling like two rocks to feeling soft and supple again.'

'Where's the babby now?' I asked with an edge in my voice. 'Buried in Dean's Grange cemetery on the outskirts of Dublin,' said Ma.

'Where's the grave?' I wanted to know.

'It hasn't a grave. Yer daddy an me didn't have the money to buy a plot to bury it in. It's buried with other poor babies in a pauper's grave.'

'Did ye put it in a coffin before ye buried it?' I asked her.

'Yer daddy, God love him, and some of the soldiers in his army unit scraped-up the money to buy the babby a small white coffin.' Ma looked towards me as if to determine whether to continue with the story or not, then she went on. 'The coffin was the size of a shoebox. Yer daddy carried it under his arm as if it weighed nothing at all, as if the coffin was as light as a feather to the grave site, and me following beside him.'

Lally opened her mouth and said, 'What happened then, Mary? Ye don't have ta say if it stings.'

'Well, Frank—yer daddy,' Ma noted in my direction, 'explained that lots of others would be buried with ours. The dead babbies of the poor who died in the hospitals around the city were collected twice a week and buried all together. Ours would be buried with the pile.'

'When we got to the gravesite, some of the young soldiers from yer daddy's outfit were waiting at the gravesite where sunshine shone off the rows of brass buttons on their shamrock-green uniforms. Wan of the young soldiers handed me a twig of white apple-blossom to put on the babby's coffin.' Ma's eyes filled when she explained that when all the small coffins were put into the open pit, the gravediggers took sacks of quicklime and poured it all over the coffins before shovelling in the grave. Added Ma, 'the quicklime would burn through the babbies under the sod.'

Lally, in an attempt to cheer Ma, exclaimed, 'Wasn't it well Mary that the babby lived long enough to be baptised and could go straight to Heaven and wouldn't be stuck in Limbo for all eternity.' Ma told Lally that whether baptised or not, all babies who died went to Heaven 'where the light a God shines on them'. Ma reminded Lally that the pope still wasn't God. Ma tucked the covers up around Lally and her baby, warning Lal not to let the bedbugs bite. We washed out the baby's soiled clothes in the washbasin, wrung them out and hung them over the back of the chair to dry. Then we tidied the room, banked more turf on the fire, and after Ma ran a final eye round, she took me by the hand and we left Lally to slumber in peace with her baby. Two of our neighbours, Mara and Lucy, would be over later with a bit of grub for Lally.

As we walked back to our building, the worn down cobblestones under our feet were slick from morning drizzle. I hesitated awhile before going back into our room. I wanted to go over in my head the idea that Ma and Da had a baby before my brother Frank, and that the baby got buried in a pit. When I closed my eyes to picture such a thing, I saw Ma's baby trembling like a leaf beneath the earth.

The pigeon-coloured sky overhead looked about to shake itself out. It seemed only seconds before the sun burned away the overcast to blast the earth in light as lemony as the skies over Montana, a world away from O'Brien's.

On the way back to our room, I said to Ma in Gaelic, '*Tá airgead agam* (I've got money). I'll take ye to a film playing at the Regal in Ringsend. I know ye don't like bang-bangs, but this one's in colour.'

'Where did ye come by the *airgead*?' she inquired.

'Old Rafferty gave me all his empty porter bottles and I traded them in for a shilling at Ryan's Pub. He expects me to buy a notebook and pencil with the money from selling the porter bottles. He told me not to waste me pennies on picture shows or drop any pennies in the slot machine in O'Dwyer's.'

'I'll go on one condition which is when ye're a *cailín mór* you won't leave me and Ireland to go to America.'

'Am I a magician, Ma?'

'Where there's a will there's a way, love. Little by little a bird builds its nest.'

Poor young Irish men and women were expected to leave Ireland if they hoped to have a better life. They went to England, Canada, and the favourite place, America. The neighbours in O'Brien's talked at length about the young lads who left or were leaving their native land to better their lives. Anyone who managed to get to America or was planning to go, was looked up to. They were considered to be smarter, more Irish, and more ambitious than those who went to England or Canada. With all the talk about emigration, little chatter focused on young women venturing afoot.

I knew more about America than I did about Ireland from all the films that played at the local cinemas. It cost two pennies for a kid to get into the picture houses and the places were always packed with kids.

The films we saw from America at the Regal and the Shack offered a better life for all the people in the world if they could only get to America. Going to see the films lifted us all out of the shiteholes we lived in day after day, year after year. Hollywood made our misery go away for a few hours.

Ma thought I was getting too mesmerised by all the Hollywood stories, and that I might believe they were all true. She dreaded the thought that her only daughter might leave her. But I loved the films that showed poor people getting rich, having a nice house to live in, and all the food they could shovel into their faces. After the cowboy and Indian films, my favourite picture was *Little Women,* starring Margaret O'Brien. Granny Martin loved the picture too. She went to see *Little Women* every night it played at the Shack and took me with her. We cried and cried when little Beth died. I wanted to be like Jo who acted smart and didn't mind what anyone thought. She did the right thing when she refused to marry Laurie even thought he had plenty of money and a big house. I liked the professor because he told stories, and Jo loved stories. Granny Martin thought Jo should have married the lovely lad, Laurie. I told Granny Martin that I wanted to travel to New England and meet the March family.

The exposure

I was always on the lookout to make a few pennies to take home to Ma. The grannies in O'Brien's gave me a penny here and there for running to the shop for them. I thought that some of the old ladies who lived on Bath Avenue might want a girl to carry messages for them. I had seen Mrs L, looking out her window any time I went to the shops. One afternoon she called to me from the window, and beckoned for me to come to her hall door. She said that she had noticed me hauling things back and forth along the street, and asked if I ran messages for people. I told her I did. She asked me if I would be willing to run errands for her. She never left her house because of being crippled with lumbago. I learned a painful lesson about life from my acquaintance with that family.

Mrs. L paid me a shilling a week to do her shopping after school and on Saturdays. She spent most of her time sitting curled in a chair like a cat, looking out of her front window at people passing by.

Mrs L told me she had been a dressmaker, years past. She wore her hair braided into two circles over her ears. She liked to tell me funny tongue twisters, that I remember to this day. 'Say after me five times and as fast as you can, this twister,' she challenged: 'I put me foot in the bucket and I footed the bucket about.' I tried it, and soon got the meaning. It seemed a strange type of a tongue twister to teach me, but I went along.

Another twister you have to say five times and very fast went: 'Kiss me ask me over to your house.' Again, the old woman surprised me. I wondered where she learned the twisters. None of the old grannies in O'Brien's ever talked to a child like Mrs L did me.

The kids in O'Brien's loved the tongue twisters I learned from Mrs L and taught to them. For a week, all the kids in the laneway were going around getting everyone to repeat after them, 'I put me foot in the bucket and footed the bucket about,' and 'kiss me ask me over to your house.'

Mrs L seemed lonely in the big rented house. She talked with me about all kinds of things before she ever got around to telling me what she needed from the shops. I often thought she just made it up that she needed something at the shops.

She said that millions of black beetles carpeted her kitchen floor during the night and that if a person came down early in the morning to the kitchen and quickly turned the light on, armies of black beetles covered the floor like a black cloak. I had no intention of ever visiting her early in the morning and seeing such a strange sight.

She asked me one afternoon if I had any clothes to my name other than the rags on my back. I was taken aback by her remark and did not know if she had intended to hurt my feelings or if she had asked a normal question. Ma dressed me the best she could. My dress and jumper were old, but Ma made sure they were clean. Mrs L told me that she was going to make me a new dress. She said that she had some red velvet material on a bolt left over from her time as a dressmaker, that had sat in a cubbyhole for years. Ma said that I should be more than delighted to get a new frock.

Mrs L took all the measurements. It took her a long time to pin and sew the dress together. I loved the red velvet material. I had no idea what kind of a dress it would turn out to be.

The dress turned out to be a fright. She had fashioned it in the style of a 1920s pattern with a long body and a short pleated skirt. She put a white lace collar on the neck of the frock. I had to hide my disappointment when I tried on the dress in front of her eyes. I knew that when I wore the red velvet flapper's frock, all the kids in O'Brien's would go in stitches and I'd be the laughingstock of the lane. When I wore the dress to mass, the kids wanted to know if my granny had left the dress to me in her will. I thanked Mrs L for the dress, but I'd die first before I ever wore it in daylight again.

Mrs L had two grown sons and one daughter. Her youngest son, Pip, lived in England. Mrs L told me all about Pip coming back to Ireland and she could hardly contain herself thinking about his return. I continued to run errands for Mrs L and then one day I met Pip. It was one afternoon when I went to see if Mrs L needed anything at the shop. Pip answered the door. He knew who I was, and asked if I had come to see his mother.

Soon after that, one afternoon he came to the door with his trousers unbuttoned, and I just looked the other way. I thought that he had forgotten to button them up. The next time he opened the door at my knock, he exposed himself completely to me. I knew it had been deliberate. I knew what a man's thing looked like—how many times had I seen my brothers pee in the slopbucket?—but this thing with Pip was beyond my comprehension. I was shocked and disturbed at the sight of his rat's tail.

I ran home and told Ma, very embarrassed in myself. Ma said, 'The man is an exposer,' and she forbade me to go near the house again. I never told his mother on him. Ma noted with anger, 'If yer daddy knew what happened, he'd knock his balls off.' I missed my friend Mrs L and my pay for running her errands. I often wondered why her son, Pip, had acted bad.

Barky Dog

It had been nice having an extra penny to spend on sweets when I worked for Mrs L Sometimes, I took Noely Joseph to the shop and bought him a lollipop. He shared his lollie with any dog he met on the street. Soon Noely wanted a 'goggie' of his own. Our room, packed with the six of us, could hardly squeeze in a mouse let alone a dog. But Noely Joseph begged to differ.

One day, Noely Joseph came home with his arms full of a dog. He told Ma that the dog was lost and had followed him home. It wasn't like any other dog that we had seen. It wasn't much bigger than a cat. Noely could hold all of the dog in his arms. He ran across the hall to Granny Martin's to show her his new dog.

'Cler'ta God, Noely, is that a dog or a cat? It's not like Lassie down the lane nor it doesn't look like Wilfie Noon's wolf dog, Prince. Is it a dog, d'ye think?'

'It's a dog a course,' he answered her. 'Does it have whiskers on its face, huh, Granny Martin? Does a cat have a pair a whiskers, huh?' he wanted to know.

Granny Martin, wiping her face off with her bib, chimed on, 'Well, these days with everything going on, and everything else, who can tell any more what dogs look like? Dogs anyway are bigger than that thing in yer arm, Noely,' she noted.

'THIS IS A DOG, can't ye tell?' he pleaded. 'This is a barky dog. Did ye ever hear a cat go "bark, bark bark"?' he asked her with his eyes like saucers. 'This is a barky dog,' he repeated.

'Well, what'll ye call it then, Noel?' she asked, put off.

'His name is Barky Dog. That's its name, Barky Dog, 'cause it barks, and cats don't bark. Isn't that right?' he asked Barky Dog. Noely had to keep himself from squashing the daylights out of Barky Dog, because of love. He found a rope and made a leash for the dog, and the two of them were to be found running up and down O'Brien's Place from one end to the other. Noely would be ahead of Barky Dog, as far as the rope leash allowed, with Barky Dog skittering after him on seemingly invisible legs.

Noely collected old wooden boards from around the lane and got some nails off someone and a hammer, and he made a doghouse. He collected grass from the field by Beggar's Bush, and lined the doghouse with it, to make it cushy for Barky Dog. Ma gave Noely two pence to go to the pork shop to buy two pence worth of black pudding for the dog. The dog went mad for the black blood sausage pudding. He ate it as if it were caviar.

We were all happy to have the small, hairy, big eyed dog, who looked more like a monkey than a dog, living with us. Noely ate, slept, and talked with the dog, like it was another Christian, observed Da.

Three weeks later, a tall man all dressed up in a suit came to O'Brien's Place and went around to all the neighbors. He carried a white envelope in his hand. He opened the envelope and took out a photograph of a dog that he said was missing or lost that belonged to a lady who lived on Haddington Road.

The dog in the photograph was a dead ringer for Barky Dog. 'This is a high breed of a dog. A Japanese Chin, quite valuable,' he told the crowd gathered.

'That's a picture of Noely's Barky Dog!' screamed out the kids with excitement.

'There's a one pound note reward for the return of the dog,' the man said, so someone quickly found Noely and the dog. 'Yes, that is the dog that got lost from the front garden, although the lady can't understand how it ever got out of the fenced garden,' the man explained.

Noely had to part with Barky Dog, and he nearly went mad for a while, sobbing himself dry. Da told Noely that as soon as he could he'd get him a new dog even if he had to find one on the moon. Da told the manservant to pocket the reward for the wee dog.

Leaving O'Brien's Place

In 1950, when I was twelve, the tenements in O'Brien's Place were condemned as being unfit for human habitation. Dublin Corporation sent every family living in O'Brien's Place a letter informing them that they were going to be moved into council housing.

The good part about leaving O'Brien's was to get out of the cramped room I'd lived in for twelve years, never having a corner to call my own. I looked at the double bed that I had shared for all those years with five other people. Being able to sleep in a bed by myself and stretch my legs would be a blessing. It had became harder to keep my legs crunched up while I slept in the bed. If I stretched out my legs, my toes touched my brothers. They yelled out for me to mind my bloody feet and stop kicking them in the balls.

I hated it when my toes accidentally made contact with Da at the bottom of the bed. He'd turn on his belly to sleep, making every attempt to protect me from doing such an embarrassing thing. Tinges of sexual curiosity leaked into my mind about why the bodies of men and women were different. However, any questions of that kind about either Da or my three brothers got overpowered by claustrophobia, which was stronger than any sexual curiosity. Having a little space, a place to sleep, and some privacy to call my own would be a gift from heaven.

The families in O'Brien's were sent to various council houses that had sprung up on the outskirts of Dublin, in Kimmage, Drimnagh, Inchicore, Ballyfermot and Ringsend. The remaining grannies and elderly bachelors who had lived in O'Brien's for as long as I remembered were told by the housing authorities to find a relative to take them in or else they would be put into an old folk's home. A few lucky grannies, like Granny Martin, had relatives who took them in. The remainder of the elderly were moved out of O'Brien's and scattered like a fistful of feathers among the old folks' homes in the city where they stayed 'til they perished.

The neighbours were sad to be scattered from each other, but they were also anxious to take their children out of the shitholes in O'Brien's.

We got a letter from the Dublin housing authorities to inform us we were allotted a new flat in George Reynold's House, in Irishtown, about a mile from O'Brien's Place. We were both sad and glad to be leaving our room in O'Brien's and all the neighbours. Our room held many memories, happy and sorrowful, but we were eager to fly the coop.

My brother Frank borrowed a wheel-cart from a fellow he knew. We piled the bed mattress and kitchen table on the cart along with some odds and ends. My brothers pushed the piled-up wheel-cart from O'Brien's to our new home in George Reynold's House.

Ma took down the picture of the Sacred Heart of Jesus from over the fireplace. She intended to hand-carry her treasure to its new location. I wrapped my belongings in a handkerchief to carry to my new home at George Reynold's. It didn't take long to clear out the room. When we had gone, any horse or cow or pig would have felt right at home moving into the dim cave.

Part 2: George Reynolds' House

Moving in

My older brothers pushed the cart from O'Brien's to our new home in George Reynolds' House. Ma, Noely Joseph and I walked behind them. Ma carried the framed picture of the Sacred Heart cuddled in her arms. The walk from O'Brien's Place to Irishtown Road seemed a good distance. We were unfamiliar with this part of town. As we drew closer, we could see the four blocks of four-storey buildings standing on the naked green field. The blocks were identical. Our new home would be in the block of flats that backarsed onto Irishtown Road.

After we got to George Reynolds', Frank blocked the wheelcart against the kerb and he, Da and Bob began to unload our stuff. Ma, Noely Joseph and myself flew up the three flights of stairs to the third balcony, turned right along the balcony until we came to flat number twelve.

Ma beamed as she inserted the new brass key into the keyhole, opened the door and pushed Noely and me into the hallway before her. Everything smelled of new paint and plaster. We could not believe that we had such space to live in. We went into the family room and right away Ma took a nail and a stone from out of her coat pocket, walked over to the fireplace and, with the stone, pounded the nail into the wall above the mantelpiece. She carefully hung the framed picture of her man on the nail. 'We're ready to move in now,' she said, as energised as an electric wire.

I walked around the two bedrooms, wondering which one Ma and I would call our own. Ma said it would be the front one that faced onto the balcony. We heard Da, Frank and Bob huffing along the balcony with the bed. Da asked Ma where she wanted it put. She and I got the bed, and the other four would sleep on the floor in the adjoining bedroom until we got another bed. All I could think about as I roamed from room to room was that God must finally have arrived in Ireland.

The bathroom had a door that could be locked from the inside which ensured privacy. It had a flush toilet, a big bath, and a small sink for hand washing. An irresistible urge to pee in the new porcelain toilet took hold. I gingerly sat down on the spotless commode and with the utmost pleasure and sense of freedom I expelled a flood of piss remembering the effort it took to even dribble in the former vomit pits in O'Brien's Place. I didn't have the heart to do number two in the sparkling bowl. I reached for the overhead pull chain above the toilet and yanked on it. The pull on the chain caused a gush of water which whisked the pee away as if by magic.

Noely banged impatiently on the bathroom door calling for me to get out. He looked over the bathroom, climbed into the bath with his street clothes on and lay down. 'I'm a "dicky-diver",' he laughed, flapping about in the bath like someone about to drown.

The big family room had a built-in fireplace. It also had a large picture window that looked out over Irishtown and towards the open sea. We could see plumes of smoke in the far distance from ships on the horizon.

The flat also contained a tiny scullery with a gas-stove and a sink with running water. The whole place had electric light which to me seemed the most divine light in the world.

Da and Frank plonked the kitchen table in the middle of the family room, and Bob placed the chair by the fireside. Ma took from Da the box which contained our cups, plates, knives and forks, the washbasin and the teapot. She put the utensils in the scullery. After things were arranged, Da asked if anyone knew the location of the neighborhood pub. 'Dwyers,' said my brother, 'is across the street.'

'Thank Christ,' said Da.

None of us could sleep the first night in the new setting. Ma and I tossed and turned in the bed sorely missing sleeping with Noely, Da, Frank and Bob. We could hear the four of them, in the other room, tossing about on the floor. Ma whispered that she'd have to find another bed soon because a skinny bag of bones like Da needed a cushier nest. The next morning we were in a daze as we drank our tea. Da said we were like newly separated Siamese twins. He also said that we would have been separated long ago had it been possible, adding that other families in the flats must be going through similar feelings.

Families who moved into George Reynolds' came from various parts across the city and the four blocks of flats were full in no time. We met the families who lived on our balcony. They had lots of babies, toddlers and kids my age and older. The women on the balcony continued to talk about their former neighbourhoods and how they missed their old neighbours, although they were glad to be living in their new places. The majority of the incomers to George Reynolds' had little furniture for their new homes. The women were soon talking about how they would furnish their new places if only they could afford to do so.

Because the flats were all identical, some mammies, daddies and kids got mixed up about which flat they lived in, on which balcony and in what block. It took time for everyone to figure it all out. Even after a few weeks, Da with a jar under his belt had trouble finding his way home. Half the time he didn't know if he was on the second or third balcony. Mrs O'B from underneath teased Ma about Da going into her flat and making himself at home.

'There he was sittin' down in the chair be the fireplace with a corkscrew in his hand pullin' on a bottle. He'd no idea he was in the wrong flat. He nearly put me back a week with fright . . . as contented as ye please, having a bottle at the fireplace.

'"Mr Kearns," says I, "Get outta that. Ye're in the wrong flat. Ye're up on the next balcony up," I told him.

'"God save me, Mrs What's-your-name," he apologises. "Glory-be-to-God I thought this was our flat."'

Da turned beet red when Ma slagged him about going into the neighbour's flat by mistake, but the old fella wasn't alone in getting the flats mixed up.

John Joe, the old-age pensioner, who lived with a granddaughter on the second balcony in our block of flats, continued to get lost. He got lost when he went for a walk or when he was coming back from the pub. The old man would standd on the street and roar, 'Someone take hold a me arm and lead me home. Be the jingo! I wish I was back in me room in Ringsend.'

His granddaughter, her husband and kids spent a lot of time hunting for the old man in the buildings, but as time passed we all got used to finding our way home, with only an odd one remaining mystified about their new location. Toddlers learned to manoeuvre their way up and down the steep stone stairways. They bounced down the stairways on their bums and slithered back up on their bellies. Older sisters and brothers kept an eye on them. But God help the kid of any age who dared to even accidentally shite or pee on the stairway. Their mammy got told in no uncertain way by other mammies that their kid deserved a box on the ear and should have their bum blasted for committing such an act.

In the past such behaviour might have been overlooked because of bad conditions, but not now. The women in George Reynolds' were determined to keep their new homes spick and span, inside and out. From the beginning, Ma and the other women made an agreement to take turns sweeping the balcony and scrubbing down the staircase with soap and water. The only bone of contention that emerged among the women had to do with sharing the clotheslines.

The communal clotheslines were located down in the courtyard on the ground floor. Tubs and tubs of family wash needed to be hung on the clotheslines to dry. Older housewives blamed the younger ones for hogging the lines for themselves. Blame also got placed on the women who lived on the lower floors who could run out sooner to the courtyard and claim a free clothesline before someone from an upper floor could make the trip down.

Mrs M, one of the younger housewives, lived on the ground floor and filled every free clothesline with her piles of wash. She'd wash the eyeballs right out of her head, said some while others huffed that even on Good Friday and Christmas Day she'd be out there, with her half-washed wash, claiming the lines.

Mrs D complained bitterly about how she tried for a week to find space on the clothesline to hang out her Mica's overalls and workshirt, all without success. Cora from the fourth floor cribbed how she nearly killed herself carrying down a basket of wash to the courtyard only to find that gunner-eyed bitch from the second balcony swiping the empty clothesline.

Baby nappies by the dozens constantly snapped back and forth on the clotheslines thanks to the stiff breezes that blew over the flats from Sandymount Strand, nearby. I hung out Da's shirt, the tea-towel, brothers' trousers and socks on any space I could find between the baby napkins.

But of all the things hung on the clotheslines to dry, none ever included a woman's underwear. Any girl who dared hang out a pair of knickers or a slip to flutter in the breeze, got looked upon with suspicion. Ma made me dry my underwear in our bedroom. She nearly went into conniptions when she saw me about to peg my knickers on the clothesline beside my brother's unmentionables. It just wasn't done.

And after school, just as it had been in O'Brien's Place, the courtyards at George Reynolds' filled with the sound of kids playing games until their mammies called them home. The voices of the mammies calling from the balconies to their children continue to chime in memory.

'Jimmy, Patrick, Anthony, Maureen, Ann! come up for yer tea,' ordered one mother.

'Get up here this minute, Larry, Teddy, and Maura, before I send yer daddy down with his belt,' warned another wornout woman.

'Do ye hear me calling ye, Mary Foley, Mike Foley, Dolly Foley?' another mother bellowed down.

Then we'd hear, 'Billy, Brendan, Brian, Janet, Bruce? I'm calling yez to come up.' This in the voice of the most beautiful looking mother in all of George Reynolds' public housing.

But when the voice of Mrs C erupted it captured all ears. Mrs C had a lisp. I can still hear her distinctive voice hovering over the balconies as she called down to one of her sons, on Saturday afternoon. 'Ja-woam, Ja-woam, catch dis shiw'in, and get me a talf-a-pound of tsausages at the pork shop. Get ta fat tsausages not the tskinny tsausages.'

Jerome threw a hell of a fit if he detected titters coming from anyone he thought was making fun of the way his ma talked. He warned everyone he'd knock their shite out if he thought they were snickering at his ma!

The flats were a toss away from the small shops that bunched together on Irishtown Road. Most of the families in the flats bought their groceries in Coadys' across the road. Mr and Mrs Coady let some in George Reynolds' buy their groceries on credit. Considering the high rate of unemployment at the time, the credit they offered seemed a godsend.

Doin' up the place

As if out of nowhere and to the delight of most of the mammies in the flats, streams of salesmen began to show-up in George Reynolds'. The salesmen offered to furnish every flat in the four blocks of housing with everything from a needle to a Persian rug for the fireplace, and all could be had on credit, on the 'hire purchase plan' that later came to be known as the 'never never plan'. Salesmen were sent into the flats by the Dublin Gas Company, the Electricity Supply Board and from the new furniture shops like Cavendish's, Boyer's and Radnor's that were springing up in the city. The salesmen discouraged mammies from talking over any potential new purchases beforehand with daddies, and were the daddies surprised when vanfuls of new furnishing got unloaded and carried into their flats: living room sets, bedroom sets, electric stoves, electric heaters, bedding, dishes, pots and pans, framed pictures, chalk statues, carpets, radios, record players and mirrors.

Ma, like others, furnished our flat from top to bottom on the available credit. And thanks to the credit, Da slept like a lord in his own bed complete with a box-spring mattress.

Mammies for the first time in their lives became preoccupied with interior decoration. 'Doin' up the place', it came to be called. And some mammies tried to outdo each other in the decorating department. There were women like Mrs McD, on the bottom floor, who showed a flair for 'doin' up the place' like nobody else in the flats. Her arrangements brought wild raves from the other women.

'Julia's flat is gorgeous. It's lovely. It's a showplace,' were some of the praises heaped on Mrs McD for her artistic ability. Jinny on our balcony suggested to Ma and me that we take a look at how Mrs McD had furnished and decorated her flat.

'Mary, go down and just see what Julia did. She's letting everyone in to see her place and she doesn't mind who copies her ideas.' Soon Mrs McD invited Ma and me to come in and see her flat, and over a cup of tea and buttered toast she told us how much she loved doing up the place. I let my eyes wander in wonder around the flat.

Mrs McD had hung 'feather and fan' wallpaper in her family room and in her hallway in colours of red, gold, green and blue. She had laid down high gloss green linoleum on the floor that matched the green in the wallpaper, and she picked-up the blue with her furniture. She had an oval mirror framed in gilt hung over the mantelpiece. And scattered here and there were an assortment of small figurines and delft springer-spaniels.

'All I can say,' said Ma to Mrs McD, 'is the flat is that gorgeous!' I echoed the praise with the same utmost feeling. And Mrs McD's brilliance didn't stop indoors. She went on to create a tradition in George Reynolds' that continued for as long as I recall. She had the inspiration to take a tin of Cardinal Red Furniture Polish and use it to create a red half-moon crescent on the ground outside her front door.

The makebelieve welcome-mat caught the imagination of the other women on our block, and in no time Coadys' shop had sold every tin of red furniture polish they had in stock. Overnight, poppy red half-crescent moons appeared in front of every doorway, adding whimsy and colour to the plain block of buildings.

Sounds of American music blared out from all the new wireless sets. Young people tuned into Radio Luxemburg to hear the latest songs sung by Kay Starr, Rosemary Clooney, Teresa Brewer, Frankie Lane, Johnny Rae, Pat Boone and Elvis Presley. Radio Eireann continued to play Irish music. Da told my brothers and me to tune into Radio Eireann instead of Radio Luxembourg. We told him that we were tired of having to listen to old fellas raving on the radio about the life of the cuckoo or curlew; or talks on how Bord na Móna (The Turf Board) harvested, stacked and dried the turf they got from the bogs of the West of Ireland; or to another priest going on about the 'mysteries of faith'.

Everyone in George Reynolds' enjoyed the new radios, and the other new furnishings our mammies purchased on the never-never plan. However, increasing debt began to pile up, and take its toll on families. The once sweet-talking salesmen who sold our mammies everything from shoelaces to living room furniture, demanded payment on the goods. When the choice had to be made between paying off the debt or putting food on the table, mammies went with the grub. The firms who sold all the stuff knew that unemployment ran high, and that most of our fathers were out of work in this new decade of the 1950s. Ma used to send me with a payment, sometimes late, to Radnor's furniture shop in Mary Street. I would give the payment along with the payment book to Mr Radnor who marked the amount in his large ledger, and in our payment book. He would warn me, and others in line, not to let the payments get in arrears, 'or else'. A new word 'repossession' began to make its way into the conversations of the people who lived in George Reynolds'. I soon learned the meaning of 'repossession'.

On a Thursday afternoon, I happened to be alone in our flat listening to the radio when someone nearly rattled the mailbox off its hinges. I opened the front door to find two big brutes stomping back and forth, with a slip of paper in their hands.

'Is yer mother in?' asked one.

'No,' I replied like a gobshite. The other brute said they had been sent out by the owner of Radnor's furniture shop to repossess the furniture that Ma had got on the never never plan.

'Well, me mammy is not here. You'll have to come back,' I told them as calmly as I could.

'Mr Radnor wants his furniture back 'cause yer mother is behind in her payments,' said the boxer lookalike.

'We've a list here in our hand of the things we're supposed to repossess: a sofa, two fireside chairs, a pair a statues, and a bed with a box spring mattress.

'Well, me mammy isn't home,' I repeated.

'Git out iv our way,' they barked and marched right into the flat. In the flash of an eye, they carried away the sofa, fireside chairs, and the pair of umbrella girl and boy chalk statues that Ma loved. They asked me where the bed and box mattress were. Awareness finally set in. I told the brutes that my brother, sick with TB, lay in the bed in the next room. When I mentioned TB, the pair did a bunk out the door in fear of the dreaded tuberculosis.

As I gazed around the empty living room, I realized what a flittermouse I'd been to let the bullies in. At least I'd saved the bed for Da, Frank, Bob, and Noely Joseph. The kitchen table, the one chair along with the framed picture of the Sacred Heart were all the room held now. I dreaded the thought of Ma coming back and finding all the cherished possessions gone with the wind. I knew Ma owed money on the furniture, but she paid on it weekly or as often as possible. She'd lose all the payments on the confiscated furnishing: gone up the chimney like smoke.

I heard Ma turning the key in the door, and I felt sick in the belly. She called out my name in greeting. I watched her face as she strode into the living room and saw it bare. 'In the name of God what's happened to the furniture? Where's the sofa, the two fireside chairs and me lovely pair of umbrella children?' 'They've all been repossessed,' I told her brimming with tears. 'What does that mean?' asked Ma, dropping the shopping bag down on the floor with a thud.

'Radner sent out two brutes to repossess everything,' I told her. 'They said you were in high arrears and ye'd had yer warning.'

'The auld fixer,' exclaimed Ma. 'I've more paid off on the furniture than what I owed in the first place.'

I kept my mouth shut, because I suspected that she owed more on the furniture than was needed to pay it off. I believed that the two bullies sent out to take back the furniture should have waited to face Ma instead of marching over me. 'Well what's done is done, no use crying over spilled milk,' said Ma in an attempt to make me feel better.

When Da got back from another fruitless search for a job, and walked into the living room, he thought he'd made a mistake as he took in the naked surroundings. 'Is there somethin' different going on in here or am I in the wrong flat?' he inquired of Ma and me. Ma explained that old Radnor had sent out two fellas to repossess the furniture and that if Da needed to sit down he'd have to sit on the floor. 'Who let the buggers in?' inquired Da as he looked at the floor. Ma's face drew a blank. He shifted his eyes from her to me, and I burst into tears.

'I didn't mean it. I didn't mean to let the buggers in. They pushed me aside and came in. I didn't know the buggers were after the furniture or I'da tried to shut the door in their faces.' Da gave me a blank look. I wondered if he remembered how I'd let the sanitary lady back in O'Brien's Place enter our room to find him and Ma in the midst of a passion wrestling match in the bed?

All Da said was, 'Titch, don't ever get yourself a job as a jailer.' He looked at our crestfallen faces and recited,

'Little apples will grow again,
Birds will still sing their song,
Your mammy is still the greatest girl in the world,
And Titch! watch out for the quicksand.'

A month hadn't passed before a cocky salesman from a newly opened furniture shop in Dublin rapped his knuckles on our hall door. He inquired if Ma had ever seen pictures of the new kind of furniture his shop sold. 'The furniture,' he said, showing Ma pictures in a book, 'is modelled after the latest furniture in America!' Our newly furnished living room with the latest up-to-date American lookalike furniture, outdid Radnor's.

It became more and more obvious that the heavy rate of unemployment among the men in George Reynolds' was taking its toll. The grim faces of unemployed men carried the story. Their muffled talk and sharp coughs caught the ear, as they clung to the corner of Irishtown Road, trying to crack a joke or fling a curse. The men gathered on the corner in hopes of hearing word about getting hired on the docks to unload ships or on a building site as labourers.

My brothers Frank and Bob found work as messenger boys and handed their wages over to Ma. The sight of the passing ships from our window had delighted Bob who, after seeing the high smokestacks, had set his heart on being a seaman. Da talked about us all moving to England if we could scrape up the fare for the six of us. In the interim, Sandymount Strand offered a respite from everyday care.

Sandymount Strand

It seemed a miracle to live within a ten minute walk of the strand. In summer, loads of kids from the flats went to the strand to play and take a swim in the sea. Florrie Pepper, who had the only girl's bathing suit in all the flats, let us borrow her suit to go dipping in the sea. She never got upset at us pestering her for a turn to swim in the togs. She loaned the suit to thin girls, heavy girls, short girls and tall girls. By the time we had all had a chance to wear the bathing suit, its shape had changed ten times ten times.

We followed Florrie to the strand and waited until she had finished playing and swimming in the sea. She dashed from the water as soon as a raw breeze picked up. We'd hold a towel like a tent around Florrie, as she slid off the dripping suit and flicked the wet bundle with her foot to the next person in line to wear it.

'It's my turn after her,' went the refrain for the afternoon as we each waited impatiently for our turn to don the suit, run forth to meet the incoming tide and belly flop into the expanse of green.

An unwritten rule existed that girls and boys did not to go swimming together. Adults believed allowing girls and boys, even under the age of twelve, to go swimming together, could lead to acts of indecency. My brother Bob, (Robbler to his friends), hiked to the Pigeon House, on to the Red Lighthouse, then on to the Shelly Banks to swim, far away from the sight or sounds of girls splashing and dancing about in the tide pools.

Only men and older boys were supposed to swim at the Shelly Banks. Rumour had it that the men, young and old alike, liked to skinny-dip to experience the freedom of the sea, and they could only have such freedom away from the glare of females of all ages. Thus, only the screeching sea birds were allowed to get a glimpse of the milkwhite arses and crimson balls being slapped and caressed by the sea.

The only women I had ever seen wearing a bathing suit were in Hollywood pictures. On the odd occasion that our mammies had the time to accompany us to the strand, the only parts of their bodies they revealed were their feet as they soaked them in the surf. Some outrageous mammies dared to tuck up the skirts of their dresses into the elastic legs of their knickers, as they frolicked like young girls in the sea. Some of them laughed at the sight of each other's bare thighs, and teased each other about such wanton exposure. The sea made them lighthearted and they laughed and sang as they kicked their feet in the water, dipped their hands in the sudsy surf, and let the wind unpin their hair.

'Watch out for men who might walk this way down the strand and see us with our skirts rolled up,' warned the women to their daughters adding, as if in jest, 'we don't want them or a priest from the Star of the Sea, seeing us half-naked!'

The rare times we went to the strand with our mammies got stored away in memory. I never saw any da take his daughters to the strand. Da said the sea made men mad and that I only had to read about Moby Dick to find that out.

The Star of the Sea on the Sandymount Road became our new parish church. Ma missed going to mass at Saint Mary's Church on Haddington Road, the church she'd belonged to since being baptised there. The Star of the Sea drew in a lot of toffs and few tinkers. And though the well-off church would be a new spiritual home for all the poor families that lived in George Reynolds' House, our new parish did not put out a welcome mat for us; toffs would continue to be the favoured flock.

Whether mass was on Sunday or on holy days of obligation, the favoured sermon centred on how hard it would be for the rich to get into heaven. We knew the priest and his recruits went over such mumbo-jumbo to pretend they were on the side of Jesus, who supposedly favoured the poor over the rich, but one had only to take a gander at the well-fed priest and recruits to see that they had never had a hunger pain that lasted longer than a fart.

Such thoughts and accusations could never be voiced by a girl unless she was a gillygoose. It was much easier for a girl to turn a deaf ear to the men's blathering. The love of God still stuck to my soul as taffy did to my teeth, causing a similar rot. I didn't need to be reminded Sunday after Sunday that I should be thankful for being poor.

On the way home from mass, the smell of Sunday dinner drifted from the parish house of the Star of the Sea, causing me to buckle in my belly as I walked past. Hopeful, I prayed as I walked back to George Reynolds', that Ma had created a miracle and she'd have a plate of mashed potatoes with a few sizzling sausages waiting for me to eat. I had yet to experience the luxury of having three square meals a day, and I wasn't getting any younger.

The gasman cometh

The gasman who got sent out by the gas company to collect the money in the meters in George Reynolds' every two months became a dreaded figure. He had the power to cut off the supply of gas into any flat if the tenant hadn't put enough money into the meters. Both the cooking stoves and built-in gas fires in every flat were fuelled by gas, and the meter boxes had been carefully designed by the gas company only to accept shilling coins.

When it came down to putting the last shilling in the house into the gas meter or using it to buy food for a family, the gas company usually lost out. People came up with various ways to fool the meter and keep the gas running. The meters could not tell the difference between a well filed washer or a religious medal or a filed down half-penny. If any of them got snagged in the slot, all that was needed was a hit with a hammer, and the meter swallowed the dud. The duds kept the gas on, the stoves burning and the bedrooms warmed in winter.

But when the gasman opened up the meter and found all the duds instead of shillings, he had the gas turned off. Ma, along with the other women, dreaded the sight of the gasman, because they knew all he'd find in the meters were washers, holy medals and filed down half-pennies. Keeping the gasman out of the flat became the goal, so an early warning system got set up. Kids were put on the watch out for any sight of the gasman making the rounds. If four bangs rattled the letterbox, it meant the gasman had been spotted on the ground floor. Three raps on the letterbox meant he was headed for the second balcony, and a flurry of raps meant time to draw the front curtains, latch the front door and hunker down 'til the collector had his fill of pounding on the letterbox, and walked off in disgust to try his luck at another flat.

A couple of days later, a letter would arrive from the gas company complaining that their collector had been unable to collect the money from the meter, and if the occupant of the flat did not show up at the gas company soon all kinds of terrible things would be inflicted. Ma and the other neighbours would show up the day after the letter arrived hoping to get a reprieve so their gas would not be cut off.

Ma and the neighbours wanted to pay the gas company but they could not draw blood out of a stone: if no money was coming into the house, how could slews of shillings go to the gas company?

'It torments the heart out of people,' said Ma, 'when they can't pay their bills or put a bit of grub on the table for their family.' With so many families living hand to mouth in the flats, it's a wonder any of them survived the times. Mrs D had fifteen children to look out for. Her husband found part-time work on the docks. She wore a look of weariness about her like a mantle. Her husband, the fucker, treated her like a slave. We heard him chase his kids out of the flat at noontime when he came home, and order his wife indoors. Sometimes she ran back out into the courtyard with him after her. Mrs D told one of the women that her husband acted the way he did because he only wanted her for 'her Mary'. With a flatful of kids, she tried to shield her 'Mary' at all costs. So the story went.

One of the younger married women spouted off to ears all open, 'Why does he chase her like that? What's does he see in her? She looks dragged out.'

'Well,' noted an older one to 'Gawky Eyes', 'men like him don't look at the mantelpiece when they're stoking the fire, if ye get me gist?'

At the time, Gawky Eyes' remarks about Mrs D were over my head. Gawky Eyes, who imagined herself as a model mammy, had no qualms about slagging others who did not fit her notions of propriety. Another woman—I won't name her—was called 'the Queer One' by Gawky Eyes and others of her ilk. I realised later the woman kept her family alive by letting questionable men stoke her flame with their burned out pokers.

The Queer One had a flat in the third block of George Reynolds' and had a houseful of children to support without the help of anyone. Her husband, the mister, had been put in jail. Talk had it he had been sent to jail for meddling with his oldest daughter. His wife found herself alone in the world to care for the troubled daughter and the rest of the children. The amazing thing about her was that despite the bombshell over her daughter, the mister rotting in jail, and having to find the wherewithal to pay for rent and food for her seven kids, she remained a smasher, unlike a lot of other wives who looked old before their time.

To some in the flats—both men and women—the Queer One represented the evils of vice, immorality and unholy womanhood. They cast their eyes to the ground if they met her on the street, as if by looking at her they might be led astray. They often referred to her as 'that redheaded whore'. The redheaded whore wore her mop of orange coloured hair in the style of Lauren Bacall, the sultry American film actress. Madam's perfectly coifed orange hairdo topped off the rest of her fashionable appearance. She wore a two-piece suit, fawn nylons on her long legs, bare-toed alligator platform shoes and she carried a long, envelope-shaped fawn-coloured handbag under her arm. She wore Max Factor type makeup, plum coloured lipstick and did up her eyelashes until they stood out like spikes. She constantly smoked cigarettes in a long cigarette holder as she walked along the street, tall and straight as any man in uniform.

Some exceptional neighbours didn't cast their eyes to the ground when the Queer One passed them by on the street. Instead they gave her the time of day, and she replied in turn. If I caught her eye, she gave me back a faint smile and a knowing look of some kind. Ma and her friend Jinny didn't join in with others by flinging their eyes on the ground when the woman passed, either. Gossips whispered for others to hear how she earned her wages by illgotten means. I asked Ma what the gossips meant by such a thing?

'By the mother of Christ, that woman earns every penny,' said Ma, with more than mercy sounding in her tone.

'By the mother of Christ,' I thought to myself, 'the Queer One could not earn her wages any harder than the girls who work in the animal slaughter house in Ringsend.' They made the casings and stuffing for sausages and other meats for the pork shops around the city. The girls earned only shillings a week instead of the pound notes that the Queer One supposedly made by the fistful. And the girls who worked in the slaughterhouse smelled like pig shite as they walked home from the factory.

Whatever the Queer One did for a living that prevented her from making sausages and smelling like pig shite seemed smarter to me all the way. What was it she did for her wages? Our nextdoor neighbour, quite by accident, nearly filled in the blanks for me.

An unfamiliar man, seemingly a toff, came up to our balcony, and rat-tat tatted on the letterbox of our neighbour. Everyone knew how religious our neighbour was. She went to mass every morning in rain or shine and practised nothing but virtue. If the redheaded whore passed her on the street, our neighbour responded by making the sign of the cross with the rosary she kept constantly in the left pocket of her coat.

To this day, it remains a mystery how the stranger mistakenly mistook our neighbour's flat for that of the Queer One's. As merry as you please, he commenced to rattle our neighbour's letterbox, the grin on his face about to split his ears.

The neighbour opened her front door, bibbed as usual in a floral apron, arms folded across her ample mother's breast. She asked the man what he wanted rattling the letter box nearly off the hinges. He told her that he was here to pay Mrs X a visit. He got her name, he said, from a friend.

'Ye're lookin' for who?' asked the neighbour, and he repeated the refrain again, word by word. All the talk came in through the open bathroom window, as I lay in the bath soaped to the nose.

'What's that ye're handing me?' ripped the neighbour.

'Two crisp Irish pound notes,' said the unfamiliar voice beginning to sound a little hesitant.

'This is the home of a Christian family,' I heard the neighbour shrill. 'The cheek of ye comin' up to this door, rattlin' me letterbox and looking for that redheaded wan who lives in the other block of flats. You must be one of the dirtbirds who go to her flat. Answer me. Are ye one of her dirtbirds?' roared our neighbour letting the whole of Ireland in on the man's woeful ways.

'Ye bloodsucker, ye dirty dirtbird! Git out iv here. Ye bloody fancy-man. If me husband was in, he'd throw ye over the balcony. Ye wouldn't be walking back down them stairs!'

I could hear the stranger telling the neighbour that he was sorry, that he had made a terrible mistake. A terrible mistake. Afraid that the stranger might come flying through the bathroom window, I got out of the bath, dressed quickly and went out on the balcony. Some of the other people who lived on the balcony were standing outside their doors watching and listening to all the commotion.

The man kept trying to apologise for making the mistake. He pointed out he'd picked out the wrong corner flat on the wrong third balcony, in the wrong block of flats and that he would never make the mistake again.

'Ye skuttebully!' she continued to roar in his face.

Ma came walking down the balcony and stopped to see the up-roar outside our bathroom window. Mrs H beckoned for Ma to come over and hear what she had to say about the man in front of her face. By this time, he looked as if he'd been dragged through a ditch. When he saw Ma approach, he told her of his mistake. With that, he gave the neighbour one more mortified apology and offered her the two crisp green pound notes along with the box of choco-lates he had kept under his arm.

The neighbour flung the man's pound notes to the ground along with the big box of Black Magic chocolates. The man picked-up the money and the chocolates, handed both to Ma and took off down the balcony still protesting his mistake.

The neighbour looked at Ma standing in front of her crinkling the pound notes in one hand and breathing in the smell of the sweet chocolates with her nose.

'Ye're not thinking of keeping that dirtbird's trash,' said the neighbour to Ma. With that she walked over to the rubbish chute and opened the hatch. 'Throw in that filthy money and that spoiled box of chocolates,' demanded the neighbour, the cheeks on her face as red as a cock's comb. She kept opening and shutting the rubbish hatch with a bang waiting for Ma to dump in the illgotten loot. Ma took a step forward and tried to give the neighbour the money and the box of chocolates one more time.

'No! I would not soil me hand by touching those things,' exploded the neighbour, sweat now drenching her top lip.

All eyes were on Ma to see what she would do with the fortune in money and the delicious contents in the box of Black Magic. Ma cast her eyes over us all, and said, 'I'm sorry that fancy-man upset you, but I see the money and the box of chocolates as a godsend,' and with that she handed over the box of chocolates to Andy to pass around to everyone gathered. Ma said she'd share the two pounds with any woman who needed a few shillings like she did to feed their kids and husbands.

Our neighbour bashed the chute shut for the last time, pushed past Ma and me, walked back into her house, and slammed the door nearly lifting her letterbox off the door. Ma and the other women on the balcony were aware that the neighbour's husband had a full time job and that two of her sons were also working, and compared to the rest around, she stood in gravy.

After several weeks passed, the next door neighbour got over her grumble and was back talking to Ma asking Ma if she thought Da would ever find a job, and didn't he look a bit drawn most of the time.

The milk-fed chickens

The only time our family got into a terrible row with anyone in George Reynolds' House was because of Da. The old fella, home alone at the time, answered the postman's knock. The postman had a brown paper, rain soaked parcel to deliver in George Reynolds'. The rain had made the address label blurry and unreadable. The postman told Da that the name on the address label could be either 'Kearns' or 'Kiernan'. The postman said the parcel had been sent from somewhere in the country and had Da any relatives in the countryside who might send him a parcel?

Da told the postman he had a mother and two sisters living in the countryside and maybe the parcel came from them. With that, the postman handed over the parcel to the old fella. Da became convinced that the blurry address label on the parcel read 'Kearns'. He opened the parcel and found two dead dressed chickens all ready for the oven. He told Ma and the rest of us that his mother must have sent the parcel to make up with him after all their years of estrangement. We feasted off the chickens as if they would be our last meal for years to come. In between bites of the birds, Ma asked Da if his mother had put a note in with the chickens.

'Ah, she didn't put in a note with the chickens because she didn't know what to write in order for us to make up,' said Da.

'I can see a thing like that happening,' affirmed Ma. I never saw Da so happy; I never realised how much he loved and missed his mother. We were all delighted that Da's mother had made contact with us by sending the chickens, and we expected a letter to arrive from Castleblayney any day. Ma checked the letterbox every day, but no letter ever arrived from his mother or sisters in Castleblayney, County Monaghan. But Da kept believing a letter was due.

A week later, we heard a voice calling through the letterbox, 'Yoo hoo, in there. Yoo hoo!' Ma opened the door and there stood Mrs Kiernan who lived in the flat above us. Ma never thought anything was amiss with Mrs Kiernan from the sound of her blithe Yoo hoo! through our letterbox. Mrs Kiernan asked Ma if the postman had given them a parcel recently. Ma told her that Da had got a parcel from his mother in Castleblayney. 'Were there two milk-fed spring chickens in that parcel?' asked Mrs K, with high emotion in her voice. 'Yes,' said Ma. 'How did ye know that?'

'From other eyes and ears,' noted Mrs Kiernan. 'Who took in the parcel from the postman?' she wanted to know, her voice getting higher in register.

'Me husband, Frank, took the parcel from the postman.'

'Did he bother to read the label on that parcel? Did he bother to notice that parcel was addressed to a "Kiernan," not a "Kearns," or was he in his usual condition?'

'And what condition is that?' asked Ma getting edgy herself.

'Drunk!' said Kiernan. 'Ye know ye're married to a drunkard don't ye, Mrs Kearns? Well, was the mister drunk or sober when he read the label?' Mrs Kiernan demanded.

'It's hard to tell whether he's drunk or sober any more, or sick or well. God only knows,' explained Ma.

'Well, he and you and the rest of yez ate two spring milk-fed chickens that were meant for us, the Kiernans. They were sent from County Cavan by an aunt of my husband's. God help that poor mother in Castle what-ever-ye call it having a son like the drunkard ye're married to.' Mrs Kiernan left Ma speechless.

Da had been a fool to think his mother had sent him a pair of chickens as a peace token, but he continued his wishful thinking. He couldn't accept or face the fact that he'd been hacked off the family tree, and could be tumbling head over heels in hell for all his kith and kin cared.

Mrs Kiernan told interested parties how Da had diddled her family out of two country milk-fed chickens. Most of the neighbours believed Da had made an honest mistake; nevertheless, Mrs Kiernan refused to bid the time of day to any member of our family. She passed Ma going up and down the staircase without a nod or a wink. Ma felt bad about the whole mix-up because she liked the Kiernan family. My brother Frank had taken a shine to the Kiernan's only daughter, but because of the episode of the chickens, the daughter only gave him a drop dead look.

Tension between the Kearns and the Kiernans continued until tragedy struck: the oldest Kiernan son, who lived with a grandmother, came to see his mother early one morning. The mother went into the scullery to make him some breakfast, and as she worked, the son went into the bathroom, took his father's long bladed razor and slit his throat. He managed to walk out the front door and then threw himself over the balcony.

Someone in the courtyard below saw the body topple from the balcony and hit the ground. Then we heard the neighbour's scream. Ma and I rushed to see what had happened. We leaned over our section of the balcony, directly underneath the Kiernan's, and got the front of our frocks stained with blood.

'Merciful God,' said Ma, looking at the fresh blood stain. 'Someone just killed themself.' We heard the screams of Mrs Kiernan from up above. Ma ran down our balcony and charged up the flight of stairs to Mrs Kiernan. She grabbed the hysterical woman and locked her arms around her and took her inside.

A crowd gathered around young Kiernan's crumpled body on the ground. The police from Irishtown station were called to the scene. Then the priest arrived and prayed over the body, complaining on and on, 'Why would anyone kill themselves on such a lovely Irish summer morning?' A lorry from the morgue arrived and two men dressed in white hospital clothing put the body on a stretcher and lifted it into the back of the lorry.

The sight of the men in their white hospital gear set my heart rocking. For an instant, my mind struggled to bring back a memory, but my will would not allow it. Feelings of black despair began to float up from somewhere inside me but were forced down.

A pool of blood remained on the grey ground from the body. George, the caretaker of the flats, hosed off the blood with water and women sprinkled the death site with holy water. Some kids circled the spot hoping to find leftover guts. They were shooed away with a warning.

The neighbours in George Reynolds' speculated over why young Kiernan had killed himself in such a fashion. Rumour had it he had been mixed up with the IRA and was on the run from the British government. Kiernan became the first to die in our new flats, and as time went by, his ghost appeared on the stairway, as neighbours had assured all that it would.

Despite all the love and concern shown by her own family, Mrs Kiernan latched onto Ma while in her grief. In the process peace got restored between our two families, and life limped on.

Shame

Limping from George Reynolds' to Saint Mary's school in Haddington Road got more painful for me day by day. I hadn't been confirmed yet, that is, I hadn't made my confirmation in the holy Roman Catholic Church, so there was no way out of the fix. Frank and Bob had already left school, for the same reasons I soon would.

Frank got a job as a bicycle messenger boy picking up deliveries for a shop in Powerscourt. He gave Ma part of his wages. Bob learned how to go fishing with a long-line for flounders, sand dabs and silver salmon that came in on the tides on Sandymount Strand. He went off to the strand at low tide to dig for 'hairy bait' which he used to bait the fish hooks on his long-line.

He let me attach some of the dozens of fishhooks that he fastened onto the long-line. I let him bait the hooks himself with the long, squiggly hairy-bait maggots that looked for all the world like hairy caterpillars only with added legs. After Bob got his line ready he looped it carefully into a bucket making sure that none of it tangled.

He came to know the tides like the back of his hand: the high tides, low tides and ebb tides, and he set out his long-line according to them. Some mornings he got up at the crack of dawn to go out and unload his fishing line before any of the seagulls got first choice. The gulls went after the eyes of the fish and picked at the flesh. When Bob went to sell the catch at one of the shops, he would get less for the catch if they had been scarred by the gulls.

The lovely fresh fish that Bob caught on the long-line supplemented our meals at home. The money he made from selling the fish did not amount to a lot but it helped nevertheless. From time to time the parish priest at the Star of the Sea saw Bob coming along the sea wall with his bucketful of fish and he would ask Bob if he could have a look at his catch. As Bob held up the sand dabs, the flounders and the pink salmon the priest told Bob that he loved to eat fresh pink salmon. The priest would only pay for the middle section of the salmon, however, so Bob had to cut the tail and shoulders and head off the fish before the priest dished out the money, paying Bob two shillings for several pounds of the firm red flesh. Obviously, diddling Bob out of a fair price for the prized delicacy didn't interfere with the priest's digestion.

Noely Joseph and I walked from the flats to school in Saint Mary's in Haddington Road. On days without much food in our belly, the road seemed very long. I don't know why we bothered to go to school at all. The shame and abuse the nuns inflicted on us for being poor hurt more than hunger in the gut.

The shame began each day at being called up to the front of the classroom and chastised for coming to school without a uniform. Ma and Da could not afford to buy me the navy blue gymslip, white blouse, black stockings and shoes, green tie and green sash that we were ordered to wear in order to look 'respectable'. I had one dress that Ma washed and ironed for me to wear to school. I never had the luxury of looking 'respectable'.

After putting me on display for not looking respectable, the nun would announce time for our morning prayers. She fingered her jet black rosary as she prayed out loud, her face taking on an ecstatic expression which supposedly revealed her love of the saviour. After saying the rosary, we were ordered to take out our reading books. Just a few books appeared because, like myself, most of the children had no money to buy school books. So we sat at our desks like perched birds unable to fly. The nun read from her reader. Then she did some sums on the blackboard. After that it came time for the class to say the noontime angelus, and then head home for lunch.

Noely and I ran all the way home to George Reynolds' hoping to find something on the table, even if only a cup of tea and a slice of bread and butter. Most of the time, Ma somehow scrounged something up. After lunch, the pair of us headed back to school.

On Wednesday afternoons, the nun passed around the 'black baby box'. All in the class were expected to have a penny to put into the collection box for the African missions. I loved the small white box with the figure of a black child kneeling down on top. When a penny was put into a slot in the box, the little kneeling figure nodded its head in thanks.

The nun eyed each child to see if she had dropped a penny into the collection box, and accused those who did not of being selfish. Had I a penny, I would have gladly dropped it into the box just to see the little figure nod its head upwards and downwards in gratitude.

I would also have gladly paid the two pennies that the school charged for elocution lessons. Someone, somewhere, had made a decision to offer paid elocution lessons to national school children so that they would speak the King's English correctly. Every Thursday an outside teacher came to the school to teach elocution.

Any kid who could not pay for the lessons, which lasted an hour, had to stand outside the classroom until the lesson was over. Ma scraped up the two pennies now and then not because she didn't like the way I talked or believed that trying to sound like an English toff offered an improvement over Dublin street speech, but because she knew I ground my teeth at the idea of having to wait outside the classroom for an hour every week like a beggar.

I began to rebel about going to school and having my head dunked in shite for being poor and unable to buy a school uniform, buy school books, drop a penny into the collection box, and having to wait outside the classroom, week after week, because there wasn't any money for elocution lessons.

And confirmation loomed up ahead. I told Ma and Da I didn't care if I got confirmed or not. But mostly I didn't want to go though the shame and embarrassment of not having the expected new outfit required for confirmation. But Ma and Da would not hear of me leaving school at such a young age and especially without having been confirmed into the Catholic Church.

The Church placed the burden of making sure that we all made our confirmation on the shoulders of our parents, though the indoctrination process would be in the hands of the priests and nuns. All civic lessons were thrown aside in preparation: day by day and week by week we were drilled in religious doctrine, in the laws of the

Catholic Church and the teachings of Christ. In my mind the laws of the Church and the teachings of Christ were like night and day, but what child could pose such a thought to any priest or nun, for fear of getting skullcapped?

We were all expected to bring money from home to buy rosaries, confirmation medals and confirmation certificates that would be signed by the bishop. As usual, like so many other children in my class, extra money could not be had for such things. The nuns complained and slapped some of us for not bringing in the money for the necessities. One of the girls in the classroom, Gracie, driven by desperation, screamed at the nun that she did not care if she made her confirmation or not, whether she went to heaven or not, or if she died or not.

Exhilarated at her outburst, I unknowingly cried out with glee. Silence fell over the classroom. The nun walked to my desk and slapped me across the head, and told me to wait after school for my punishment. She never laid a finger on Gracie who could have levelled her like a log. Compared with Gracie, I was a shrimp.

After the class had been dismissed, I waited at my desk to have my ears boxed again. The nun told me in a cold controlled voice to kneel before the class altar for two hours without moving. After the two hours, she told me to clean the blackboard, sweep the floor, then change the water in the jamjars that held the flowers on the altar. I took down the two jars filled with flowers and carried them to the cloakroom. I filled one of them with fresh water, and I pissed in the other before returning the flowers. I stiffly walked back into the classroom and placed the jamjars on the altar.

The nun dismissed me with her hand. For the rest of the week, a faint smell of piss caressed the classroom. To the nun's nose the smell of the piss resembled stale fish. She asked the class if anyone had been so bold as to take fish and chips into the classroom unbeknown to her. We shook our heads and said, 'No, Sister!'

Saint Vincent de Paul

One morning the nun read us a note she had received from the Vincent de Paul. The nun told the class that the good people of the Vincent de Paul were passing out vouchers for free clothing to those in need. We all knew what Vincent de Paul clothes looked like. Not even the dead would be caught in them. The charity had all the clothes made in the same colour and the same style. The badly made clothing was the colour of horseshite gone green. On our way out of class, the nun handed out the vouchers with the warning that our mothers were to come to the church and have the vouchers signed by the parish priest or else the vouchers would not be accepted.

The parish priest met our mammies in the church vestibule where he asked them who they were, where they lived, how many children they had, the amount of money coming into the home, and if the children were being brought up as good Irish Catholics? The desperate mammies fed the parish priest all the information he wanted to know.

Noely and I told Ma that under no circumstances would we wear those clothes. Most of the mammies had no intention of putting the prison-like garb on the backs of their children for all to recognise as charity cases. Everyone in the city of Dublin recognised the uniforms issued by the Vincent de Paul.

The horseshite brown coarse wool uniforms the girls got were all identical, and the horseshite gone green uniforms given to the boys were also identical and the boys' and girls' clothes fitted like sacks. Girls also got a pair of navy blue knickers that they were supposed to wear under the uniform. The tight elastic bands in the legs of the knickers left purple welt marks that lasted for the life of the drawers. The bullet-proof knickers took ages to wear out and couldn't be blown off with a cannonball.

The mammies had no intention of making their kids wear the hallmark of the Vincent de Paul. They had other plans for the cheerless drab garments. But first they had to get the stuff from the

Church charity. The school let us off for the morning to go with our mothers to pick up the free clothes.

We all had to line up and wait outside the vestibule where the clothes were passed out. The long line of mothers and children stretched from the hall to the outside of the church. As we drew nearer our turn, I could see the piles of the brown scutter-coloured uniforms piled on the plank tables like piles of shite. The ladies of the Vincent de Paul stood behind the tables passing out the clothing.

The ladies of the Saint Vinnies were attired in flounced, well-made dresses with cardigans tossed casually over their delicate shoulders. Their cheerful clothes contrasted sharply with the shabby apparel our mammies wore. While we waited to enter the room, the parish priest strolled up and down the long line asking if all the vouchers were in order to hand to the ladies. Kids complained about having to wait in line for so long to get the doled-out spoils. Mammies knew that kids who complained out loud or seemed to lack the right gratitude for the uniforms ended up getting nothing so they cautioned their offspring with remarks like, 'Take that look off yer face or ye'll get nothing. The ladies and the priest expect yez to be all smiles for gettin' somethin' for nothin'—so buck-up or we'll get nothin'.'

The ladies beckoned Ma and me to come forward with a wave of their hands. They checked and rechecked the voucher to make sure it had been properly signed by the nun and the parish priest before things went further. I sucked in the gut as one of the ladies placed a uniform in my arms that would have fitted a cow. The one beside her handed me the pair of navy blue knickers that both Ma and I could fit into and have room left over.

As the ladies passed out the uniforms to our mothers, they issued a lecture—a catechism on how our mothers were supposed to take care of the uniforms:

'As soon as your child comes home from school the first thing you need to tell them is to change out of their uniform and into their play clothes. You are to tell your children to hang up the uniforms to prevent any creases. And mothers, remember you must never use too much soap when you launder the uniform. When you launder the uniforms be sure to wash them in cold, soapy water. Rinse them out under cold running water for a good ten minutes to get the soap out. Then rinse them out again for another five minutes under more cold running water. Squeeze the uniforms out gently with your hands making sure not to pull them out of shape. Place a large towel over the clothesline, and gently place the uniforms over the towel, and let the water drip from the garment naturally. Iron the clothes while damp with a hot hand-iron. Make sure that the iron you are using is not too hot. Test the temperature of the iron with your finger. If the flesh sizzles, that means the iron is too hot. Let the iron cool off, then carefully iron inside out.'

Ma helped me carry the uniform home. She teased me over the pair of navy blue knickers, saying the knickers would fit 'Lucy Moore', in an effort to change the mood of her grumpy daughter. Our mammies, smart as they were, bundled up the uniforms and headed off for the pawnshops to pawn the ugly habits for ready cash. Brereton's pawnshop in Mount Street or Rafter's pawnshop on the way to Ringsend gobbled up the uniforms which they resold back to the church. So none of the uniforms appeared on the backs of kids in George Reynolds'. Their parents, in spite of their wants, had too much pride to allow their children to wear the garments of stated and avowed deprivation.

Once in a great while the Vincent de Paul gave out vouchers for free children's shoes. Again the voucher had to be signed by a schoolmaster or a nun or a priest before they were issued. The voucher could only be used in certain shoe shops around Dublin city, that were approved by members of the Saint Vincent de Paul.

The shop owners were only allowed to exchange the voucher for 'sensible shoes' with thick soles and heels, that laced up the front. A person like myself who wanted the red leather double-cross-strap sandals with light soles and heels instead of regulation clodhoppers, had to make do with whatever she got or else the voucher went back to the church. The Shirley Temple pumps that would tap-tap-tap on the footpath or the pair of silver buckled black patent leather horn-pipe-shoes, displayed in the window, were both out of the question. The heavy dark brown clodhoppers felt like a ton weight on my feet. Ma said the clodhoppers made my legs look like two matchsticks.

Ma got wind that a Jewman who had a shop in Mary Street in the heart of Dublin city had money to lend. Ma and Da decided that they would ask the man for a loan and used the money for my confirmation outfit. They had both felt bad about not being able to dress me for my first holy communion.

Da acted astonished when Ma got back from Mary Street with two five pound notes in her pocket. She had promised to pay the loan back out of Da's army pension. Da said the man who loaned out the money, without any guarantee of getting it paid back, had either a heart the size of an elephant or brains as big as a pea. We all knew that no Irish bank would loan a penny to people like us, let alone two fivers.

I picked out a red coat with a black velvet collar and a matching Dutch hat to wear for my confirmation. I also picked out a pink dress and a pair of black patent leather horn-pipe shoes with silver buckles, a round black shoulder bag, pink ankle socks and frosty white underwear. With the money left over, Ma bought me a sterling silver confirmation medal with a chalice on the front of the medal and writing that said, 'In memory of your confirmation'. And she got me a small prayer book covered with mother-of-pearl, that bore on the front in gilt letters, the title, 'The Little Key of Heaven'.

Ma and Da turned me out for confirmation as if they had all the money in the world to spend. I knew that had it not been for the Jewman, I would have been confirmed in my washed-out frock instead of my lovely new outfit. I only got to wear most of my new clothes for a week after my confirmation. Ma had to take them to the pawn to get money to buy food and to go towards the rent.

A year passed before I saw the red coat and Dutch hat again, and by that time, neither fitted. I felt sad about having to give up the new clothes. I felt sadder when the confirmation medal had to be pawned. Ma paid off the interest to the pawnshop for over a year, but there was never enough money to redeem the confirmation medal with the chalice on the front and the writing on the back. I cried over the loss of the medal that was gone forever more.

Some time later the nun called me aside behind the blackboard to tell me that I must already know that heaven only held Catholics, and hell was filled with the heathens among whom were those Protestants who refused to accept the teaching of the holy father in Rome. I wondered why she went on so, and behind the blackboard too.

Finally, she got to the point, and said that a new girl was going to enroll in our class, a Protestant girl, who would need lots of help in learning her catechism before she could be converted to the Catholic Church. I was to teach the catechism to the Protestant girl because I had been selected by God, through her the nun, to help bring about Beatrice's conversion to the true faith. I was to spend two hours every morning for the remainder of the year teaching Beatrice her catechism. I soon realised that my tormentor demanded that I torment the soul of another, the soul of a Protestant girl.

The Protestant girl

Right off the bat, I could tell the Protestant girl didn't hail from around our part of Dublin city nor did she look like a national school girl. Anyone would have taken her for a toff's kid. She sat at a desk in the front of the class. She had on a new school uniform. She wore her blonde hair in plaits, the ends tied in green bows. The green tie around the collar of her long sleeved white blouse underneath the gymslip set off her very blue eyes.

She had a small turned-up nose and a mouth as red as blood. She gave the sour nun a smile, and the smile parted the blood red lips showing a set of small even teeth. The nun beckoned me to come and meet Beatrice. The girl stood up at the desk. She and I were about the same size, and she was also twelve years old. We gave each other gassy smiles, then the nun directed us both to the back of the classroom where I was to teach the Protestant her catechism for two hours, non-stop.

We sat down at the same desk, and she opened her catechism at page one. 'I'm supposed to go over all the catechism with ye. Do you want to read it yerself or do ye want me to read it with ye?' I asked her. She looked at me and said that she could read it herself. She began at the first page as I ate what was left of my fingernails until she stopped reading because of her eyes watering.

'I don't have my new glasses yet,' she said.

'I'm supposed to question you on what you have read in the catechism,' I told her, feeling put out that I could not participate in the sewing lesson that all the others were now involved with, and that I was stuck with her for two hours every morning, whether I liked it or not, for the rest of the school term.

After about two months had gone by, the nun gave me a list of questions to ask the girl. I told the girl that if I had my way I'd only ask easy questions because I hated hard questions. I read from the list:

Who made the world? Who is God? Who are the three divine persons of the blessed trinity? How many gods are there? How many divine persons are there in the blessed trinity? Is the father God? Is the son God? Is the holy ghost God? What is sin? How many kinds of sin are there? What does sin do to the soul? What is a mortal sin? What is a venial sin? What is confession? What are the seven sacraments of the Church? Say the ten commandments of God. Who is the pope? What is the role of the holy father on earth?

After I had quizzed her on the catechism for another two weeks, our minds began to drift above such fray.

'Why did ye come to Saint Mary's School, Beatrice?' I asked, getting away from the catechism.

Blink went her eyes. I continued, 'Where are ye from originally?'

Beatrice looked me straight in the eye and said, 'NO! I'm not from around here, and I did not want to come to this school. And I am a Protestant girl not a girl like you,' she spat. I hadn't suspected she had a temper.

'I'm from County Kilkenny. My stepmother lives in Dublin and that's why Daddy and my brothers and sisters and I are here, and I am in this place and learning this catechism. Daddy converted to get married and now my stepmother and Daddy want us all to become Catholics.' She blistered my ears with her revelations.

'What happened to yer real mammy?'

'She became ill and died two years ago. She and Daddy and the rest of my family belonged to the Church of Ireland, a Protestant church.'

Until now the only other person I knew who had a parent die was my best friend Dolores. Mammies are not supposed to die, I thought to myself.

'Can I ask ye another question? Are ye becoming a Catholic because of yer stepmother or what?'

She nodded her head, Yes! Then her eyes filled with tears that spilled onto the catechism, and I smudged the writing on the page as I blotted the dollops up.

'I want to stay the same religion as my own mother,' she said, 'but I can't.' Her revelations caused a cramp in my belly. By helping her learn the catechism, I also was making her do something that she did not want to do. We both pretended to go ahead with the lessons, but I knew they were over as far as I had a hand in it.

After a while, I asked Beatrice, 'Did ye ever hear of a place called Australia? I know every stick and stone about that place. I'll tell ye about a small Australian girl who got carried away by an eagle, if ye want me to.' I began to tell her Da's story about Hanna Banana, the story he told me long ago.

After Beatrice and I came back from Australia, I turned to her and said, 'Now it's yer turn to tell me a story, any one ye want, but don't begin with, "It's just a fairy tale." I don't want to hear stories that begin with, "It's just a fairy tale."'

'I know,' she said. 'Mammy read stories from *The Arabian Nights* nearly every evening in our old home,' she said.

'Well, g'wan then. Let's hear.'

Beatrice began with stories about Ali Baba and the forty thieves. Then she told stories about Sindbad the sailor and his voyages around the world.

'Don't skip nothin', Beatrice,' I implored her. And she didn't skip anything. She told stories of Ali Baba and of Sindbad so well that I thought I saw them both in the classroom and by the way she described the thickness and lushness of the magic carpets I could barely keep my shoes on.

Baghdad, Ali Baba, the forty thieves, the Arab merchants, tall jars of hot olive-oil, Morgiana, the cave, and the secret words, 'Open, Sesame', were all there in front of our eyes at Beatrice's telling. I could tell the Arabian tales matched Irish stories nut and bolt, then I told her what Peggy Noonan told Ma and me as we drank a cup of tea by her fireside in her flat in George Reynolds' House.

Peggy Noonan worked as a cleaning woman for some toffs in Ballsbridge. Peggy said the woman of the house told her the family was going off on a holiday. The woman told Peggy to scrub down the 'geezer' with cleanser and water every day, while the family was away. Well, Peggy had only heard the word 'geezer' used as a name for a tomcat. After the toffs took off, every day at the end of a day's cleaning Peggy did as the old one had told her: scrub down the geezer with cleanser and water.

By the end of the week, Peggy told us, pointing to her hands and arms, there were scratches all over her from washing the geezer. The family cat, declared Peggy, protested like a demon at being doused with water and scrubbed all over with cleanser. Peggy couldn't put up with the cat so she stopped going to work until the toffs came home.

When the toffs returned, Peggy went back for her wages that were due. The woman of the house asked Peggy what had happened to Mousie, her tabbycat. She wanted to know what caused Mousie's longhaired fur to go mangey and lacklustre. She asked Peggy if the tabbycat had got out unbeknownst to shuffle with allycats who might have the mange? Peggy told the woman that she had kept a close eye on Mousie and scrubbed the geezer down with the water and cleanser like she'd been told to after finishing her other chores. And that the cat hated the scrubbing. Peggy showed the woman all the scratches and clawmarks the cat inflicted when she tried to scrub it down. Instead of receiving sympathy, Peggy got told to leave the premise and never to return or the police would be called.

On hearing the true yarn, Beatrice bubbled to the brim.

Beatrice's telling of the Persian tales, Da's yarns, and Peggy's true story lifted our spirits more than all the stories combined in the catechism: the yarns about heaven, hell, limbo, purgatory and the pope in Rome became dull as dust. I slapped the catechism shut, and said to Beatrice, 'Stay a Protestant girl. Shag the nun, shag the pope, shag heaven, shag hell, and shag all the dull and dusty. Stay a Protestant girl.'

The following morning I told our nun that my mother had complained that I should be learning how to sew latch stitches like the other girls in my class instead of trying to twist the head of a Protestant girl.

I had made up Ma's story. The irritated nun told me to get out my sewing box. I gave Beatrice the eye knowing she hadn't a trace of green in her. Maureen Duffy took over teaching Beatrice her religious instruction. Maureen's face turned purple at being selected to stuff the Protestant girl with supposedly the stuff of life until the end of the school year. I was glad to be back to my knitting.

I knew when school reopened that winter that I'd had it. I had the same nun for another year, and I hated her. If nuns and priests were representatives of God, it didn't show much, except in the demeanour of the aged Sister Mary Thomasina. Sister Mary Thomasina washes back in memory on wave after wave of boiled milk.

Unlike the others at school, she liked all the impoverished kids who attended school at Saint Mary's. She never called us 'a bunch of ignoramuses'. She didn't see us as being deserving of ill treatment because we were the children of the poor. She did not make the kids feel they were a disgrace or shameful because they lived in adverse circumstances.

One day Sister Thomasina came into the classroom to fetch me and take me with her. She told me to wait on the staircase until she returned, carrying a small milkcan in her hand. She lifted the lid off the milkcan letting steam rise in the air. She poured some of the hot milk from the can into a tin cup and told me to drink it. I tasted the skim coated boiled milk and nearly gagged.

'Drink every sup of it,' ordered Sister Thomasina. 'Every sup! I heard you coughing in the play yard and didn't like the sound of it. Drink every sup!'

She informed me that for the rest of the winter months, I'd be fed the boiled milk for extra nourishment. While I drank down the boiled milk thick with skim from the boiling, the nun complained that our school and other national schools should be providing poor children with sandwiches and milk, in order to offer them nourishment. 'The Protestant schools do it,' she noted with the nod of her aged head. Sister Thomasina kept her promise about the boiled milk to drink. Consequently, my nose picked up on the smell of boiled milk a mile off. The old sister's sincere kindness wedged into my heart.

I had completed five years of national school education by the end of the winter. I could see no point in going any more. Who would pay for my schoolbooks, the uniform, give me money for the missions, money for elocution lessons, or money for anything else? I'd been made to grovel enough. Most of the kids I knew left school before they were fourteen. We were all supposed to attend until the mandatory age of fourteen, but exiting school at thirteen took place all the time.

The government couldn't care less and the Catholic Church which really ran the schools was only concerned that we didn't exit before being confirmed, then to hell with us. Ma and Da cared but they understood how national school children were put to shame. So I left school at the age of thirteen.

The cockle cook

Some of the women in the flats got an idea to have a neighbourhood 'cockle cook'. On the day of the shellfish party, a handful of women and a swarm of kids set off for Sandymount Strand carrying gunnysacks, knives, forks, spoons and buckets.

Upon arriving at the strand, the small army waited for the tide to go out. The outgoing tide gurgled its sweet time in laying bare the mudflats. Mothers and kids took their shoes off, tied the laces of two shoes together and slung them over the neck. Mrs Cashel, shading her eyes from the bright sun, looked in the direction of the Pigeon House and told stories of how it had once been the site of a TB hospital, adding that 'anywan who got sent t' the Pigeon flew out in a coffin'.

As we walked and spread out over the mudflats looking for cockles, Ma reminded us that only the cockles still buried under the mud could be eaten. Ma knew how to spot the whereabouts of cockles. Her da, Joseph O'Connor, had taken her as a child to the strand to cockle and Joseph O'Connor, Ma said proudly, never left the strand without his bucket full of shellfish.

Ma stopped in her tracks, knelt down on the mudflat and pointed out all the tiny mounds circled with darker sand.

'That's where the cockles are, see the gurgling? Dig into the hole with yer spoon or knife or fork or bit a stick and ye'll root up the cockle,' instructed Ma.

Everyone fell to their knees and found the tiny mounds dusted around with the darker sand and began to dig the cockles up by the dozens. The beautiful white-ridged double-shelled cockles were dropped in the cans and buckets and into the gunnysacks. One of the mothers suggested that I fill my bucket with the dark green seaweed that would go into the pot with the cockles.

After about two hours of collecting, the gunnysack sagged from the weight of the cockles, sand, and seawater. It became too heavy to carry. Jinny said we should all take an edge of the gunnysack and carry it home the way pirates carried a treasure chest. Big hands, medium sized hands, and small hands gripped the sack for the journey home to George Reynolds'. In order to cut the road short, one of the kids broke into a song and everyone joined in. The made-up song borrowed the melody from 'In the Shade of the Old Apple Tree'.

In the shade of the old apple tree
Where Mary got stung by a bee
She was milking a cow and she didn't know how
And she started by tickling its knee.
The cow lift his foot off the grass
Gave Mary a kick in the arse.
Poor Mary she fell and the cow ran like hell
To the shade of the old apple tree.

The women who couldn't go to with us to collect the cockles volunteered to cook them for us. After getting back to the flats, the cockles were scooped into the pots by the handfuls, with a fistful of seaweed going in each pot for good measure. The seaweed would act as a cushion to prevent the cockles from breaking as they tumbled in the pots of boiling water. The cockle cook got underway in earnest after all the daddies and older brothers were served their tea and the daddies had headed for a gargle at Dwyer's pub. Daddies and older brothers weren't interested in a cockle cook. They scoffed it off like dogshit off their shoes.

All the mammies and kids in the flats gathered on the stairway and the balcony to await the word that the cockles were cooked. After they were cooked in several different flats the women brought out the pots brimmed to the top with cooked cockles. Ma and the other women roared out on cue, 'Boiled cockles, boiled cockles! Come and get them, as quick as ye can. Who wants boiled cockles to eat?'

The still hot pots of cockles were placed on the stairs, and while the cockles cooled, mammies scurried in and out of their flats with half-emptied bottles of vinegar, plates of sliced bread, pots of tea, glasses of orangeade, and the odd bottle of porter. The pungent smell of the sea rushed over everyone when the mammies lifted the lids off the cooking pots to show off the wide-open cockles nestled in green seaweed. The smell of the cooked shellfish lured mammies and kids from all the blocks of flats to our block. Ma called out, as big hands, medium hands, small hands reached into the pots, 'Dip-in-the-dip and leave the herrin' for yer da.'

Ma made cockle sandwiches, and passed them around. She got a thick slice of bread and loaded it down with a handful of cockles, a bit of the seaweed over the cockles, then a squirt of vinegar, and a toss of salt. She smacked down another slice of bread over the lot and passed it around.

'Thank ye very much,' said hungry belly. Digging the teeth through the chewy cockle sandwich, seaweed and all, let loose the flavours of life. The cockle cook lasted until late evening, and men on their way back from being with their cronies walked past the women and children, and tippy-toed around the pots and buckets full of empty seashells perched on the stairs, as if the end of the earth were in sight.

Da eventually made his way up the stairs as the night wore on, three sheets to the wind as usual. He tipped his hat to the women and kids, and asked if we were all enjoying ourselves, stopping long enough to say, 'Aren't little occasions just as grand as big occasions?'

After every single cockle had been eaten and everything else in sight, it was time for a few stories and songs. When we went back to our flat after the cockle cook, Da looked up from the newspaper and said, 'Don't the two girls I love most in the world look and smell grand after shovelling fistfuls of cockles into their gobs?'

The statue factory

Da tramped the city looking for work til he was worn out. The jobs that became available in places like the bottlehouse or the ironworks hired the more rugged looking men. Da hadn't a rough and tumble side to him. Sometimes it seemed as if a strong gust of wind would blow him away. And even though he had lived in Dublin city now for years, it still seemed as if he had just blown in from the country.

If it had been left up to him, he'd have kept his eyes glued to a book and out of sight of the world. He hated going to the unemployment office, and having to be on the dole caused him to throw his hands up in the air. With so much unemployment all over the city, Da and the other out of work men in George Reynolds' were disheartened, in spite of now living in better accommodation in which to raise their families. Then a new factory opened up across the street from the flats in what had once been a horse stable. The new factory, owned by an Englishman, made religious plaster statues. The owner of the factory only hired workers between the ages of fourteen and forty, which left workers like Da out, but the younger workers were paid twenty shillings a week for a six day week.

The 'statue factory' as it became known, made plaster statues of all the Catholic saints and angels, of the virgin and of Christ. Some of the statues were sold in religious shops, and others were made as special orders for churches around the city. At noontime the young workers emerged from the factory plastered in white dust, and could have been mistaken for statues themselves. The fine white dust lodged in every crevice of their faces, including their eyelashes and eyebrows. When the workers sneezed, they sneezed out particles of white dust.

They laughed at the sight of each other sneezing and coughing chalk dust. The young girls and lads, on warm days, ate their lunches outside. They perched on the stone wall that squared off the factory. On Fridays (payday) they were to be seen sitting on the wall digging into their fish and chips that were wrapped in newspaper.

The fish and chips were the treat of the week for the factory workers, and the smell of them must have carried on the wind, because swarms of seagulls swooped in from the strand and alighted on the stone wall near the workers enjoying their Friday feed. The gulls skipped up and down the wall, from one foot to the other, patiently waiting for someone to drop a piece of fish or a chip on the ground, but they waited in vain.

When the factory whistle blew, the girls and lads scrunched their newspaper wrappings into balls and pitched the vinegar and grease soaked newspages into the barrel on the corner. The factory workers left chalk imprints of their behinds on the wall, and created a pattern of footprints on the pavement that led to the factory gate.

As soon as the workers departed, the gulls all flew to the barrel where they picked and pecked at each other for the chance to sniff the newsprint.

The owner of the statue factory parked his motor car in front of the factory gates. He got some of the girls to come out and wash down his car every afternoon, but by afternoon, white dust had settled on the black motor car again like sifted flour.

While husbands, fathers and brothers searched for work, the women in George Reynolds' chipped in to help each other over the rough times, as the women in O'Brien's Place had earlier done: borrowing or lending a shilling here and there, sharing food, loaning each other things to pawn, passing on outgrown clothes, and making an effort at cheer. As far as the bigwigs were concerned, we were still considered undeserving of assistance because we supposedly had bad habits that had brought ruin on ourselves. Our men had a penchant for the gargle, and were incapable of finding work, and our mammies were not hardworking enough, even though they kept house on half a shoestring.

Down in the dumps

Children like me, boys and girls who lived in George Reynolds', worked as errand runners for stores, became newsboys, sold bundles of kindling door to door, while others, myself included, joined the groups of scavengers working the Irishtown dump site.

The Irishtown dump banked up against one end of Sandymount Strand. The landfill served as a repository for the city of Dublin's refuse. The site would be my home away from home for a year, or until I turned fourteen, old enough to get a job as a factory girl. The dumpsite had walking trails crisscrossing it, just like trails on a mountain side. The trails on the dump were tramped by the feet of those who roamed over the site looking for a bite to eat or something to sell for money. Kids like myself roamed over the wasteland to scavenge for a living.

At eight o'clock each morning, rain or shine, I met with other kids from our buildings to walk over to the dumpsite. The boys never wanted to walk with the girls, they huddled by foursome as they shuffled off for the wasteland. Lulu, Patricia, Bernadette, Josie, Maisie, Phyllis, Bridie, Kathleen, Peggy, Ann, Patty and Mary were the girls I walked with. From the eyes of onlookers, few could distinguish the girls from the boys as we walked from Irishtown Road to the edge of Sandymont Strand. The early risers on Strand Road, making their way to morning mass, pinched their noses as we passed. Obviously, the sight of walking bundles of smelly rags affronted their senses.

When we got to the dump, boys and girls split off in separate directions as if by some unwritten rule. Any girl who made an attempt to salvage in the boy's area, got told to 'shag off'. We knew the boys passed the time telling each other dirty stories, sang dirty ditties, smoked cigarettes, and swore their heads off.

Girls wore their brothers' cast off long trousers or their das' old rags under their coats to keep warm, and also for modesty's sake. We had to cover our heads with a kerchief of some kind to keep the wind whipped up from the strand from flinging our hair in our faces as we rooted through the rubble. We all wore plastic goggles to cover our eyes from the constant blowing dirt and debris. We wound strips of rag around our wornout shoes to hold them in place, and also for added warmth. And we tiptoed gingerly over the zillion pieces of broken glass scattered everywhere.

In order to root out each morsel of coke from the loads of garbage of every description, we had to sit down on the fermenting filth. Each of us used a small stick to poke through the rot to uncover the cinders. In the process, we rooted through reams of old newsprint, broken beer bottles, broken dishes, odd old shoes, rotten produce, dead rats, dead cats, dead dogs, turds of calcified dog and human shite, hospital and factory waste, and every other imaginable stuff.

We also encountered the odd large dead animal illegally dumped on the site; nobody liked to see a large unburied animal, although a dumped donkey or horse sprawled sideways on the landfill, legs pushed up in the air, stiff as pokers, proved an eye catcher. We were drawn to these carcases like a swarm of insects, and were anxious to observe a large beast up close. One of the boys would find a long stick to poke into some part of a carcase, causing girls to scream out in protest, and the more we screamed, the more the boy poked. Yapper Lynch liked to poke a stick into a dead donkey's mouth. He used the stick to lift up one side of the donkey's mouth so it gave us a cockeyed grin, a grin that reminded me of the slanted smile Clark Gable gave Scarlett O'Hara in *Gone With the Wind*. Yapper continued to fiddle with the donkey's mouth telling it to give us a bigger, wider smile.

We marvelled at the size of a donkey's teeth stacked like two layers of ladyfinger biscuits one upon another. From the discolouration of the donkey's teeth, it could have been a heavy cigarette user all its life, or old age had browned the choppers.

We squealed wildly as Yapper took the stick out of the animal's mouth to poke into one of its eardrums to test if the animal were really, truly dead. 'If it feels the stick poking its brain and doesn't twitch, it's dead,' he declared. Everyone glued their eyes on the animal's body as Yapper poked deeper and deeper inside the eardrum. We watched for any slight movement, feeling relieved the donkey remained as stiff and still as Nelson's Pillar.

'It's dead, Yapper. It's double dead. Dead as me granny,' affirmed Tommy. The girls' response came in one word, 'Yuk.'

The dead donkey's eyes remained wide open and unflinching. The eyes were rimmed with stiff spiked eyelashes similar to the stiff hairs of a scrubbing brush. The animal eyes held a faraway look similar to the faraway gaze of a crucified Christ looking down from the cross above an altar. Unlike the eyes of a statue, swarms of long legged bluebottle flies daintily scurried round the rims of the donkey's eyes.

Cries of anger and disgust arose from the men who unloaded their cargo on seeing an unburied horse or donkey. With a sense of disgust at the sight they ranted, 'Lazy bastards, could have covered it up, had they respect for anything.' The men backed up their trucks and dumped the contents over the animals in an effort to cover them but it took several loads of rubbish to bury a large animal. The animal's stiff legs remained visible until flesh withered off and someone, bothered by the lingering sight, hacked the bones off and flung them helterskelter into the sea.

While I rooted among the garbage, I entertained myself by recalling a story Ma told me about Jesus and an ass. According to her, before Jesus went into Jerusalem, he halted by the wayside and told his disciples, 'Go into the village and you will find an ass and bring it back to me.' The disciples went to the village and found the ass just like Jesus said. They took the donkey back to him, and he jumped on its back and rode it into Jerusalem. Everyone in the place come out to shout at Jesus saying, 'Blessed is he that comes in the name of the Lord.' 'And because of that story,' Ma iterated, 'people to this day in Ireland believe the ass bears a sign upon its back in the likeness of a dark cross, in memory of Christ's crucifixion.' Lucky Ma imprinted the roadmap into my mind or else I'd have thought the markings on the ass were caused from its harness. I favoured Ma's explanation.

The stench from rooting through all the rot often caused me to gag, especially when I disturbed masses of white maggots with my stick.

Each titbit of the volcanic-like fuel needed to be hand-picked. I put each morsel of coke into an empty paint can I kept by my side. After filling the can, I emptied the contents into my gunnysack. It took thirty-eight paint cans full of cinders to fill a gunnysack; it took the livelong day; it took my heart; it took my mind; it took my spirit; it took love for my family to fill every gunny with cinders. By the end of the day, my fingertips and the fingertips of the other children were seared red from picking up the hundreds of pieces of coarse coke.

While I rooted through the dirt, I called out loud to the other girls scattered about. We called back and forth to each other for reassurance. We joined voices in singing out loud. We made as much noise as we could in hopes of keeping the dog-sized rats who roamed the landfill at bay. Hunched rats, unseen by us, sprang out to bite the fingers of boys and girls when they reached down to retrieve the pieces of coke. I silently asked God, as I reached out my hand to pick up the pieces of coke, not to let a rat bite my fingers. The thought of a huge rat latching my fingers with fanged teeth seemed unbearable. I asked God not to let it happen because even the thought caused the inside of my head to roar like thunder. Sometimes, as I reached down to pick up a lump of coke, I felt a warm hand covering mine.

Rats were not the only things that pounded a girl's head and heart on the Irishtown dump site. Feral men from across the city also scavenged on the dump. They collected empty bottles, bits of scrap metal, bald rubber tires, old rags, coke, and anything else they could sell for cash. They were ferocious men whose sole survival depended on what they could salvage from the discards. They demanded first choice of going through each and every newly arrived lorry load of trash. Any kid, girl or boy, who made the mistake of getting in the way of the scavengers was threatened with getting their 'bleeding fucking heads cleaved off' with a pitchfork.

The men used long three-pronged pitchforks to root through the rubble. They had no reservations about using the pitchforks as weapons to fend off any intruders who broached their self-proclaimed territory. Desperation marked their faces and their eyes glinted with hatred towards others like themselves, who were also trying to live. These were the lords of the wasteland, the head buck cats of the rat-infested landscape. Children quivered in their wake.

Some of the children uncovered other finds besides cinders. Bingo-Bongo, one of the boys from our buildings, uncovered the greatest treasure ever uprooted on the Irishtown dump.

While I was rooting for coke to fill my gunny, there was a scream that could have been heard in New York. We knew the roar came from Bingo-Bongo, and that he must have dug up something fierce. His roar reached all our ears. We stopped rummaging and made our way over the filth to where Bingo-Bongo stood waving his arms like a windmill. Before I got to where he stood whirling his arms in the wind, a bunch of kids and some lorry drivers had formed a circle around him. They were directing their eyes to a bundle on the dirt that Bingo had dug up. Bingo, stomping from one foot to another, blubbered 'I want me mammy and daddy. I want me mammy and daddy.' A tricoloured snot hung from Bingo's nose which he sniffed up and down like a flag, in his fit of agitation. I thought he must have dug up a stash of weapons hidden in the dump by the IRA, knowing the IRA were viewed by some in the flats as great men of Ireland. Bingo must have fumbled into finding rifles or hand grenades. What else could cause such a commotion? We'd seen everything from a dead mouse to a dead horse, from potato skins to swirls of shite.

I lowered my eyes to look at what lay at Bingo's boot-top. He'd uprooted a brown paper parcel under some rot, opened it up with a penknife, tore apart the layers of wrapping, and inside the layers lay a dead baby.

The ashen baby looked and smelled like a dried spray of flowers that one might uncover between the pages of an old book. A handknitted dusty white bonnet remained the only stitch of clothing intact on the infant. One of the baby's big toes hung down from its foot on a sliver of cartilage like a loose front tooth. Its bonnet, I could tell, being a bit of a knitter myself, had been knitted in the smallest and evenest of stitches (like baby teeth) on extra fine knitting needles that only someone with the patience of a saint could endure to use.

It seemed likely the baby had been loved, judging from its painstakingly knitted cap, and the way someone had gone to all the trouble of wrapping it up. First, in a striped tea-towel, then in layers of newsprint then layers and layers of sturdy brown paper (the kind used by pawnshops). Then the whole caboodle had been carefully crisscrossed with strong cord and tied all together with a trillion tight knots.

One of the adults called for a policeman and a priest to come over to the dump. The copper took down particulars from Bingo-Bongo and any other kid who felt a need to jump in. The priest, after taking a peep at the dead baby, looked crestfallen, turned to the rest of us and said, 'How un-Christian it is for another human being to throw away a precious human life on the dump.' The priest's eyes misted as he lectured, then he began to fiddle with the strap of his wristwatch, and soon took off in his motor car. The priest's eyes must have been so blurred from sorrow at the sight of the dead infant that he failed to see the plight of us children standing there in a state of hunger, mired in filth, and cloaked in shame.

I wished it had been me that had found the ashen baby. I would have kept it a secret and taken it home to Ma who would have cooed over it, cradled it, and hummed it a hundred lullabies, before seeking assistance to bury it. I would have put the mummified baby under a pane of glass, framed it, and decorated the frame with painted-on white roses and blue forget-me-nots. I would have made a glass coffin for the baby as sweet as the one made by the seven dwarfs in the film, *Snow White*.

Back in George Reynolds', where neighbours were told about Bingo-Bongo's find, some of the women said, 'Ah, its poor mother. Maybe, she's just a girl? Maybe, she came up from some part of the country to have it, unknown?' They knew if the authorities persisted in tracking down the mother of the dead child, the clergy, not the coppers, would be the throatcutters. My mother told me that a police officer had taken the baby to the morgue, and judging from the tone of things, uncovering a dead baby on the dump would remain a hush hush affair in the name of charity.

Thus the most precious thing ever found on the Irishtown dump got a second burial. The second best thing uprooted on the Irishtown dump, got dug up by Brian, who lived with his family in one of the flats on our balcony in George Reynolds'. His find is gabbed about yet.

Brian dug up a metal box full of old jewellery and medals. He brought the box home to his mother who told all within earshot, 'The box contained the ugliest auld jewelry I ever clapped an eye on, and even Woolworths wouldn't be bothered with it.' She gave a pair of earrings from the find to Rosie, her aunt who lived in Ringsend, handed over the shiny bracelets to her baby to play with in the pram, and tossed the rest of the junk into a kitchen drawer. Somehow, word got out about Brian's find and it wasn't long before a copper from Irishtown police station strode over to the flats seeking information on the lad who had dug up a box of jewellery on the dumps.

The guard told Brian's mother that the jewellery had been thrown out in error by a housemaid who worked in one of the big houses on Sandymount Green. The owner insisted on having it back. The copper informed Mrs C that the jewellery and coins in the box were antique.

'What does that mean?' asked Mrs C, her lovely face tinting pink.

'What your son found on the sanitary landfill is valuable and worth a lot of money.'

'Ye mean to say this auld stuff that Brian brought home from the dump—the medals and bracelets and necklaces—are worth somethin'? Worth money? The baby has the bracelets in the pram,' Jinny told the copper as honest as you please.

'Be a good woman now and round all the jewellery up and put it back in the box,' said the copper, in his rural Kerry baritone.

Mrs C rummaged through the kitchen drawer looking for the coins and medals she had dumped there. She stepped to the baby's pram and took the shiny beads and bracelets from the babe, and put everything into the box the copper held open.

'That's the whole lot then?' asked the garda.

He held up each piece in the air for us all to see, and described each item as he lowered it into the box: a string of rare amber beads, silver and gold bracelets, ruby earrings and rare gold sovereigns.

'I thought them sovereigns ye're holding were funny looking holy medals,' exclaimed Mrs C, looking downcast.

'Is everything accounted for now? Everything returned?' demanded the brute.

'All, but a pair of dangle earrings, like Rita Hayward wore in *Song of the Gypsy,* that I gave to me Aunt Rosie.'

'Get someone to go and fetch the earrings back,' ordered the wellfed lawman.

Mrs C sent one of her seven children to Ringsend to find her Aunt Rosie. Everyone waited with the guard until Billy and Rosie showed-up. Aunt Rosie, a woman in her sixties, could hardly talk when she got to our balcony after huffing and puffing all the way from Ringsend to the flats. Mrs C met her half way down the balcony, and told her all about the goings on with the copper and the 'auld jewelry'.

The ashen-faced Rosie stood like a statue in front of the policeman. She sniffed him up and down, then began to fiddle with the earrings in her ears.

'I don't think they're going to come off. Me ears has grown around the holes since I put them in,' said Rosie. The copper stepped up to her and began to reach for the earring in her ears. 'Don't ye dare pull off me earrings with yer big maulers,' huffed Rosie. Rosie asked the Kerryman, 'What about finder's keepers?' But he overlooked her question.

'Yeah! What about finders keepers?' everyone asked in a chorus. Rosie jerked the earrings off and flung them into the big outreached hand, vexed as a doused cat.

Everyone raged at the cop for taking the treasure from a poor family and returning it to some greedygoat who had everything.

Later, Brian got word to go over to the police station for a reward. He received a pound note for giving over the treasure. We made a pact there and then among ourselves that we would keep mum about anything valuable we uncovered on the dump, and to shite with the loser.

There were kids on the dumps who got narky with me because I wouldn't eat the leftovers thrown out by the city's three large bakeries, Johnson, Mooney, and O'Brien's, Kennedy's Bakery, and Boland's. Instead of giving the unsold bread and cakes to the poor to eat, all three bakeries had their unsold bakery items taken by lorry to the Irishtown dump. Hungry kids waited patiently for the bakery lorries to arrive at the dump and unload the goods.

I couldn't make myself eat the throwaway food, because for some reason the thought entered my mind that if I ate the dumped food meant for rats, that was that. I'd slink away when the kids saw the bakery lorries coming. The sight of them gorging on jam cakes, cream buns and bread made my mouth drip like a tap. After the feast, the kids broke into a made-up jingle:

Don't eat Kennedy's bread.
It sticks to yer belly like lead.
If yer mother don't wonder,
You'll fart like thunder.
Don't eat Kennedy's bread.

Singing songs and telling stories helped to pass the time away on the dump site, and looking at the hundreds of seagulls that flew in from the sea to feed on the site took the breath away. The seagulls, as thick as February snowflakes, hung trembling in the air before they curved their wings to hover down on the piles of rot. The birds seemed endlessly patient, feeding on whatever life provided, and seemingly remained pure as the driven snow.

Some boys who picked coke didn't have as much patience to fill up their sacks as the girls did. Such boys diddled by adding 'clinkers' in with the coke to fill their gunnysack, hoping the buyer of the fuel would not know the difference. For those who weren't well up on it, clinkers are a lookalike for coke, but did not burn. If the the truth be known, we all diddled on desperate days.

The hardest part of the whole ordeal of collecting cinders came at quitting time. Trying to figure out a way to carry the sack home, a distance of a mile, took mulling over. Small girls, like myself, asked bigger boys to load the heavy sack on their backs, crosswise, while they stooped down. After taking the heavy sack on my back, I would straighten up as best I could under the load, firmly grip the dog-ear ends of the gunny, and commence to babystep home. The homeward trek broke tears from my eyes.

Sometimes lorry drivers gave the kids and their sacks of coke a ride home in the back of their trucks. The men laughed at our get-up, and brushed off our vile smells. Sitting on our sacks in the back of the truck seemed like heaven. We whipped off our kerchiefs, shook out our hair, removed the goggles and wiped the grime from our faces. When we got to George Reynolds', the lorry drivers stopped their trucks at the kerb, jumped from the cab and came back to help us unload our sacks of coke. Some of the drivers would shout out in surprise, 'Jaysus! Ye're girls back here! I thought yez were boys. Jaysus, what kinds a girls would collect coke on that no-man's land?' After we got out of the lorry, we pulled our sacks of coke onto the pavement and waited for some other poor person to come along and buy it to burn in their fireplace. I sold my sack of cinders for a shilling.

When all is said and done, the little bit of money we earned selling our cinders put an extra loaf of bread and an extra pint of milk on the family table. We all prayed our daddies would find work, in the meanwhile we'd help feed the fold.

While I was at the dump, Ma washed and ironed my collection of hair ribbons and hung them on the back of the chair for my eyes to see. As soon as I walked in the door, my eyes searched for the coloured ribbons in desperation. The sight of my hair ribbons in colours of blue, pink, green, yellow and violet lifted my spirits and helped me to re-imagine myself as a 'child of God'.

Ma and Da didn't like the idea of me scavenging on the dump for cinders because of the stigma associated with such work. They told me to stay home, but I refused. Earning some money by selling the cinders made me feel useful and worthwhile.

My brother Frank still worked in a low paying job, Da still paced the streets, Bob earned a bit of money doing odd jobs. Mr Mullen who worked in Dublin Port and Docks, and lived in the flats, got

Bob a job on a coal boat that ferried back and forth from Dublin to Liverpool. Mr Mullen's generosity paved the way for Bob to go on and become an able-bodied seaman. Bob sang like a lark at the thought of going to sea full time, because he loved the ocean in all its elements.

I'd have jumped at the chance to go on a coal boat or a fishing trawler, but girls were not allowed to set foot on a boat because legend had it that it was unlucky for a female to set foot aboard a seafaring rig. Girls were not allowed to plough the stormy sea.

Showing respect to a father

After Bob took off on the coal-boat, Da became more hunkered down. We knew he missed Robbler, his favourite child. He said to me that boys, all boys, were more valuable to their families than girls. He thought that more than one daughter in a family was wasteful. I'd never heard him say such a hateful thing before to anyone. I knew other fathers in Ireland thought the same. He said that he expected me to marry someone who would load me down with a half a dozen snotty gets who would trail behind me in bare feet. That's what the future would have in store for me. His comments made my blood boil. I swore there and then that I'd show the bastard. The cheek of him telling me that I would be only fit to be at the beck and call of other men like himself!

Well, if I had my way, he'd be in for a surprise, the grumpy old billy goat who ran me off my feet doing his beck and call: 'Titch, go down and get me a newspaper, run over to Dwyer's and get me two bottles of porter, brew me a cup of tea, wash out my old shirt, sing me a song, recite me a poem, keep me company, put more coke on the fire, fry me a fluffy egg.'

On top of that, I had to listen with sympathy to all of his sad stories about his mother. Any happy stories he had to tell about his youth he saved for my brothers. Da talked about his youth with forcefulness and yearning that could wring out the heart. I loved to hear the stories he told about going fishing growing up in County

Monaghan. Da's youth hadn't been sordid. He hadn't grown up in slums, or remained half-starved all his young life. The old fella could yap about going trout-fishing like a pro.

He pointed out that he knew the trout-fishing waters of Ulster like the back of his hand. And he told how he and some of his pals tried their hands at dry-fly fishing. He'd fished in and around Lough Erne, Da recalled, where the inlets and streams that ran into the lough were stiff with brown trout, silver pike, eight pound salmon and shoals of dollagham.

I interrupted Da, and told him that I had never heard of a dollagham fish. I asked him if he had made it up. Annoyed at the interruption, he told my brothers not to pay attention to a girl who had never set either a wet or a dry fly in all her life.

'What did ye use on yer hook?' asked one of my brothers. 'I made most of my own dry-fly flies. Let me scratch my head a minute, to recall some of the names we gave to our dry-fly flies. While I'm scratching my head, Titch! make us all a nice cup of tea.'

'Let me see now, boys—some of the flies were named Daddy Longlegs, Hare's Ear, Brown Wagtail, Peter Ross and Grenwell's Glory.'

'Here's the tea,' I interrupted.

'Whisht Titch! Every time you talk, when ye're not supposed to, you steal my memory. Och! I nearly left out of the picture other flies, like Wickam's Fancy, Blue Witch and Olive Witch. But the best fly of all was the Goat! The Goat was a curious looking production. I'd make it from goat's hair that I tied and dyed. Everyone living in Castleblayney at the time, including your grandmother Kearns, had a goat in the backyard.'

'I wish we could live in the country,' we all said. And listening to Da tell all about the ins and outs of fly-fishing in Ulster waters, living in the country seemed a lovely thing to me. I wondered how he'd been able to go from his old life to his life now.

At every chance, Da drank himself into a stupor. He sat by the fireplace until late in the night or until he had wrung every drop of liquor out of the bottles. After draining the contents, he'd lift the bottle and say, 'Another dead soldier.' He scattered all the empty bottles about his feet like shell-casings.

While drunk, Da would talk about his old home in Castleblayney. It still hurt him to the quick that his mother never made any effort to see him. And he believed that the reason his two sisters never looked him up had to do with his mother's order.

It appeared that Granny Kearns possessed a steel heart and because of Da's distress over her, I steeled my heart against her. My brothers and Ma gave up on the old fella as he sat night after night drunk at the kitchen table demanding that someone keep him company. God knows why I cared about the drunken scut who badgered us to death with all his drinking and his constant demands. He'd sit on the chair in front of the table surrounded by liquor. As the evening wore on, he dropped his head down on top of the table and let the rest of his body slide under the table. Only the head remained in view. The orb lay on the table and continued to talk and talk. I'd look and listen to the talking head as it jabbered on about no one caring if it had a bit of grub in its belly or how it needed a cup of tea or how it would appreciate a few fried sausages and a few fried rashers put in between a few slices of bread with a bit of mustard slathered over the lot.

The head now turning to the right and to the left on the table wanted to know if a daughter still had a sense of duty in these days in Ireland to show respect to a father who only wanted to love and look after her and never expected even a drop of drinking water from the girl. The bleary eyed head stilled its rolling to wait for an answer.

'Ye don't think me such a fool as to believe all of that nonsense ye just spluttered out? Sit up in that bleeding chair or I won't say another word to ye.'

The head remained still on the table and took in the tone of the voice, then slowly lifted itself off the table to join the neck and shoulders, then the rest of the body reconnected.

'Light this Woodbine for me would you, Duck?'

'What do ye think I am—yer servant? By God, I'm not yer bloody servant. Ye may think Ma's a servant but don't think ye can carry that over with me.'

'Whisht that noise. Ye're giving your father a headache. Do you want to wake up your poor mammy?'

Poor mammy, me arse. If the auld shite cared about Ma would he be dead drunk every chance he got? Then with an air of baffled innocence, the drunkard would say, 'Titch! I'm beyond the beyond.'

But I knew that. I worried about the old bollox setting fire to himself or setting fire to the flat, as he nearly did on several occasions.

Even at midnight, he expected me to sit with him and listen to him sing and recite until the dawn. He kept a sixpence in his pocket to pay me to recite poetry and sing the songs he liked. It always went, 'Sing me songs of old Ireland and the tanner is yours. Ah, sure, I know I'm a disgrace. Don't look at me like that.'

'I'll look at ye any way I want to. Ye're a disgrace for a father,' I added for measure.

Still insisting that he had a right to my attention he said, 'Sing me "Down By the Glenside" or "Last Night She Came To Me".'

'No, I won't sing "Down By The Glenside". I hate "Down By the Glenside". Do ye remember when ye insisted that I sing that song in the amateur hour competition at the Queen's Theatre? Who in hell's blazes cares for songs the like of the songs ye like to have sung?'

'You may not care for the great songs of Ireland, my girl, but ye can be doubly sure, I'm not giving you a sixpence for singing clattering songs from America—old rubbish that has no meaning to it.'

Dickering with the shagger for a lousy tanner seemed hardly worth it. I told him that he could sermonise away about the rubbish in modern songs but modern songs about real people made more sense than the old rubbish he wanted sung. I also told him to stick the tanner where the monkey stuck its nuts.

Sheepishly, he said, 'and now where is that?'

'UP ITS ARSE!' I'd shout.

He continued to dicker. 'This sixpence is getting hot in my hand waiting for you to open your mouth and sing a song of Ireland or recite a poem about your native land.' I could clash like a warhorse with the old fella and it did not do a bit of good. And finally, I wanted the sixpence. So I sang.

Last night she came to me, she came softly in,
And so softly she came that her feet made no din.
And she placed her hand on me and this she did say:
'It will not be long, love, 'til our weddin' day.'

Singing songs and reciting poems for sixpence scratched the throat. In spite of Da being splattered from the drink, he knew immediately if I cut a verse short and made me restart. After he wrung all the songs and poems out of me, he handed over the tanner with a smile that almost split his ears apart. Then off he went with, 'Duck, make your daddy a nice cup of tea before he heads for bed.'

I'd point to all the full cups of tea standing on the table that Ma had make for him and he'd let get cold. 'If ye want a cup of tea at this hour of the night then get it yer bloody self.'

'Titch! It's easy to see that you're becoming like a common fish-wife, a street hawker.'

'Ma made ye all the cups of tea standing in front of yer face and ye let the line of them get stone cold.'

'Angeline, you're not a bit like your mammy. You'll never be as lovely looking as your mammy was when she was young. You'll never walk on the ground that she walks on. You'll never hold a candle to her. Wisha! It's hard to believe you're a child from the pair of us.'

I expected the litany of comparisons between Ma and me. The scutter did it all the time, just to unglue me. Most of the time, I made up my mind not to let Da puncture my heart, but often his spiteful jabs caused a wound. He knew he near slitted my wrists by telling me I'd never measure up to Ma in any way. He knew Ma shone in my eyes and that I'd cartwheel around the world for her.

'What did Ma ever see in a drunkard like you when she was so beautiful and could have had the pick of the litter?' I challenged him. He'd pull in his horns at this remark.

'Ah, Duck make your Da a cup of fresh tea and he'll be off to bed.'

How could I have filled the teapot one more time to make him more tea?

Then it was, 'Titch, Titch, sit beside your daddy while he drinks the best cup of tea he ever tasted and let an old soldier sing his song.'

'I heard all yer soldier songs a million times and yer stories of being an Irish soldier in the stupid army.'

I'd leave the room and walk into the scullery to wash the cups before heading for bed. Even when out of sight he continued the chorus.

'Titch, remember you can't beat or better an Irish song. Titch! Delia Murphy married a rich American. Are you making me the tea? I don't know what kind of a girl you are at all. I often wonder who you take after. Are you listening to your Da in there? And another thing, Titch, always remember to rise up the green, white and yellow flag, the flag of Ireland, over your head. You can tear down old John Bull's flag, the Union Jack, if you want. The flag of old stuttering George and giggling Maggie. You can wipe your arse with the Stars and Stripes of America, but always honour the Irish flag. That's an order.'

Da's sour puss towards England made sense but his sour puss towards Hollywood made no sense to me. I know he hated it when Ma and I left him home alone to rave to the walls. Whenever we could, Ma and I went to the pictures at the Shack or the Regal. Da saw one film in his life, a film with Fred Astaire and Ginger Rogers, and that was that.

'For God's sake,' called the scourge, 'What's holding you back with the tea? Your mother would have it made in no time. Ah well. Are you listening to me in there with that tap water running full blast in the sink? Remember when I die wrap the tricolour flag around my coffin. I want to be buried as an Irish soldier—one of the Free State's first soldiers, so make sure you and your mammy wrap my coffin in the Irish flag, or else I won't die happy. Did you hear all of that? You're wasting an awful lot of tap water in there.'

Then it went, 'Ah, you're a great girl getting me a fresh cup of tea. Now get that sour look off your puss and listen to what I have to tell you.'

Long after midnight now, Da remained oblivious to the needs of anyone else. Hardly able to contain my anger, I told him that if he let the tea get stone cold again he would not get any more. I'd rail at him, 'Do you hear me? Cause if ye let that tea get cold one more time it'll be the last for the rest of the night. I swear ta God and on a stack of bibles, I won't make ye another cup. May I may get struck down stone dead by lightening if I do. Get that into yer head. Get it into yer drunken skull.'

'You're an impudent young girl. The way you talk to your father who loves you every day of his life. You're worse than any of your three brothers. After I drink the tea with you sitting down here beside me, I'll be off to bed and into the arms of Morpheus. Stop looking at me like a cat. Duck, do you remember to say your prayers before you fall asleep at night? I pray every night to Saint Roc. Who watches over your mother and brothers every day of your lives? Has any harm ever befallen your mammy or Frank, Bob, and Noel? No! And why? Because your Da prays for all of you every night no matter how tired and run down he feels. He never lets his head, or never will, let his head fall back on the pillow until he prays for you all.

'Answer me! Has any harm ever came to you or any trouble lit upon your head? No! Because your father loves you and prays for you every night of his life.

'Your father may be an old drunkard and a disgrace to himself but that doesn't mean he makes up saints or fish that are not already in existence. Ah, you're a hard young girl. Ah, sure you can't help your strange little tinpot ways. I think you must take after your grandmother, Minnie, in Castleblayney, instead of your ma who has a heart of gold and a kind word for everybody no matter whether they are drunk or sober. For the love of God, this cup of tea is cold from blathering with you. Make Da a fresh cup?'

'No! By God, I'm not making ye another shaggin' cup.' And a curtain of silence would fall between us, a curtain of silence tasselled with rage.

'OK, I'll make ye another cup of tea, but this time it's the last cup of tea that I'm making for ye tonight. Do ye hear me? I swear to God that I'm done making tea for tonight, no matter what ye say, so don't try to get around me with yer auld soft soap. And I'm going to bed right after I put a fresh cup of tea in front of ye. I'm bloody well tired and fed up with yer going on about tea, and so is me Ma. I know she is, although Ma won't tell ye that. But I will, and in a hurry. What's more, who do ye think ye are, expecting us all to stay up half the night listening 'till we hear yer head crack down on the table. And waiting too for the sounds of empty porter bottles bumping into the others as they roll about the floor? I'm getting fed up with it all, with yer drinking. If Ma can put up with yer drinking 'til ye're stupid, I'm not going to. And don't forget that.

'And another thing, I'm tired of hearing ye moaning about not having a speck of food in yer stomach or a drop of nourishment in yer body. I hate yer drinking. I hate it. I hate it. I'll never have a bottle of porter in my house if I ever get married. The rotten stuff will never enter the door. And one more thing, the kids in the flats say ye're a drunkard in front of me face.'

'Ah! let the kids say what they will to you, Titch. Turn a deaf ear. Sit down now and I'll sing a few bars from a Thomas Moore melody. Oh! Breathe not his name. . . .'

'Oh! fuck off and make the tea yerself, ye madman.'

'Titch, I can't stand to see you in such a rage. I'm gone too far now with the drink to turn back. I hope one day you will forgive me for putting all of you through this. If only you knew how I feel when I haven't a drop. Maybe if you knew of the terrible pain and sadness that fills my mind you wouldn't be so hard. I can't shake off such a terrible feeling. It's unbearable and the feeling only shuts down with the drink.'

I wasn't going to let the old fella's sob story about why he drank soften the stiffness I was stuffing in my heart against him. He'd remind me then that in spite of his drinking, he never spent a penny of Ma's money, either when he had a job or was on the dole, and with that, he'd slide his shoe towards me and pull down the top of his sock, and say, 'See, the first thing I did when I opened my pay packet or got money from the dole, I'd take out your mammie's share, and stuff it into the top of this sock.'

Sometimes the thought ran through my mind that maybe Ma could have put a stop to his drinking. Ma told me when they were first married he never touched a drop. Somewhere along the line, it seemed to her, something triggered the drink in him and ever since he couldn't stop drinking. She told me that she thought about leaving him years ago because of his drinking and some other things.

'Who could I have turned to without a penny and the four of ye to feed?' said Ma. She reminded me that although Da had his bad side she still cared for him because deep down she still had memories of their time together before he drank. In spite of what Ma had to say, it became harder to put up with the sight of Da drunk every evening. Like Ma, I'd have good and bad memories of Da for a lifetime. Da the storyteller, Da the folksinger, Da who helped put food on the table, but most of all, it was Da the fucking drunkard who left me cross-eyed.

The sight of Da drinking himself to death began to fill me with desperation as did the realisation that life offered little to girls like myself.

One afternoon, rage and desperation seeped in every pore of my being. Christ, the blessed mother, the angels and saints couldn't dampen the feeling of rage and hopelessness. I took Bob's pocket-knife in my hand and headed for Sandymount Strand. I didn't know what I intended to with the pocketknife. I wanted to destroy something. I wanted to kill something. I took the knife and knifed all the crabs I could find under the rocks or peacefully lounging on the rocks against the seawall. I stabbed the crabs again and again with the pocketknife until each crab went rigid. I knifed the mother crabs, I knifed the father crabs, I knifed the brother crabs and I knifed the baby crabs.

After the slaughter, after littering the beach with dead crabs my mind and body felt refreshed. My act of murder comforted and confused me.

That night, images of the slaughtered crabs filled my dreams and I awoke to their screaming and crying. I felt so ashamed of what I had done, that Saturday afternoon I walked up to the church to go to confession. In anguish, I told the priest about killing all the crabs with my brother's pocketknife and then hearing the crabs crying in my sleep. I told the priest that I wanted God to know how sorry I felt for doing such a thing. I asked the priest if he would ask God to forgive me for the killings.

After listening to my heartfelt remorse, the priest said, 'You're a silly girl to be going on about dead crabs on Sandymount Strand when you could be examining your conscience about impure thoughts or desires or offering prayers to the blessed mother for the reconversion of Russia to Christianity.'

A factory girl

I found an ad under 'situations vacant': fourteen-year-old girls were needed to work in a knitwear factory in Rathmines. I took the bus to Rathmines and found the factory. I told the manager that I had read the ad and had come looking for a job. He asked me how old I was. I told him two months away from being fourteen. He said that the law stated that no-one under the age of fourteen could be hired to work in the factory. I told him that I would work like a slave if he hired me. He decided to slide back the law. 'Be here early on Monday morning,' he ordered. Ma and Da were surprised that I had got hired to work in the factory being underage and, in their eyes, still a child.

I knew that when I went to work in a factory, I'd be leaving childhood behind. I'd worked on the dump site for nearly a year but the few shillings I managed to earn from selling the sacks of coke didn't go very far. I asked Ma if she could borrow money from someone to buy me a new headscarf and a pair of nylon stocking to wear to my new job. All the factory girls covered their heads with a scarf and wore nylons. I still wore the gear of childhod, even anklesocks. I wanted to look as grown-up as possible on my first day at the factory. I gave the little girl down the balcony my bunch of hair ribbons that I had loved and kept for years. I'd not be needing such childish trappings anymore. I saw myself on the way to becoming a young woman: a woman of the world.

Ma packed me a bread and butter sandwich and put some milk in a bottle for me to take along for my lunch. I'd be going to work five and a half days a week from eight am 'til five pm. I'd earn nineteen shillings and two pence a week. I had no plan to bank the wages for later use, they would go to Ma to keep us all going. And part of my salary would get eaten up by bus fares going from George Reynolds' to the textile factory in Rathmines, way over on the other side of the city.

The Keltic Textile factory operated out of an abandoned warehouse. I vividly recall the clattering noise of the knitting machines and the haze of lint the machines generated all over the place. I coughed like an old codger at having to inhale the milky sea of lint, but nobody could hear me over the noise.

An Englishman owned the factory and an Englishman managed it. A German woman supervised the workers; she was nicknamed Brunhilde by the girls. She armed me over to the cotton-spinning machine and told me in a strong German accent that anyone who could knot a broken thread could work on such a machine. She turned on the switch that operated the big machine and it roared into life. The row of bobbins on the top of the machine spun round like swirling demons. I took in the scene, and wished I were back on my perch on the Irishtown dump.

The electric bobbin machine measured at least twenty feet in length, and I had to feed hanks of unwound yarn into the machine which spun the loose yarn onto the bobbins above. Friction constantly caused the yarn to break as it wound around the bobbins. It was my job to rejoin each break and get the bobbin swirling again. I ran up and down the length of the machine all day long making sure that all the bobbins were spinning the yarn.

It took a week before I got the hang of the machine and what I had to do. The spinning machine had to be kept running all the time. The supervisor told me I could shut it off to use the lavatory once during the morning and once during the afternoon. I had an hour off for lunch.

During the lunch hour, I became acquainted with the other girls who worked in the factory. We ate our lunch in the factory. The older girls, in their early twenties, were looked up to by younger workers. The older girls worked as piece time workers sewing the garments together on sewing machines. Younger girls worked as finishers and inspected each garment for flaws. Then the garments were handed over to girls who ironed them and folded them into boxes. A salesman picked up the boxes and delivered them by motor car to various shops in the city and to areas of rural Ireland.

As the last girl to be hired in the factory, I got the job no one else wanted: working the spinning-machine. I thought I'd never make it through the first week because I'd never worked so hard in my life not even on the dump. I could hardly wait until Saturday noon came around and the work week ended. Saturday was also payday.

At noon when all the machines were turned off, I picked-up my paypack. A girl from the front office gave out the paypacks. She handed me the brown sealed envelope without even a smile. It was small and felt heavy to the hand. I opened it and counted the money inside: one ten-shilling note, four two-shilling coins, one shilling and two hen pennies. Ma said before I started the job to take two shillings out of my wages to spend on new clothes for myself, the rest of my pay would go for household expenses. The rent for our flat cost nineteen shillings a week, as much as I earned in a week at the factory. Ma promised that as soon as Da found work, I'd get to keep my pay for things I badly needed. But I needed work clothes and clothes to wear for going out after work, and I knew that if I waited for Da to find a decent paying job, I'd be an old woman.

There were some women in George Reynolds' who had set themselves up in their homes as 'docket women' for clothing and shoeshops in the heart of Dublin city. Theshop owners, in order to generate business for their establishments, selected these women to be their standins. They sold dockets to other women who used them to buy clothing and shoes, paying off the dockets on a weekly basis, including high interest. The docket women were paid a percentage of the dockets. They were also responsible for collecting the weekly payments made on the dockets and for taking the money to the shopowners. Dockets were the only way to get new clothing or shoes, so going to the docket women and being approved for the credit, meant a lot. Dockets were not given out to anyone under sixteen years old. I asked Ma to get me a couple of dockets to buy new clothes and shoes, otherwise I would have to continue to wear my childhood dresses.

Mrs T, a docket woman living in one of the flats in George Reynolds', willingly issued two dockets to Ma, who handed them to me for a shopping spree. I thought about what I would buy, it being the first time in my life that I had ever had a choice about such things. I envisioned which film star I wanted to look like, and Audrey Hepburn came to mind.

Ma accompanied me to the shops that accepted the vouchers; these shops were considered second rate, but beggers can't be choosers. I'd seen the film *Roman Holiday* with Audrey Hepburn and Gregory Peck. I fell in love with Audrey and the way she dressed, so simple and modern. I used the dockets to buy a tight fitting black skirt with a slit up the back of the leg, a pink fluffy jumper, black underwear and a pair of wedge-heeled black shoes for wearing after work. I used the remainder of the vouchers to buy stockings, a pair of cheap flat shoes, a cheap blouse and skirt, and a coat for wearing to work, along with a new headscarf.

The girls in the factory were from different parts of the city. Some of them rode their bikes home for lunch, and the rest of us ate our sandwiches around a work table. The two favourite topics discussed during lunch time were menstruation, called 'Charlie', and the mysteries of sex. Both topics were new to my ears. During the lunch hour, Rita asked me out of the blue, if I had got my Charlie yet? I hadn't a clue what she was talking about. Ma had never mentioned anything about a Charlie to me. I was still in the dark regarding the deeper mysteries of life which were now about to unfold.

'*You* know,' said Rita. 'The thing girls get each month? The curse! Boys get jelly stuff and girls get the other thing? I can see ye're still a kid,' she said, buttoning her lip.

Lily, on the other hand, insisted on making sex as clear as could be when she told me, 'Look, it's like this, yer father puts his thing into yer mother's and that's what causes babies.'

Then Eve jumped into the conversation and went a step further. 'It's like this, yer mudder has the head of the mop and yer father has the handle. He screws the handle into the mop, and that's it. Get it?'

'Ah!' said Josie, 'Leave her alone now. Are ye fourteen yet?' she asked. 'Listen. I have a better way of explaining the difference between men and women. It goes like this—there used to be a tune that went along with it, but I forget the melody—anyway, here's how it goes:

When God made man he make him out of string.
He'd some left over so he left a little thing.
When God made woman he made her out of lace,
He didn't have enough so he left a little space.'

After work one evening, I told Ma what the girls had told me about sex. Obviously embarrassed, Ma told me not to listen to the rossies (brazen girls). By the look on Ma's face, I knew the girls in the factory had truth on their side. As the truth about sex settled in my mind, I recalled the longago image of Ma suffering with the festering ulcers under her armpits, under both breasts, and the excruciating pain when she peed. It dawned on me then how she had acquired the unnamed secret disease. I realised that when Da served in the army away from home, supposedly protecting our green shores from invaders, the bugger had been humping and bumping among the rushes O!, and carried carnage home to Ma.

After I had worked at the factory for a while, I began to menstruate. I could hardly wait to tell the other girls that Charlie had flooded my knickers. After I let them in on the tale, Rita cut off a piece of knitted material and offered it to me to use as a sanitary napkin.

'We use this soft stuff for pads, but don't let Brunhilde see ye with it or we'll all get the sack.' The girls discussed their Charlie in great length. They talked about how long it lasted, how heavy the flow was, the degree of any pain, and they wondered if what they had heard about washing their heads while they had their Charlie could be true: a person could lose their mind. They showed a lot of concern and kindness towards each other during the time of their periods.

Finding and dating fellas became part of the conversation after the discussion about Charlie ran dry. Some girls were going with steady fellas while others had their eye on someone special, or were on the watch out. The girls who were planning on getting married in the future would be expected to give up their work in the factory because married women were not supposed to work outside the home, even if they needed the money.

Some of the girls set up a signal when they wanted to meet in the lavatory for a talk or a quick cigarette. We were not supposed to leave our workplace or else Brunhilde would come over to give us a talking to about what earning a pay cheque was all about. I gained great control over my bladder because I could only empty it once during the morning and once during the afternoon, but I was ready at any time to meet with some of the girls in the lavatory to have a chat or a fag.

If we were missing for more then a few minutes from our work station, Brunhilde would pound on the bathroom door and order us to get out and to get back to our work stations. She made some of the younger girls cry after she gave them a lashing for not working fast enough or for talking with another worker alongside, or for having to pee more than twice in the work day.

She told me more than once that I was not keeping up with the bobbins on my machine, though I did the best I could threading and tying every broken knot. After one of her outbursts, I stuck my tongue out at her as she headed towards the office; when she turned around and caught me giving her the raspberry, I nearly collapsed. I didn't want the bitch to have the satisfaction of sending me packing. I packed it in myself, as soon as I found another factory job elsewhere.

Now that I was fourteen, jobs were to be had across the city for similar wages and working conditions. I worked for a while in Carroll's Tobacco Factory in Pearse Street until they laid off half the workers because of some new machines. Then I found a job at Wilton's Confectionery. Wilton's made marshmallow wafers, hard rock candy souvenirs of Ireland, hen's eggs and marshmallow mice. Two brothers owned and operated the factory. I got hired to work with Big Mary on the mould table.

Big Mary lived up to her name. A strapping girl of about six feet tall, Mary had a round pink face, piercing blue eyes and dish-blond hair. She asked me if I'd always been a pipsqueak.

The mould table measured about twenty feet in length and five feet in width and had edges on the top. Big Mary and I poured bags of cornflour onto the top of the table and spread it crosswise and lengthwise. Then we each took the end of a plank of wood and scraped it over the cornflour to form a smooth base.

After that, Mary and I got the mice mouldboard or the egg mouldboard and laid it down carefully on the cornflour the width and length of the table. When we got an order for marshmallow mice, we worked with the mice board, and vice versa. It took patience to make good moulds. Each time we pressed the board down into the cornflour we tipped it gently with the handle of a hand brush to make sure it had formed an impression. Then we carefully lifted up the board, brushed it off, set it down again into the cornflour, and repeated the same thing the length of the table. When the mould table was set up, the piping girls took over.

The piping girls had the sought after job because they got to pipe hot melted marshmallow into every mould we had made in the corn flour on the table. Piping jobs were given to the nicest looking girls in the factory, and piping the right amount of sticky marshmallow into each outline required a fast and steady hand. Speedy piping, with exact precision, prevented the marshmallow from cooling and going stiff in the bags. Cooled marshmallow wouldn't flow rapidly enough to fill each mould, and the stiff fluff, heavier than the warmed fluff, collapsed the cornflour into unrecognizable shapes. Piping girls did everything right.

Big Mary pointed out, 'It's a good job for the two of us that the piping girls don't get the sneezes while they work or we'd be redoing each and every mould.'

After the moulds were filled with the marshmallow, they were left to set and dry. Mary and I kept watch over the moulds to make sure they hardened and kept their shape. After the eggs and mice had set, we collected them in a sieve and gently shook off any excess cornflour. After that we put the delicacies on trays.

It was my job then to mark make-believe eyes on the mice with a three-pronged metal gadget. I dipped the tips of the gadget into a cup of black dye and branded each marshmallow mouse. The idea was to make the penny mice look like Mickey Mouse so the kids would buy them after they were delivered to the shops. Sometimes the mind wandered, which meant that dozens of the penny mice ended up getting eyes branded on their arses instead of their heads.

My friend Dolores from O'Brien's Place also worked in Wilton's. Her job was to dip the plain marshmallow eggs one by one into a container containing melted chocolate. Dolores stood behind a gas boiler which contained melted chocolate. She fed the big pot chunks of chocolate all day long. She told me that by the end of the day she felt sick from the gas fumes and the smell of simmering chocolate. Doloro did a great job at dipping. She hand dipped hundreds of marshmallow eggs every week. While she dipped each egg into the chocolate, she had also to keep an eye on the chocolate in the boiler to make sure it had the consistency of silk. She picked the egg, slid it into the palm of her hand, dunked it quickly and completely under the chocolate, flipped off the excess, and slid it onto a waiting tray to dry. Inexperienced dippers ended up with scrambled eggs or odd shaped eggs or eggs that still had dribbles of chocolate, instead of the fine hand-dipped work done by Doloro.

Before we left to go home for the day, Mary and I would cover the mould table with some flour sacks. Every morning when we came to work and lifted the flour sacks we saw the lines and lines of rat tracks. It took us time to filter out all the rat shite out of the cornflour before we began to make our moulds for the marshmallow delights.

Not surprisingly, neither Big Mary nor I had any desire to sample the marshmallow eggs or the marshmallow mice, even though we both had a serious sweet tooth. By the end of the working week, we were as stiff from our work as the eggs and makebelieve rodents we stacked on the trays. We hated how we were constantly covered with cornflour from the tips of our eyelashes to the soles of our shoes.

We looked like a pair of graveyard ghosts as we headed home from work each day. Instead of heading straight home on a payday, we headed for Caffolla's on O'Connell Street, to gorge ourselves on Melancholy Baby, a mixture of ice-cream, canned fruit, half a banana, custard, heavy whipped cream, shaved chocolate and a red cherry.

Big Mary also had an eye on a fella who worked in the restaurant—an Italian—the spit and image of Tony Curtis, only taller. Tony Curtis kept topping our half-eaten Melancholy Baby until we nearly busted, or heaven forbid, belched or farted.

I had to listen first thing in the morning to Mary's mooning over her Italian boyfriend. I asked her what she wanted most in life, trying to get her off the love chants. 'Framed and nailed,' she replied, meaning she wanted to get married. I asked her if she'd heard the rumour that Italian fellas had to be literally cut away from their mothers in order to marry a girl? Rumour had it that the Italians were a hundred times worse than Irish fellas when it came to getting them to leave their ma in order to marry. Big Mary's eyes went tick-tock back and forth on her platter face like a wall clock, while she contemplated the dilemma. After several minutes with the tick-tock, she told me I was the slowest worker she had ever had on the other end of the mould-board and the biggest bejabber (talker) she'd had to put up with. But we were off again the following payday for our Melancholy Baby, and to meet with Rocco.

Mary and Rocco asked if I were going dancing at the Claro later. I left the dickiebirds, and took the bus home to Irishtown. With the two shillings I had kept out of my wages for myself, I'd enough money to go to the Claro. It cost a shilling to get into the dancehall. Loving to dance as I did, I toed it off to the Claro every Friday and Saturday night.

The Claro

Unlike the large formal dancehalls scattered about Dublin city, the Claro was considered to be a hole in the wall. It was off Leeson Street, an out of the way location for most young factory workers, but they discovered it. It attracted working-class girls and boys under the age of twenty, a young crowd that would not be seen dead dancing in the more well-known establishments. The Claro had featured the first rock n' roll band in Dublin city, I'd been told. It only played rock n'roll music from the United States. Now that every household in Ireland seemingly had a radio, the airwaves blasted out the new music day and night, and young people loved it. The film, *Rock Around the Clock* with Bill Haley and the Comets, had played in the largest cinema in the city, and each showing sold out. The Roman Catholic hierarchy spoke out against rock n'roll. The fathers saw it as a bad influence on the young. The new music appealed to young factory workers, like myself. The holy fathers expected us to embrace *Rince Gaeilge* (Irish traditional dancing) with its *Fol dol de di do* instead of dancing to the rock n' roll beat of, 'One two three o'clock, four o'clock, rock!' or 'Giddy up a ding-dong, Giddy up a ding-dong, Giddy-up a ding-dong. Rock!'

The Claro had been a warehouse of some kind before being turned into a makeshift dance hall. The place had no windows, or toilet, or anywhere to hang coats, so everyone piled their coats in a corner of the long room. A mirror hung on the wall over the pile of coats for girls to check themselves before strutting out onto the dance floor.

A small stage stood at the end of the long hall like an altar, an altar to rock'n roll instead of adoration to on high. Three musicians, a drummer, a guitar player, and a singer stood centre stage dressed in Teddy Boy outfits. Two lines of people formed along opposite walls. Teddy Boys stood stiff-backed along one wall and droopy-headed girls lined the other. Glancing around the dance floor at all the boys who looked like Tony Curtis and Elvis Presley, and the girls swooping around in their poodle skirts, we were American lookalikes. As young factory workers, the clothes on our backs had been purchased on dockets. Every girl I knew paid into a docket club weekly; if it hadn't been for the dockets, not many of us would have a stylish thing on our backs. Getting decked out to go dancing at the Claro meant serious business. Myself and my friends favoured the Teddy Girl look as modelled by May May in George Reynolds' who never let a Friday or Saturday night fly past without going to the Claro. May May wore a black pencil tight skirt, slit up the leg, a yellow or black turtleneck jumper, and a wide black elastic belt round the waist. For a dash of Audrey Hepburn added on to the Teddy Girl look, I wore a wisp of chiffon tied round the neck, making sure the points did not entangle my long, loop earrings. I preferred to dance in high-heeled shoes, the higher the better, even if it meant risking a broken neck.

Certain procedures were expected for selecting a dance partner. As always the stylish sought out each other. As soon as the band got going, two or three fellas would rush across the floor to ask May May to dance. To anyone with good vision, May May was not only the best dancer she also filled out her turtle neck jumper more firmly and fuller than any of the other girls. Girls who filled out their turtle neck jumpers always got the pick of the litter, the rest of us shrank even smaller than usual. Some of the fellas cracked out loud their preference for 'girls who won't fall on their faces if they fall on the floor. Huh, huh.' Hearing the singer sing 'Giddy up a ding dong', 'Blue Suede Shoes', 'Rock Around the Clock', made our young blood bubble.

I learned some of the art of seduction at the Claro. I paid attention to how a fella clicked with a girl. Girls who were good clickers were second in popularity after the sweater girls. Since I was still undeveloped, I figured if I weren't to be a wallflower, the solution was the click. Serious clicking got underway after the first band break. The click took place in the eye, but first it needed to rove.

I blinked several times to make sure that my black mascara still clung to my eyelashes like thick mud, keeping in mind that the wider the eye the wider the scan, and the wider the scan the better the catch. I made a distinction between the men who ogled with their eyes and open-mouthed drool, and the beamers who steadily searched around the dancehall with their peepers. As a beamer met my eyes, and I found a gleam in his, I would try to intensify the luminosity in my eyes as a signal of come-on.

My fierce lock-on worked on occasion because of its boldness; at other times, I might as well have been trying to thread a couple of narrow-eyed needles in the dark without a pair of specks. After our eyes held steadily for more than a blink, the click was in the bag. I'd bagged myself a dance partner for the rest of the night, and hopefully someone to walk me home, or even someone who could afford a bottle of orange crush.

Of all the music that stirred me, none affected me like the sound of rock n' roll from America, and to cuddle in the arms of a lad as we danced around the dance floor to a slower song like 'Young Love' was to fill the soul with deep emotion. But there were always the inner voices of the priests and nuns and Da in my ear, so I never let my emotions take over, especially those that clicked and throbbed between my legs.

Jesus, Mary and Joseph and God forbid that any girl in Dublin city of the late 1950s, would go to school before the bell rang. Any girl who got 'knocked up' by a fella had Christ to pay for her mistake. An unmarried young mother in the flats had the heart cut out of her, not only by her own family, but by other older married women who wagged their tongues like clappers every time the unfortunate girl passed by. And the rage some of the older mothers levelled at the girl's mother for as they said, 'not keeping a proper eye on the daughter'. Nothing would satisfy such guardians of Irish morality; even when the girl got married, she got fingered for having a kid out of wedlock. We were told to live our lives like the virgin mary in conditions that the blessed mother never found herself in. Fellas, on the other hand, got a pat on the back from older men for 'getting a bit' and getting away with it to boot.

I never forgot how T, a young factory girl, got forced by family members to take the mailboat across the Irish Sea to England to have her load undelivered. Some pious Irish thought it more OK for English doctors to fix up the dirty work of some Irishmen overseas, than to make the men bear the blunt of their actions at home in the bosom of the family.

Ma told me about girls who had been told to take the boat to Liverpool, and how the unfortunate girls were thrown into terrible situations when they arrived in Britain to have an abortion. Married women around the place were burdened by one birth after another, as many as fourteen births to one mother she knew of, whose husband bragged how much he loved his little wife. Ma also told me about desperate women who for one reason or another—only a woman knew her own mind—were forced to seek an end to their condition at the hands of butchers in dirty rooms or filthy alleyways. 'Everyone turns a deaf ear when it comes to poor women having loads of children,' added Ma. Most priests ordered poor women to bear their pain, obey their husbands' desire for sex, and should a women refuse, she got tarred with tempting her husband into sinning with someone else.

My mother told me to be careful about falling for a fella and maybe getting into trouble. She told me that Da would never forgive me should such a thing happen and that he would scourge me, because he wouldn't be able to undercut his upbringing. Ma told me that Da would expect me to leave the house should I get in the family way without a husband. Ma told me she'd never leave me in such a plight, and if it did happen, we'd leave together. During the course of the conversation, I got up the nerve to ask Ma why she had only four kids, unlike most of the other wives? I knew in the back of my mind it had something to do with what had happened to her years ago but I'd never brought it up.

'It's a miracle Noely didn't come into the world born blind or backward or even worse. After Noely, I didn't want to take any more chances on bringing a deformed babby into the light of day.'

'But Ma, why did ye think that such an awful thing could have happened to a baby born after Noely?' Ma stared into my face. I asked her, 'Did it have anything to do with the terrible sores ye had all over yer body, years ago?'

'Yis,' she said.

'Da gave it to ye!'

'Yis. He had other women,' said Ma, 'and brought the disease home to me.' I said, 'and now the same auld bastard thinks he's a saint, huh, Ma?'

'Yis,' she said.

After clearing the air, we both laughed at the thought of the auld fella fancying himself to be a saint. I loved Ma more than ever, and especially for never scourging Da about his past sin, which I might have done. While we were talking about men, I told her about the priest who tried to put his hand down the front of my dress when I was a young child in school. I told her about the priest who asked me to put my face closer to his in the confession box so that he could stroke my face as he muttered and fiddled with himself. I asked her if it were true that priests were supposed to be a substitute for God in the confession box. She replied the priests were not God, for God's sake, and for me not to muddle the two in my mind. And she noted that some men, no matter what their station in life, are a gang of dirty auld bastards tarred with the same stick. It became more obvious to me that girls were to arise without any blemish or trace of sin from hellholes.

The old fella began to give me a weekly sermon on the importance of purity. He raved that I was to keep myself as pure as the driven snow and become like God's holy mother or like Ma, the two women, according to him, who never dirtied their copy books. Knowing what I did about him and keeping mum about it all my life, I wanted to slap him for yapping on about me preserving my purity. I wondered how many other fathers, some drunkards like my own, raved themselves into the notion that girls had nothing more on their minds than the constant preoccupation with the 'hairy lariats' that hung down between the legs of some buggers?

JoJo, the steam cleaner in the factory, referred to the thing that men had between their lets as the 'hairy lariat'. I told her what an apt description for the sausage it was. One Saturday evening after working eight hours in the factory, to gain a little overtime pay, I sat by the fire hoping for a bit of peace. The old fella took my silence for a good time to hammer home another piety lesson. He had borrowed a book written by A. J. Cronin, and to make a long, long story short it is about a young priest who hopes to rise high in the Catholic Church. Anyway, on the way up, he comes up against a brick wall. He finds out that his sister has been sleeping around, finds herself up the pole, and goes into labour. The young priest, Stephen, gets word that the sister is having complications delivering the baby due to the size of the infant's head, as big as a turnip, I must have assumed. Stephen is called on to make a decision about the life of the mother, his sister, and the infant. He struggles with the image of his sister who went wrong and the innocent babe stuck in her belly. His Catholic faith has taught that only a baptised person can enter the gates of heaven. If the child dies in the sister's womb, not having a chance to be baptised it won't go to heaven and see the light of God. If the mother dies, already baptised, she will go straight to heaven, because all mothers who die in childbirth, goes the faith, go straight to heaven. He tells the doctor to save the infant and lets his sister die. I hoped any of my brothers, in a similar situation, wouldn't act like the shagger Stephen, and let me die. I didn't have to wonder why Da thought Cronin's book would be one I should read, slowly and carefully. Cronin's book carried a threat and I'd be buggered before I'd take the time to read it.

The obsession men apparently had with the hairybush that flourished between a woman's legs bordered on the ridiculous. Judging from overheard snippets of conversation, they either loved or hated the thing that tantalised under the skirt. And all the pet names the men had for the thing that flourished under a woman's skirt! Pet names like mop-head, ball a yarn, the rent book, a crack, her muff, Mary Jane, cunning cunt or dirty cunt, the treasure, the downfall, little pussy, her gee, the rag, her sty, sliddery-slit, mop, and my favourite, soft moss.

As a young factory girl, like most of the others, it was dancing, working for a wage, not humping, that kept misery at bay. The small wages I earned paid for my keep, and when there were layoffs at the factory, as there were frequently, a sense of despair set in. The layoff at Wilton's sweet factory due to the owners not making enough money, or deciding to shut down for a while, sounded like a broken record. The real reason, I concluded, why so many of us got laid off was that we had been promised a pay rise after some time on the job. We got the boot because they hired a constant supply of new girls for lower wages. An endless supply of girls drifted from one factory to another looking for jobs, girls desperate enough to work for a pittance and the companies knew it. If ever the day dawned when Ireland's capital city became prosperous, the city fathers would have the hundreds of factory girls and boys to thank. I would have had to leave the sweet factory in any case, because my bronchitis kept getting worse from inhaling the cornflour into my lungs. Someone told me that they were hiring ice-cream girls in the cinemas around the city, and that I ought to apply for one of the jobs.

An ice-cream girl

I applied for the job of an ice-cream girl at the Regent Cinema in Blackrock. I was interviewed by the manager of the picture house. Mr B appeared to be in his middle thirties, stood about five foot six in his elevated shoes, and at first glance it seemed to me he must have deformed feet to wear such shoes. His narrow face inched all the way up to his high forehead, and he wore a charcoal grey suit that wouldn't get a fiver in the pawn. He asked me my age, where I lived, and my last job. Then he told me to walk around his desk. I felt like a fool parading in front of the prick. His eyes rounded on me, a sneer tipped up his lip, and his droopy eyelids went up and down like windowshades. He acted like a liontamer inspecting an untamed animal.

After he had had his fill of gawking, he pretended to wrestle in his mind as to whether I had the right appearance to sell sweets in a dark picture house. He wanted 'a girl with a colleen's face', he snickered. And at fifteen, of course, my face lacked even one wrinkle.

The manager rubbed his hands together, tipped his fingers into a pyramid and said, 'You're lucky. You've got the job of being the ice-cream girl for the Regent.' I knew with him for a boss, the job wasn't going to be peaches and cream!

My ice-cream girl outfit consisted of a white wraparound smock set off with a royal port collar and cuffs. I had to wear a tiny white soldier's hat on the side of the head. My pay for the eight hour, six day week job was twenty shillings per week.

I had to become a walking shop. The manager handed me a large wooden tray with a leather strap attached. He pointed to a freezer and told me to load on as many ice-cream tubs as possible along with orange drinks.

He told me not to keep the ices and drinks out for longer than five minutes because the patrons liked their ice-creams hard and their drinks cold. After every five minutes I had to put the unsold ices and drinks back in the freezer and restock the tray with new, firmer tubs and colder drinks. I also had to arrange on the tray an assortment of sweets, bags of popcorn, cigarettes, matches, and one-penny items.

The tray also contained a built-in light that operated by a set of batteries which added to its weight, and a cash box. Work started at two in the afternoon when the picture house opened and finished at ten pm. I got a half hour break. The manager said my job was to' Sell! Sell! Sell!'

The first day of work the manager helped me on with the loaded tray and pointed me in the direction of the auditorium. I went forward like a horse with a cracked neck. Mr B thought it was very funny that I nearly lost my balance and cartwheeled onto the floor with the heavy tray. He put a torchlight into my hand and told me to aim it at the floor as I walked the aisles in the dark.

I walked up and down the aisle, except for the half hour off for tea-time. Selling stuff off the tray while holding a flashlight and making up change inside the dark interior took getting used to. If I made a mistake when it came to giving change I had to pay for it. If someone overpaid, the manager put it into his pocket. Worst of all, during the intermission between films I had to stand in front of a spotlight so that the patrons could see me.

A short advertisement film got shown on the screen as I stood under the spotlight. Mr B took on the job of aiming the spotlight on me. 'Howdy do, Miss Kearns,' he'd whisper under his breath.

After I finished work in the evening, Mr B would breeze down the stairs from his office to check how much merchandise I had sold for the day. I had to keep a written account of all the items I had sold and Mr B checked my account. If the amount of stuff sold didn't correspond to the money in the cash box, it meant I had made a mistake and the shortage came out of my paypacket.

Others who worked in the Regent included two older women in their early forties. Molly worked as the cashier and Kay worked as an usherette. The women and the male ushers all wore uniforms that represented the colours of the cinemas owned by the same concern across the city.

Kay and Molly had a cool relationship towards each other. It became clear that I was expected to travel towards one or the other. I latched onto Kay, probably because she was unmarried. She had a boy friend, however, a butcher who worked in the butcher's shop next door to the Regent.

The first thing Kay wanted to know was if I thought she looked younger than Molly. As far as I could tell they were both old. Kay took a lot of pains with looking beautiful. She plucked her eyebrows, constantly inflated her cheeks in and out to take out the creases and plastered bottles of camomile lotion over her face to keep it from getting dry. The pink lotion made the skin on her face resembled a Hafner sausage.

Kay had worked in cinemas around the city for fifteen years. She said that working indoors for so long had taken all the natural colour from her face. She let me use her make-up to plaster my face. She complained that I was too flat-chested and needed a bit of padding under my uniform. We had the same day off from work. She took me to Clery's on O'Connell Street and had me try on a brassiere—my first! I bought a padded bra and a fancy black lace garter belt. The padded brassiere did wonders for my looks and it did wonders for my sweet sales in the cinema.

Molly, the cashier, had been deserted by her husband who had taken off with another woman to London. He left Molly with a little girl of two to fend for. Molly lived with her mother who took care of the child while Molly worked. Although her husband had taken off and left her and the child, Molly was expected to live the life of a virgin mother for the rest of her life. A few men asked her out but she refused because, as she said, every tongue in Booterstown where she lived would wag a mile.

Molly lost no love on her mother-in-law. She talked about the old woman with scorn. Molly said that she and her newly married husband had spent the first night of her wedding at her in-laws' place, and the next morning after she and her husband had got up, her mother-in-law came into the room and examined the sheet for blood. The old rip said to Molly that his mother was checking up to see if her son had married a virgin. The bloody sheet would be a verification of that. No show of blood on the sheet could mean that Molly had gone to school before the bell rang and that her son had been taken to the cleaners by Molly. Opening night, said Molly, had been a big thing for the mother-in-law.

Molly kept a close eye on everyone who came into the Regent over the years. She spotted any married man who ducked into the dark picture house with a box of chocolates for some woman not his wife. She wanted to know if I had a fella.

Now that I worked as an ice-cream girl in a cinema instead of having a job in a factory, my relationships had changed. I now had to work until ten or eleven at night. Going to the Claro had to be put on the glimmer. I'd also put clicking fellas on the glimmer.

Kay and Molly didn't like girls who worked in factories. They thought that factory girls were common and loose with their charms. They kept hinting to me how lucky I was to be working in a picture house instead of a factory. Obviously, for them I was now a step above buttermilk, as they would say in Irishtown. I listened to the women rattling on about the low morality of young girls these days all the livelong day. The two viewed their jobs of being a cashier and an usherette as being on a par with secretaries and clerks.

Along with the three of us, six men were employed at the Regent besides the manager and assistant manager. Three men worked in the projection room showing the films. The chief usher, a barrel chested six footer with a nose on his face like a fox, loved his little bit of authority. Kay, Molly, Mike, Dermot, and myself were overseen by him. Every day before the cinema opened for business, the chief usher got everyone to line up in formation. Then he would call the manager in his office upstairs to come down to see the parade. In would come the manager with the greeting, 'Howdy do!' Then he'd tell us all to put our arms forward so he could inspect our fingernails. All the while he would smirk like a Cheshire cat as he prowled round us. I hoped the bastard would end up in a lunatic asylum some day and have someone smack his face with hard shite balls.

The manager, a slithery type of Dubliner, lorded it over his assistant, Mr O'B from Bray. Mr O'B was like a squire out of an English film: all tweedy and smelling of Aran Gold pipe smoke. He looked around thirty, stood at least six feet tall, had salt and pepper hair, wore wire-rimmed round glasses, and wore a green woollen cap on his head. He wore brown clodhopper shoes on his feet and carried a walking cane. He looked like a hick from the country instead of a border-edged Dubliner. The manager had him calling him Mr B this and Mr B that, as if he wasn't allowed to call his boss by his usual name. The staff snickered at Mr O'B's appearance. They wondered what kind of a 'mot' (girl friend) he had stashed away. Unlike the manager, who had a dishwater blond waiting for him after work, the assistant manager kept his love tokens out of sight.

Mr O'B looked a bit like a priest when you got close to his face. I mentioned this to Molly thinking that was why he didn't seem interested in women. 'Let me tell ye he's like all men. He knows that he didn't get what he's got in his trousers to stir his tea with.' At least he kept his urges, if he had any, to himself.

The same couldn't be said for some of the other men who worked in the picture house. Some thought a bit of manhandling for me as the youngest female on the staff was called for, whether I liked it or not! One of the ushers, a married man, liked to brush up behind me whenever I bent over the fridge to restock my ice-cream tray. He pestered me for a kiss and tried to force his mouth on mine a few times. When he stood near me, he'd sing this song for my benefit:

In sweet Blackrock I lost me cock,
In Booterstown I found it.
I left it there—beyond compare
With all the girls around it!

Whenever the battery in the light on my tray needed to be charged or changed, I had to take it to the projectionists' room. The old goat in charge would bounce down off the stool he sat on behind the camera, and offer to help me. He'd try to replace the tray-light while the tray was still hung around my neck; he'd fumble the light pretending he couldn't see in the dark and grab my breasts. It didn't take me long to cop on to the codger and figure out what he was really up to. One of the other men in the projectionists' booth, who saw what his boss was up to with me, became a friend and helped me whenever I needed a new battery.

On my sixteenthth birthday, Mr B knocked on the door of the women's staff room and stood in the entrance with a big birthday cake in his hands. 'Happy birthday, Miss Kearns—sweet sixteen and never been kissed.' He put the cake into my hands and offered his puckered lips for a kiss. I took the cake and put it on the table. After the manager left without a kiss, Kay and Molly giggled at the cake and asked me how I intended to pay for it.

I'd been kissed before my sixteenth birthday but never fucked. For double sure when I did it would not be with the quisling of a manager whose lewdness would gag a maggot.

Mr B started to invite me to meet him after work at the Four Provinces ballroom. He gave me all kinds of free tickets to dancehalls around the city. But I saw enough of his ugly face at work to last me for a month of Sundays, so I never went. He'd also summon me on the house phone from his upstairs office to come upstairs and make his tea. I'd make him a pot of tea and bring it into his office. One afternoon, I asked him why he had never learned how to make tea for himself. He didn't relish the remark. When he asked me for change from the cash register, he held my hand and squeezed it tight.

He also began to offer me a lift home in his car after work. I let him give me a lift home one frightful rainy night. Half-way on the way to Irishtown, he stopped his Morris Minor and tried to kiss me. He told me he wanted me to like him, to get to know him and we could have lots of fun. But I wasn't to let anyone in on our relationship. I told him that I didn't want any of his kisses and that if he went any further I'd tell my mother on him. He told me that he had me in mind for the first usherette's job that came up, when I got to be eighteen and that I had only two years to wait.

I wanted to tell him to bugger off, but I knew my wages made a difference for my family so I had to keep the job. I told the manager that I belonged to the Legion of Mary and that kissing and going out with men would be a sin as long as I remained a member. He replied, 'Righty-oh, Miss Kearns.'

The Regent became a courting place for a lot of young coppers out of the police station in Blackrock. Some of them brought their mots to the cinema. The courting couples made a beeline for the seats in the back of the cinema.

'They're back there playing tents again,' the chief usher would say with disapproval in the direction of the trench coats making tents over the heads of the coppers and their girl friends as they rocked away underneath. Sometimes the noisy sound of grunting and groaning from underneath the coats caused customers to complain. Kay would have to shine the torchlight over the heaps until quiet breathing got restored. When the house-lights went on after the afternoon matinee, the quiffs of hair on the heads of the garda were tussled and tossed. The men tidied their shirts and ties, flung on their trench coats and though some sheepishly left the cinema with a woman in tow, some left alone and she stayed behind.

Some Blackrock coppers who went to the Regent never spent a penny on anything but their tickets. They took paper bags full of oranges, bananas, apples and pears into the cinema with them to eat during the picture. After they had eaten all the food, most slid the peels and skins down the sides of the seats, where the cleaning woman found them causing her to mutter, over and over, 'the country bumpkins'.

I came to recognise some of the regular patrons who came to the Regent every week. We all aimed an eye in the direction of the celebrities of the time who passed through the door: Noel Purcell, Joe Lynch and Eddie Byrne.

The people who lived in Blackrock and the surrounding areas were mad about western films. Any film that had John Wayne or Gary Cooper in it filled the house. When westerns were on the bill, my floor sales shot up. It seemed that watching all the action in the westerns caused people to want to munch, drink or scoop something into their mouths. They ate with relish everything off my tray as they scooped in the blasting riflefire and ricocheting bullets from the big screen.

During an afternoon matinee I heard a familiar voice calling out, 'Miss! Oh, Miss, I want you to stop.' The voice belonged to the old fella. He sat in the middle of the row grinning like a cat. I could not believe my eyes at the sight of him in the Regent. It took two buses to get from Irishtown to Blackrock. As usual he was three sheets to the wind and then some.

He fell over everyone in the row of seats trying to reach me at the end of the row. 'I'll buy all the tubs of ice-cream and all the drinks and sweets on your tray, Miss,' he said fishing out a crisp green pound note.

'What are you doing here, ye disgrace to the world?'

'Now, now, I'm going to buy all the ice-creams and stuff on your tray and maybe then you can go home early. Don't let anyone here know that you are related to me or that you even know me!'

'Why are ye here?'

'I came to see if you are a good ice-cream seller.'

'They won't let me go home early even if ye buy everything on the tray. How did ye get here in the state ye're in?'

'Titch! Am I right or am I wrong but is that thing up on the screen supposed to be a human green pea? I've been watching the picture for a half hour or so and I think that your poor Da may be in trouble. Maybe losing his mind.'

'Did ye look on the still out front for the name of the film being shown to-day?

'Och, Titch! I only bought a ticket to come in and see you.'

'The picture on the screen is *The Invasion of the Body Snatchers*. D'ye hear me? It's called *The Invasion of the Body Snatchers*. It's all about peapods from outer space taking over the bodies of people on earth,' I told him. 'For yer ease of mind ye're not becoming a lunatic right now. All the stuff about giant peapods is not in yer head, Da.

It's just a film.' I told Da to follow me to the exit, get on the bus and go back home to Ma.

The film *Shane* for some reason caused me to feel uneasy and sad. As I watched excerpts from *Shane* while walking up and down the aisle, the lovely colours of the outdoor scenes triggered some sense in my mind. The coloured images of the sky in the movie especially caused the most disturbing rumbling in my head. It seemed as if my brain, while it took in the sight of the sky in the picture, was trying to tell me something. But what?

Shane upset me for some reason, and what was more upsetting, was that Kay took ill with TB and was sent to a sanitorium. I felt lost and lonely without her company through the long hours of the day. Kay wouldn't be back to work for a long time. After a week passed Kay was replaced by a beautiful young woman, Dolores Flann, who had just turned twenty. She looked like one of the gorgeous models in the *Sunday Independent* newspaper fashion section.

When Dolores appeared in the lobby for the first time in a new, slim fitting usherette uniform everyone gawked. Her S-shaped figure under the uniform caused lads to hoot and holler. Dolores had short curly brown hair which fell clinging around her baby-face and tossed like floss. Her eyes were as blue as the stripe in the rainbow. She shaped her mouth with lipstick into a cupid's bow demanding to be kissed.

The local young men who came to an occasional film at the Regent now came every night to get a look at the new beauty gliding the aisles in high-heeled shoes. Dolores flashed her torch here and there over the seats and in the aisle as she walked back and forth jiggling her arse like an oscillator. 'What a glamourpuss,' sighed onlookers.

Dolores decided that I needed her expertise to make me a more glamorous ice-cream girl. 'You look too much like a schoolgirl,' she lambasted. 'First we need to improve the way ye walk.' I let her know that I wanted to be just like her and wanted to wag my arse like she did as she strolled the floor.

'When ye're walking you have to bump one knee against the other. This causes the hips to go one way and another. When you do it right, yer bum will automatically go bim and bam,' she said. Making the bum go bim and bam proved difficult when carrying a heavy loaded tray around. Sometimes when my bum went bim the stuff on the tray went bam and fell to the floor.

My new walk caught the eye of the chief usher. 'What are ye trying to do walking like that, walking like ye have two eggs in a handkerchief instead of a bum?'

Fellas bought all kinds of stuff off my tray for Miss Flann. They asked me to give her the treats because they were too shy to give them to her themselves. She told me to give her the money instead, and sell the treats to others in the picture house. The manager kept tabs on my sales, and now most of the sales were for treats for Miss Flann who only wanted the money. I told her she'd have to take some of the ice-cream tubs, chocolate bars, cigarettes, popcorn and sweets the customers bought for her, or else my sales would be down and I could get the sack. Instead of eating all the treats bought for her by the men, she decided to split the money for the treats with me, and we both did well. She easily made twenty shillings on a Saturday night, with another ten shillings for me.

The fellas who bought Miss Flann all the treats were not the only ones who went goo-goo over Dolores. The manager of the Regent, Mr B, nearly toppled off his specially made high-heeled shoes every time he saw her. He'd come into the back of the picture house, smug as a cat, whisper, 'How is it going to-night, Miss Flann? Are you going to the dance in the Top Hat in Dun Laoghaire this Saturday night? I have a car if you need a ride to the dance or anywhere else. Let me know, Okey-dokey?'

Dolores, besides having half the men in Blackrock after her, had a steady fella of her own. He hated to come into the picture house while she was working. Dolores's mother favoured him, believing he had a steady influence on her daughter. The mother seemed keen on getting the pair married. Dolores's ma worried about having such a beautiful daughter, and instead of relishing her beauty, she found it a burden. She wanted the daughter tied in chains as soon as it could be arranged. Although the young man Dolores's ma favored seemed serious, sombre, and handsome, Marlon Brando would have been my pick for Dolores.

In the meanwhile, the manager of the picture-house gushed and gushed over the beauty. Dolores told me, 'I wouldn't piss on him if he were on fire.' Confidentially, I wouldn't have pissed on him either.

Working eight hours a day six days a week inside a dark picture house began to get the better of me. The union official who showed-up every fortnight to collect my one shilling union fee pointed out that loads of young girls like myself were working for almost nothing for the long hours we put in. He assured me the union was working to make sure ice-cream girls only worked a five day week instead of six days a week.

No change ever took place while I worked in the picture houses, and I'm sorry that I ever gave my hard earned shilling to such a worthless union.

In spite of the fun Dolores was to be with, a deep downhearted feeling began to set in. I couldn't shake off the feeling of being down in the dumps. Usually, I tried always to act as if things were bearable, but after working in the picture house for over a year, OK didn't cut the mustard any more. It wasn't likely that anyone would ever know how sad things seemed to me. During my half-hour break, I began to skip to the pub next door to the Regent and buy a bottle of Bulmer's cider to drink. The barman seemed unconcerned about me buying a bottle of Bulmer's cider three times a week. He guessed the alcohol was for old what's'is name in the projection room.

The Bulmer's tasted sweet and tangy. The alcohol took away the awful emptiness in my heart and made it bearable to continue to work. I'd eat some Silvermints off the tray to cover my breath, and go back to work. Sometimes the cider had more effect on me than others. I'd feel myself sway back and forth with the tray going up and down the aisles. The head usher began to roar at me for bumping into the back of the seats. 'Git yer bleeding eyes tested for Christ's sake.' 'Ah, go n' shite,' I said back under the breath. 'Ah, go n' shite,' became my verdict to everyone. I'd bang the ice-cream tray into the back of the seats and all the stuff on the tray would topple all over the place. Some of the patrons started to complain that their ice-cream tubs were all melted, others grumbled that I let the cold orange drinks on the tray get tepid, and others said that I had eaten Silvermints and other sweets from supposedly untouched packages. Others griped that the bags of popcorn they had bought had been nibbled to half the amount. What really brought the house down upon my head were the narks who complained about finding a few cigarettes were missing from a new pack.

I didn't know if the weight that hung round my chest was caused by the weight of the ice-cream tray or something else, but the realisation came over me that life wasn't worth living. Going into the dark for eight hours a day, six days a week and putting up with everything brought the weight of the world down. It became harder to want to live, but I didn't know how anyone could kill themself without making a terrible mess for someone else. I thought of those who had suffered because of the deaths of those thoughtless suicides like young Kiernan, who had done himself in in George Reynolds' flats, or the chap O'Neill who had hung himself long ago in O'Brien's Place.

Mount Merrion Strand wasn't far from the picture house, and I decided to go there one afternoon to find some comfort. I told the page that I needed a bit of fresh air. I couldn't bear to spend another afternoon and night inside the dark picture house walking up and down. My head split at the thought! I dumped the tray on the ice-cream fridge and headed for Mount Merrion Strand. The tide was coming in in the far distance.

I started to walk out to meet the tide. The wind on the strand whipped up my hair and belted my face. My whole body started to feel alive and free. I took off my shoes and walked in my nylons across the sand. The hard lined ridges of sand jerked life into my feet and up my legs, which made me run, run, run, to meet the tide. The sea birds swooped and made their screeching sounds and I spread my arms out in flight like them and let the wind stir me on. It seemed that the earth held me now like it had some other time, long ago. It loved me and I loved it. As the warning signs along the strand faded out of sight, the sea became more visible. I remember lying down on the sand to wait for the tide. Trickles of water drew in and wet the back of my body and small crabs hurriedly crossed my toes and hair. I never wanted to leave the moment that had me in it, now. What a relief to die.

The tightness in my chest was lifted, and the pain that had surrounded my mind broke away. The sky above me was silver and gold. A feeling of being cared for circled me as I waited to be lifted with the tide. It would be so easy to slip beneath the sea. If this was how it felt to die, this feeling of being at peace, then life seemed terrible, and its sharpness wasn't going to cut any more. I'd never go back beyond the signs or to the slip of the strand again. A white wave of foam backwashed over my face and settled on my chest like translucent seed-pearls nicer than the kind worn by the Saint Vincent De Paul ladies, a long time ago.

As I lay on the sand so content, Ma's voice called out of nowhere for me, 'Head back to the shore, love. Go back to the shore. What will I do without you?' Ma's voice repeated the same plea over and over in my head, and her face appeared before me. I knew Ma and Da loved me, but a trail of loss constantly followed me. The voice again implored, 'What will I do without you?' as if coming out of a dream, and I sat up.

A sense of urgency took hold as the tide came hurrying in. I rushed back through the water, my feet and legs going a hundred miles a minute and reached the slip, but not before the water had reached my waist. It seemed as if the sea had a strong desire to take me in its clutches. Exhausted, I walked home to George Reynolds' and never said a word.

I went back to work the following day at the Regent in Blackrock, the pain in my mind eased, and decided to give Bulmer's cider the slip.

Mr B got transferred to a larger Dublin cinema. He replaced the manager of the larger picture house, who, in turn, became the manager of the Regent in Blackrock. Mr B offered me a job at the bigger cinema, but I turned him down. Our new manager spent more time in the pub next door than he did in the picture house. When I checked in my tray after work, he would go over the sales with me, and calculate to his own benefit. Putting up with a diddler was as bad as putting up with manhandlers, so I decided to find work closer to home as an ice-cream girl at the Theatre Royal.

The Royal made the Regent look like a matchbox. I ran the kiosk on the second floor. The ice-cream girls and usherettes in the Royal were exciting to be with. Plenty of clicking went on in the theatre. Fellas fell for the usherettes, took them dancing, to coffee, and for rides in their cars. On the other hand, ice-cream girls were viewed as being under age for romance.

Working in the kiosk paid more money than being a salesgirl on the floor, and oftentimes a patron gave me a tip. The ice-cream girls in the Royal palled around together. After work, we'd high-tail it over to O'Connell Street to have coffee in the Green Rooster, Forte's and Caffola's. Once inside, we played the juke box for sixpence and let Elvis Presley melt our hearts by singing 'Love Me Tender' and 'Let Me Be Your Teddy-Bear' while Pat Boone singing 'April Love' dampened our drawers with desire.

Political and nationalist songs moaning about poor old Ireland and the fallen heroes, all fell under the weight of rock n'roll. As we listened to the songs from America, the girls talked about what they might become if they ever got there. We were all tired of being ice-cream girls. The only other options we had were to work in the factories; become office scrub-brushes; find a fella and get married and have a basketful of babies; or emigrate. Emigration topped my list.

Being ice-cream girls inside a cinema for eight hours a day, six days a week, we got more than our fill of films from the United States. Consequently we spoonfed ourselves on the etiquette and sexuality that the films offered. Between watching all the Hollywood films and listening to rock n'roll, a bunch of us talked more and more about finding a way to leave Ireland.

I especially loved films with spunky young women in them; films like *Gone With the Wind*. *Gone With the Wind* played and replayed at the Royal like a broken record, so we knew the story by heart. Scarlett O'Hara, a mad bitch if ever there was one, had things in proper order when it came to getting out of tight situations. Her pulling down those green velvet curtains in the movie to make a fetching dress for herself in order to bamboozle a man seemed brilliant.

Shamelessly, others might do the same with what they had at hand. First we needed to toss out all the blarney about romance in Ireland. Maybe toffs could be romantic about love and marriage but guttersnipes had to be more realistic. How many times had I heard *Tabhair dom pog, cailin og*-Give me a kiss, young girl-from some scholarly type in the cinema who though he had the right to ask for a kiss after buying a few rolls of toffees.

I'd be damned if I'd give my kisses to such likes just because they bought a few sweets. I needed to get over the horseshite about falling in love with some rustic from the west of Ireland, or waiting in hopes of finding a quickfooted Kerry dancer type with a steady job in the government who might find me attractive.

I had given up waiting for my brother Bob's friends, Charlie and Pat Mullen, to take notice of me. I'd ask Bob if either of the brothers ever asked him any questions about his sister. 'They're not going to ask me things about me sister,' said Bob, never catching on, or pretending not to catch on to my interest in the two handsome young men.

Charlie and Pat worked on the coal boats that went back and forth across the Irish Sea to Liverpool. They were both tall and handsome with sunny blond hair and deep blue eyes. The brothers looked more Norwegian than Irish, and my heart pounded at the sight of either one of them looking as rugged and handsome as could be in their seaman's gear. They gave me warm smiles if I passed them on the street, but they never went a step further in getting to know me better.

Girls with jobs like mine put up with a lot of malarkey from fellas who insisted on a kiss or a cuddle for buying an item off our ice-cream trays. I remember the gobshite who stammered, 'How many tubs of ice-cream will I need to buy to blow smoke up yer shirt?'

'G'wan home and singe the hair off yer balls,' I rapped back in his face.

'I'm just coddin',' he said, returning to his seat all smiles.

Like me, some of the girls made the decision only to pucker up for foreigners. We'd ravish their gobs with passionate kisses and maybe end up leaving with one to get away from Éireann's mangy green half-penny arse.

Having some foreigner fall in love with us became a fixed fantasy and Yanks flew to the top of the list. We thought we knew more about Americans than any other foreigners because of all the Hollywood films that we'd been watching all our lives.

By 1957, more and more Yanks were to be seen strolling the streets of Dublin, thanks to the efforts of Aer Lingus and Bord Fáilte. They used the image of the Irish colleen in their advertisements as if she was the queen of Sheba. Their constant promotion of the colleen in their brochures and advertisements made her a pin-up girl.

The US servicemen we met in Dublin talked about how they were enticed to head for Ireland after seeing the Air Lingus brochures they picked up at the military base. The men raved about their longing to meet and even marry a colleen and take her back to the States. Obviously, not all of the servicemen we met were interested in finding a wife. At the same time, they didn't come to Ireland to trace their family trees or to moon over Waterford crystal with its unequalled fire and brilliance. Nor did they come to finger and fondle bulky Irish tweed and croon over its woven warp and weft, nor to whine about the fragility of Belleek china, so delicate and precious. They wanted to sample Irish pussy. We let the young men know that we were not 'flash girls' (prostitutes) who roamed around the city, older girls who made a hard living selling sex while we made a hard living selling sweets and ice-cream. But we were interested in everything American, love, romance and a possible husband. A few Yanks told us in an indirect way that some of their buddies viewed Irish pussy as premium pussy because few invaders ever got to experience it.

Yank chasers

The Theatre Royal in Dublin city became the perfect place to meet Yanks. The cinema offered a combination of films and vaudeville. The Yanks in their civilian apparel stood out in the audience like poppies in a field. Some of the girls referred to the Americans as 'kaleidoscope buzz-heads' because of their brightly coloured shirts and shorn haircuts.

In the course of walking up and down the aisles selling stuff off the tray, eyes spotted the colourful tourists and smiles were exchanged. After the last picture show, some of the young Americans would linger in the lobby to meet us after work. They were more than delighted to go with us to dance in some of the local dancehalls.

The Americans especially liked colleens who jabbered a few sentences in Irish into their ears as they danced together. Little bits-and-pieces such as '*Tá fáilte romhat go hÉirinn*'-'Welcome to Ireland' or '*Cad is ainm duit?*'-'What is your name?' And the clincher '*An Americeánach thú?*' 'Are you an American?' This last titbit caused some Yanks to go on and on about the virtues of the United States in comparison to the Soviet Union, and trip all over the dance floor. The ancient bits of Irish melted the stranger's heart and had him nibbling out of a girl's hand like a dicky-bird.

The most popular dancehalls around the city were the Four Provinces, the Metropole, the Olympia and my favourite dancehall, the Crystal. Moral types blackened the reputation of the Four Provinces because the management welcomed Yanks, foreigners, 'blackies' and arty types to mingle together, and God only knew what they got up to went the prevailing cry.

Decent young Irish girls were not supposed to be seen in such a sinful setting. Good Irish girls were supposed to go to the National Irish dances and jig with others like themselves. And good decent Irish young women were never to be seen walking or linking arms on the street with some brown-skinned foreigner or God forbid! with a black man. And a sour glance got directed at any Irish girl who liked arms with a Yank on the streets of Dublin, especially a Yank in uniform. Those who did were labelled 'flash girls'.

Thus, the Four Provinces offered the setting where such mingling could take place without conflict. Irish fellas also went dancing at the Four P's. My friends from the Royal and I loved to dance there because of the excitement if offered. We knew of its bad reputation and ignored it, marking it off to stick-in-the-muds, and were thrilled to go and meet interesting people, especially lads from yonder lands.

My friend Ginger wanted to know, 'Are ye going to dance with one of them brown-fellas or a "blackie" if wan asks ye to dance?' She would duck out the door if she thought one of the African men seemed inclined to ask her to dance.

I told Ginger that I'd never danced with an African. The words were just out of my mouth when over strolled a tall graceful black man. 'Would you care to dance?' he said, extending his hand towards me. I took his hand, the first non-white hand I had ever clasped in mine and glided onto the dance floor.

On looking at his princely bearing, I wondered if this African gentleman attired perfectly in a grey striped suit, white shirt, striped tie and black leather shoes had anything in common with all the starving African babies I had been told about by the Catholic Church? How many hundreds of pounds had Irish people donated in the form of coins and put into the hundreds of black baby boxes all around the city? The African's tapered fingers entwined with mine and his torso rose above the top of my head. Looking up into his face took a bit of courage. As a child the nuns talked about Africans being hedonists and in need of conversion to Christianity and civilisation. And yet, how many times had the nuns landed their rulers on my hands for not having a penny to drop into the white box with the nodding black baby on the top? And, here I was, a lowly commoner, dancing with an African prince.

As if able to read my mind, the young African laughed out loud and said, 'What have you heard about people from Africa? I'm from Nigeria. I'm studying medicine at Trinity College, Dublin. Are you a student?'

I told him No. I told him I earned my living as an ice-cream girl in the Royal and hoped he didn't notice the catch in my voice. As I danced in the arms of the African prince, I daydreamed about us as a pair. Maybe, if I fell in love with the Nigerian and he fell in love with me, we might get married and I'd go back to Africa with him. Maybe in Africa, I could be more than an ice-cream girl. Maybe I could become a teacher or a writer or a brain surgeon?

If falling in love with the African didn't occur, maybe the medical student on completion of his studies would go back to Nigeria, and set up collection boxes all over his country for needy Irish children. Maybe he could convince his government and religious leaders to get behind his efforts, and before long hundreds of small collection boxes topped with a nodding Irish child begging for pennies would be as common a sight in Africa as the black baby boxes were in Ireland.

Dancers like myself showed the strangers how to 'dip' and 'lurch' while a crooner sang in the background, 'I Love Paris'. With a Yank in hand, the dance began. Two dancers sauntered onto the dancefloor arms entwined around each other's waists. The lurcher took her arm off her partner's waist and locked it around his neck crushing them closer. Next she pressed her forehead to her partner's, constantly gazing into his eyes until she sparked a blaze within.

Then she lifted her partner's arm from around her waist, slapped it against her arse as if to nail all five digits in.

For added measure, she put a foot between her partner's feet as they danced, causing him to tip backwards. Upon recovery, he encircled the girl's body more completely within his arms as if fitting for a wedding ring.

Some Americans could not bid *auf Wiedersehen* to my friends they had met. My friends from the picture house, Ann, Helen, Carmel, Mary and Sheila—all ice-cream girls and great lurchers—went to West Germany to marry Yanks. Although the young girls were leaving Ireland to marry the men they had fallen in love with, they still represented the rising tide of young women leaving Ireland in the 1950s.

There were few misty eyes or boo hoo accounts in the Irish newspapers or talks given in the parishes over the high emigration rate of young women leaving their homeland to seek a better life elsewhere, one way or another. All the laments dealing with emigration centred on the lads, or the lads who'd already booted the place.

The young handsome university educated US serviceman who fell in love with me, and I with him, came to Ireland after reading one of the brochures published by the Irish tourist office at his base in West Germany. The image of the charming colleen, not the grey dreary castles, captured his attention, and he travelled by Aer Lingus all the way to the rocky road to Dublin, where we met. He complimented me on trying to preserve the Irish language and said he admired my unique style of dancing which caused his head to spin and his heart to dance.

He made three trips back to Dublin to see me and to meet Ma and Da and proposed marriage on a beautiful summer day in Saint Stephen's Green, in Dublin. He ringed my wobbly finger with a beautiful diamond ring.

The neighbours in George Reynolds' were delighted that I had met a lovely Yank and was going off to America to marry him. Of course this being Ireland, begrudgers like Mrs D down the balcony with three unmarried daughters still living at home, was overheard to say, 'Young wans who nowadays go far away from home? Who's to say what state they're in, do you know what I mean Mrs C?'

Mrs D could have rested easy on that account. Even now, at almost age eighteen, I'd only kissed and done a little fiddling here and there, but my maidenhead hadn't been hammered. After all, had not Da told me time after time, 'Never dust my eggs with a hammer.' I certainly didn't need a professor to help me unscramble Da's dictate for God's sake.

At the age of eighteen, I had my emigration farewell party or 'wake' as some called such parties. It was given by the neighbours in George Reynolds'. I got three chalk statues of the Holy Child to pack in my suitcase along with a bottle of Lourdes holy water. My friend, Peggy Hawthorn, who was also eighteen and worked in a jewellery factory in the city, gave me a lovely shamrock brooch as a goingaway token which remains pinned to my heart.

Ma wanted me to take the picture of the Sacred Heart of Jesus with me, but the image had looked down upon me for twelve years in the room in O'Brien's Place and almost six years in the flat, and I'd had enough of the gawk. Ma kept her guy.

I fitted everything I had in the one suitcase. I had five shillings and two dollar bills to take with me to New York. Ma and Da said that if my intended did not show up at the airport to meet me, I should go to the nearest Catholic church for assistance. But I knew he'd be waiting for me because he was, and is, one of the grandest people God ever put in shoe leather, as they say.

Ma and Da, Frank and his wife Bridie, and Bob and Noely went with me on the doubledecker bus to Collinstown airport. My friend Rosaleen Byrne, who was still working in the Royal as an ice-cream girl, and her mother were at the airport to see me off. Rosaleen and I hugged and kissed each other. She called me her sister and said she wished that I would stay in Ireland.

As the time drew near for me to board the small Aer Lingus plane that would take me to Shannon airport to board an American flight bound for New York, I began to get cold feet about the whole adventure. I was breaking Ma's heart and the old fella's by leaving. I told Ma I'd send her a teddybear fur coat. I hoped to get a job in America and save some money. I'd save every penny to make sure that when Ma and Da died, a hundred years in the future, they would be buried in a real grave together in a space of their own.

As I waited to board the plane for Shannon, Da complained that he had a bad pain in his chest. He told me that he'd always love me, and that he'd write to me every day. And he said, 'Don't go!' And I knew that I had never loved him with only half a heart; it had always been with a full one although he broke it often. The goodbye to Ma is too painful to recall. My brother Bob told me not to go. Noely, Frank, and Bridie wished me luck and said I knew the way home even from America.

Crowds of young Irish people at Shannon airport were waiting to board planes for faraway places: Canada, Australia and the United States. A chap waiting in line with me to board the plane for New York asked me if I knew that half the people leaving the land were around our age. It was 1957, a banner year, he noted. He asked if I'd a job lined up in America? I told him I was off to get married. 'Marrying a Yank?' he asked tilting an eyebrow. 'Aren't you a bit young to get married?' he asked. I gave him a look. He took a slip of paper from his pocket and wrote down the place he was going to in the United States. 'If you need a friend here is an address,' he said handing me the slip of white paper. Time to walk out to the tarmac and board the bruiser for New York.

As I walked through the exit on the way to the plane, a soft Irish breeze touched my face. I had the urge to run back into the airport, and forget all about going away. But I had to go. I had to taste what the other side of the world offered. I let the slip of white paper with the address fly from my fingers, before I boarded the flying Nelson's Pillar. The plane rumbled down the runway like an overstuffed goose unsure about flight. My heart pounded as the plane sucked and pulled its way upwards into the heavens. Seemingly, at any minute the plane would bellyflop back to the ground. As we banked towards the open sea, I saw the last vestiges of the landscape below, and marvelled at its beauty. The fields resembled swatches of green felt some old granny had stitched unevenly together with ravelled cord. I thought that with the exception of my family, especially Ma, and all the old neighbours in O'Brien's Place and George Reynolds' House, I'd lived for eighteen years in battle-zone conditions not caused by the bloody Brits.

It would take a while to get over the hump of being born and bred in Ireland. Would my adopted country have a kinder heart? As such thoughts raced, the stewardess handed me a cup of black strong coffee and an assortment of sample packs of cigarettes which included packs of Marlboro, Chesterfield and Lucky Strike, along with books of matches. I sipped on the coffee and smoked one Lucky Strike after another without any effect on my nervous system.

The noise of the powerful engines racked the plane as we flew towards our destination. From my perch by the window, I saw the waves of fog drift over the plane scurrying back in the direction of home. I began to wonder about leaving all the familiar. I checked on the two dollars I had in my pocket, my fortune, my dowry, and wondered what would happen if my love failed to show up at the airport. How far would two dollars go? I'd made up my mind that if I fell on my arse no one in George Reynolds' would be made the wiser: so many had pinned their hopes and dreams to my heels. We all believed that the United States offered the greatest opportunity for poor people in the world, and only a gobshite would fail to make it in America.

Why had I ever expected my life to be any different from the lives of people back home? Why did I want to pitch my tent so far? What would making love for the first time be like? Could it cause a person to have a split personality, did the world spin, did the heavens shift? I began to wish I'd never paid so much attention to Hollywood films. I should have become a nun and gone to Africa to save the heathen. Why did neither of the Mullen brothers ask me out. I might have married either one had they shown any interest, besides being pleased to see me on the street.

If I stayed in Ireland Da might take the pledge and give up the drink. Ma will be heartbroken without me, I knew. Would my brothers forget me? Did old Granny Martin, long dead and buried, know I was on my way to America? I noticed the mists had abated, and wondered who flung the trillions of silver sparkles into the night sky. The full moon, bright as a beacon, glided alongside the plane familiar as the face of my mother.